MOBILIZING THE HOME FRONT

NUMBER FIFTEEN:
Presidential Rhetoric Series
Martin J. Medhurst
General Editor

MOBILIZING THE HOME FRONT

War Bonds and Domestic Propaganda

James J. Kimble

Texas A&M *University Press*
COLLEGE STATION

First edition
The paper used in this book meets the minimum requirements
of the American National Standard for Permanence
of Paper for Printed Library Materials, Z39.48–1984.
Binding materials have been chosen for durability.
∞

Library of Congress Cataloging-in-Publication Data

Kimble, James J., 1966–
Mobilizing the home front : war bonds and domestic
propaganda / James J. Kimble.—1st ed.
p. cm. — (Presidential rhetoric series ; no. 15)
Includes bibliographical references and index.
ISBN 1-58544-485-5 (cloth : alk. paper)
1. Savings bonds—United States—History. 2. World War,
1939–1945—Finance—United States. 3. Patriotism—
United States—History. 4. Nationalism—
United States—History. I. Title: War bonds
and domestic propaganda. II. Title. III. Series.
HG4936.K55 2006
940.53′1—dc22
20050252250

For Lucille Dubs,

who convinced a six-year-old boy
that he was an author

CONTENTS

PREFACE

If this book represents a journey of sorts, I think I can date its origins to several desperate days on the sandy training ranges of Fort Dix, New Jersey. I enlisted in the military when my student loans failed to cover my undergraduate tuition and fees; the local National Guard recruiter assured me that the army would be delighted to pay most of those school expenses on my behalf. Perhaps somewhat naively, I got off a bus at Fort Dix in August, 1987, with some fear, but also with confidence that I would overcome this series of obstacles and return to my schooling without too much trouble.

My drill sergeants had other ideas. The training, of course, was grueling, as it should have been. But what was most difficult for me were the combat skills. Firing a rifle or thrusting a bayonet were fine ideas in the abstract. Yet once on the range, firing at or attacking silhouettes *made up to look like humans,* I hesitated. What was the problem, my instructors wondered (well, shouted)? These silhouettes represented the enemy, they said, the one whose job it was to kill us. I wanted to kill the enemy before it killed me . . . right? As I fired . . . and missed . . . and fired again . . . I wondered how to go about answering such a question.

At some point I realized that I was resisting the military's indoctrination, described so well in Col. Dave Grossman's book *On Killing*. I began to recognize the dehumanization in which I was being told to participate. I started to realize that the army's approach in basic training amounted to a personalized propaganda, its aim to shape the worldview of trainees and their actions on a battlefield. Surely this would be no surprise to most people, but to that young would-be soldier, it was a revelation.

Somehow I was able to finish basic training—and my advanced training—and I served my six years in the National Guard faithfully, and even with occasional enthusiasm. The questions I had learned to ask in basic training, however, stuck with me. I became intensely interested in the process of indoctrination, about the use and abuse of propaganda, and about the ethics of dehumanization. Eventually, I came to believe that propaganda, like rhetoric, was effectively neutral. It could be used for noble ends as well as nefarious ends. Of course, the question then became, how could one tell the difference, except from a historical perspective? And who should make the judgment about the essential morality of specific acts of propaganda?

It is these sorts of questions that underlie this book. The context is not basic training in the 1980s but the federal government's attempts to shape public morale during World War II. The Roosevelt administration created dozens of rhetorical campaigns, each aimed in some way at motivating public support for the war effort. By almost any objective definition, these campaigns were domestic propaganda—large-scale attempts by the government to indoctrinate the public into a certain way of thinking. The largest of these attempts was the U.S. Treasury's war bond campaign, which sold an incredible $185.7 billion in bonds during the war years. The Treasury's massive campaign came to resemble the psychological stages inherent in military training; in short, the war bond campaign mobilized the public by attempting to convince home front Americans that they were fighting the war, too.

The aim of this book is to present a rhetorical perspective on this dramatic campaign as domestic propaganda, and to evaluate it as such. In doing so, I am well aware of the notion of "the good war" that surrounds our memories of World War II. This notion occasionally suggests that to label as "propaganda" any of the government's domestic campaigns during the war is to mislabel them at best, and to slander them at worst. I respect this perspective and, indeed, share many of its assumptions. However, to me the question is not whether the Treasury's campaign meets the definition of propaganda; I believe there is little doubt that it does (and the people who created the campaign agreed that it was propaganda, at least in private). The real question for me is whether the war bond campaign's propaganda was used for noble ends, or for ill. This book offers a viewpoint on that complex question, but readers must, of course, answer that question for themselves.

No long and perilous journey, of course, can proceed without assistance. I have been extremely fortunate to have dozens of benevolent guides on this book's travels from idea to archives to draft to manuscript, and I acknowledge several of them here. My wife, Tina Potuto Kimble, was a source of great energy, and even found time to read through many versions of the work; she is truly a "virtuous woman" whose value to me "is far above rubies." My parents-in-law, the Potutos, provided a quiet haven in New Jersey where I did my best writing. My own parents and family back home in Norfolk, Nebraska, eagerly anticipated the project's completion, and were anxious to celebrate it; so was Lucille Dubs, to whom this book is dedicated.

Most of the research for this project was completed at the Franklin D. Roosevelt Presidential Library, whose staff was quite supportive. I am also grateful for the use of several other libraries and collections, particularly the Library of Congress, the National Archives, George Mason University (GMU), and the University of Maryland. The photographers who helped secure the illustrations from various locations were also very enthusiastic; my thanks to the fine folks at Do You Graphics and to Carol Krauss of Concord, Massachusetts—who, it turns out, is a GMU Patriot from way back. My former colleagues and students at GMU were uniformly supportive, enthusiastic, and willing to lend a hand. I am particularly grateful for the encouragement I received from Gary Kreps, Kathy Rowan, and their fine staff in the GMU Department of Communication. My new colleagues at Seton Hall University have been similarly encouraging. The dedicated folks at Texas A&M University Press have also been wonderful, showing enthusiasm for the project and answering my questions swiftly and accurately.

Many people read and commented on earlier versions of the manuscript, including Linda Aldoory, Don Boileau, Jeanne Fahnestock, Robert Gaines, Jim Klumpp, Janette Muir, Star Muir, and Chris Tittel—to each of you I offer my sincere appreciation. Melissa Bannister helped with the final phases of manuscript preparation, and Anne R. Gibbons contributed her expert eye for matters of consistency, flow, integrity, and intelligibility; I am grateful for their assistance. Finally, Shawn Parry-Giles was the adviser on this project when it was just a series of disconnected ideas; under her guidance it turned into a dissertation, and with her continued encouragement has become a book. It is difficult to express how thankful I am for her contributions to this project. Any errors that survived her scrutiny and that of others, of course, remain my sole responsibility.

MOBILIZING THE HOME FRONT

INTRODUCTION

Propaganda and the Bonds of War

The principal battleground of this war is not the South Pacific. It is not the Middle East. It is not England, or Norway, or the Russian Steppes. It is American opinion.
—Archibald MacLeish, Office of Facts and Figures

[It would be] a concentrated, co-ordinated, single-impact national campaign such as would be created to launch and sustain sales of a new model Buick.
—Peter H. Odegard, Defense Savings Staff

James Gerard had very strong feelings about propaganda. The American ambassador to Germany, expelled by Kaiser Wilhelm II on the eve of U.S. entry into World War I, returned to his homeland with dire warnings about Germany's intentions. In his sensational book *Face to Face with Kaiserism,* Gerard told of the "insidious German propaganda now going on in America—propaganda that is often cleverly concealed in a guise of apparent innocence." The "far flung tentacles of Prussian propaganda," he suggested, were the primary means by which the Kaiser was attempting to achieve his "dream of world dominion." Gerard's new book, he claimed, would tell readers how they could "discover and suppress this 'poison gas' attack" of the Kaiser's propagandists.[1]

Gerard's dramatic charges were part of a loud chorus that proclaimed the dangers of German propaganda during World War I. "The Kaiser's secret army in America," proclaimed the *Literary Digest,* was producing "a hundred forms of insidious and demoralizing propaganda."[2] Such claims invited a general public watchfulness, as Americans became alarmed at the possibility that the Kaiser's propaganda might be targeting them, thereby attempting to decrease public morale. As Thomas Jewett Hallowell told the *New York Times* on May 10, 1915, "we want no propaganda of the German cause."[3]

Ironically, while Americans spent much of World War I on the lookout for the dangers of German propaganda, most failed to consider that their own government might also be targeting them with propaganda.[4] The vast machinery of Pres. Woodrow Wilson's Committee on Public Information (CPI) aroused little suspicion because the organization claimed to disseminate the war's available news without government influence, ostensibly allowing citizens to draw their own conclusions about the war effort.[5] Similarly, the U.S. Department of the Treasury's efforts to sell Liberty Bonds to the public during the Great War seemed to be nothing more than an official, albeit aggressive, fund-raising operation in support of the conflict.[6]

In retrospect, however, both CPI's information dissemination and the Treasury's bond program appear to have been strategically devised propaganda operations aimed at influencing domestic opinion on the war. For its part, suggest Robert Jackall and Janice M. Hirota, "CPI was America's first propaganda ministry, a term that most of the leaders of the organization used without embarrassment, at least in private."[7] Garth S. Jowett and Victoria O'Donnell argue that although CPI was targeting a populace that held widely varied opinions at the outset of the war, its propaganda work "turned out to be very skillful and highly coordinated."[8] Writing more than two decades after the war, James R. Mock and Cedric Larson point to the power of CPI's efforts, noting that "by and large the American people today hold the articles of faith which the CPI . . . drew up in 1917 and 1918."[9]

The Treasury's Liberty Bond drives were also designed as a domestic propaganda operation in support of the Great War, targeting "patriotic rather than commercial motives."[10] Those who purchased their bond quota wore "badges and medals as a sign of their patriotism."[11] Recent immigrants, eager to prove their support for the war, found that "buying bonds, singing the national anthem in public, and displaying the American flag became important symbols of national loyalty."[12] Treasury Secretary William G. McAdoo later justified this approach, pointing out that "any great war must necessarily be a popular movement. It is a kind of crusade. . . . [I]t sweeps along on a powerful stream of romanticism."[13] Not surprisingly, McAdoo's Treasury effort and CPI's propaganda machine often shared ideas and even employees.[14]

For the most part, home front Americans were unaware of the behind-the-scenes morale work of CPI and the Treasury. Soon after the war, however, U.S. citizens began to shift their suspicious outlook from the alleged evils of the Kaiser's propagandists to their own government's ostensibly patriotic campaigns. Several writers confirmed for Americans that during the war they had been the unknowing subjects of government-sponsored domestic propaganda.[15] By 1927, when Harold D. Lasswell wrote that modern governments could use propaganda to shape their own citizens into "one amalgamated mass of hate and will and hope,"[16] Americans were increasingly alert to the possibility that their own leaders might be using tools of mass communication to manipulate their thoughts, beliefs, and actions.[17]

By the time Europe entered a second world war, this change in American sentiments meant that the government's renewed wartime propaganda would find a more suspicious audience. The official "information" agencies this time were Pres. Franklin D. Roosevelt's Office of Civilian Defense (OCD) and its successors, the Office of Facts and Figures (OFF) and the Office of War Information (OWI). Each agency inherited the weight of CPI's now-dubious ethos.[18] Roosevelt, recalling his own growing recognition of CPI's questionable reputation after the Great War, was acutely aware of the image issue.[19] Allan M. Winkler reports that many members of Congress felt the same way, complaining that OWI was a "refuge for the derelicts" and that its domestic propaganda was "a stench to the nostrils of a democratic people."[20] By the summer of 1943, OWI was a fraction of its original size, the victim of drastic budget attacks. Although its foreign propaganda arm remained viable, it had lost much of the financial and political backing for its domestic propaganda division.[21]

The Treasury's reprise of its war bond activities, in contrast, seemed to win the public's trust. More than seven months before Pearl Harbor, the Treasury kicked off its sales effort by selling the first defense bond to the president. In theory, Roosevelt could have used involuntary war taxes to offset the full cost of World War II—at $350 billion the most expensive war in American history. Yet he recognized that such efforts would defuse the national morale so necessary to the war effort.[22] His solution, as suggested by Treasury Secretary Henry F. Morgenthau Jr., was a massive crusade inviting Americans to loan the U.S. government their money while simultaneously—and surreptitiously—using the Treasury's bond publicity machine to target public morale. The resulting war bond program ultimately became the largest and most visible campaign of the war.[23]

The massive project soon sponsored an astonishing array of appeals. Bonds sold quickly to the tune of Irving Berlin's radio hit "Any Bonds Today?" Hollywood starlets such as Lana Turner and Judy Garland sold bonds on national theme tours while Donald Duck and Bugs Bunny promoted them on newsreel clips; from Washington, Roosevelt hawked them in Fireside Chats. Even artist Norman Rockwell allowed his famous *Four Freedoms* to become war bond posters. These appeals helped form a milieu of ubiquitous advertisements, town rallies, window displays, service club drives, farm-to-farm canvasses, newsreel trailers, even a Treasury-sponsored comic book.[24]

The widespread war bond appeals were never publicly singled out as official propaganda, and perhaps for this reason they often succeeded in reaching the wary public when OCD, OFF, and OWI could not. Ironically, the intensity of partisan discourse in the Treasury's publicity rivaled that in OWI's truncated domestic propaganda. Yet Morgenthau's bond program was criticized largely in financial terms, as proponents of war taxes and enforced savings programs had their say.[25] Thus, exactly when the Roosevelt administration needed a reliable, yet reputable way to depict the war to the public, Morgenthau's bond-selling program was both convenient and available. To borrow John Morton Blum's phrase, during the war's "absence of a glowing public rhetoric," the administration was frequently able to communicate its vision of the struggle to unsuspecting Americans through the Treasury's credible messages.[26]

This book views the Treasury's credible war bond campaign as an immense domestic propaganda program, both in aim and in effect. First, ample evidence suggests that its design went beyond fundraising and into a strategic focus on national morale and self-image. Secretary Morgenthau was enthusiastic about the program's "potential unifying factor in a time of great public discord and uncertainty."[27] Blum describes the bond organization as the administration's "machinery for selling the war," explaining that Treasury critics "continuously underestimated the value placed by Roosevelt and Morgenthau on the psychological aspects of the successive sales drives."[28] As Roosevelt himself commented, "only a united and determined America could possibly produce on a voluntary basis so huge a sum of money."[29] Privately, the Treasury's staffers agreed with these assessments, pointing out that "the best way to sell Bonds was to restore to the American people faith and confidence in their destiny as a nation."[30] Perhaps most tellingly, the bond program's primary strategist in its formative years was Peter H. Odegard—an academic who was employed by Morgenthau as the resident expert in "forces that mould the public mind" and "how words can help to win the war."[31]

A second reason to view the Treasury's campaign as a propaganda operation emerges when one assesses its domestic achievements throughout the war. For example, the bond organization produced more than $185 billion for the war effort—at a time when most Americans were still quite mindful of the Depression's financial woes. A significant portion of these billions came from America's average citizens, the very people Morgenthau wanted to reach.[32] But in addition to selling bonds, the Treasury's propaganda also seems to have had an impact on domestic morale. "What we have done," wrote Ted Gamble—a central figure in the bond program—"was to provide an activity in which all 135 million Americans could . . . serve their country and achieve that sense of personal participation in the war, so valuable to their morale."[33] Another Treasury strategist, Judy Graves, recalled that "the voluntary savings program . . . has borne good fruit first by its contribution to civilian morale."[34] Lawrence R. Samuel concurs with these perspectives, arguing that the war bonds "reflected and helped shape a new version of Americanism" that acted "as a catalyst or spark toward the creation of a broader and more deeply felt sense of national loyalty."[35] The program, then, began as the war's "grand experiment."[36] It ended the war as "the greatest mass selling achievement in history," selling war bonds, unity, and a heightened nationalistic spirit.[37]

Of course, the realities of wartime life presented significant obstacles to Morgenthau's propaganda efforts. Indeed, the distractions of the war effort consistently created a challenging target audience, one plagued with both a sense of overconfidence in the war's outcome and a sense of frustration over the war's slow progress.[38] In partial response to these complications, the Treasury developed a series of highly strategic bond drives. Although individuals could purchase bonds at any time during the war, the eight drives were specific, all-out propaganda blitzes aimed at maximizing every citizen's contributions. Each drive had a sales quota, special theme, catchphrase, and logo, all targeted to the home front's current mood.[39]

The bond drives began rather simply, but grew more complex as the war progressed and as the Treasury strategists perfected their appeals. "After three years and four bond drives," writes Laurence M. Olney, the Treasury's drive program "reached the point of a carefully planned and well-directed organization."[40] The drives peaked in the Mighty Seventh war loan, which began in May, 1945. Its original objective was to raise $14 billion for the final phases of the war. Despite Germany's surrender and the lingering effects of Roosevelt's sudden death, the drive surpassed its goal by 188 percent, netting $26.3 billion in just over fifty days.[41]

The sheer numbers involved in the Mighty Seventh and its predecessor drives are impressive. Yet one cannot ignore the role rhetoric played in their success. The persuasive nature of the bond drives is evident in the strategic choices made by Treasury planners as they adapted their messages to the ever-changing context of the war. Indeed, an examination of internal Treasury memorandums and correspondence demonstrates that the strategies behind this publicity were the product of a rhetorically sophisticated group of propagandists who were eager not only to sell bonds but also to influence the public's understanding of the war and to strengthen that public's commitment to it.

To be sure, the Treasury's strategists did not operate without direction. They took their orders from Morgenthau, who in turn served the president. Although it would be folly to argue that Roosevelt micromanaged the bond operation, it is clear that he was intensely interested in its progress, often giving time to war bond speeches and appearances at the invitation of Morgenthau, his personal friend. In fact, one can understand the Treasury's bond program as the war's best example of a decentralized propaganda machine—one that was coordinated by the Roosevelt administration at the highest levels, but that appeared to operate with independence. From one perspective, this so-called propaganda of the act gave the administration an extraordinary apparatus with which to attempt to shape public opinion. From another, it simultaneously insulated the president from the potentially damaging consequences of directly sponsoring propaganda that would target the wary home front.[42]

Clearly, the president was well aware—as was Morgenthau—that to be seen by the public as a propagandist was a serious political mistake. Indeed, some sixty years after the war the term "propaganda" still tends to bring to mind the very same negative connotations. Some theorists argue, however, that propaganda is essentially neutral, and that it can function on behalf of either good or evil causes—and sometimes both at once.[43] Without question, the Treasury's staffers did not feel that their propaganda efforts were inappropriate. On the contrary, Odegard—the program's initial strategist—argued very forcefully that "the essentially sophomoric assumption that all propaganda is necessarily wicked is giving way to a more sensible appraisal of the function of propaganda in society." "This new attitude," he continued, "enables us to pick and choose among competing propagandas and also consciously to use this ancient instrument for righteous ends instead of leaving it to be monopolized by the forces of darkness."[44] Thus, even if one assumes, as I do in this project, that "propaganda" is comprised of "strategically devised messages that are disseminated to masses of people by an institution for the purpose of generating action benefitting its source," one cannot assume that all propaganda is inherently negative.[45] Such a judgment, I suggest, requires careful rhetorical analysis of the propaganda texts in question.

Appropriately, the basis for this book's analysis of the Treasury's propaganda emerges from a rhetorical perspective. Aristotle argued that rhetoric was the ability to find in any given situation the possible means of persuasion.[46] Building from this definition, it follows that my task is not to create a historical narrative, although historical context is important to my approach. It also follows that my task is not to provide a personality-driven chronology, although some of the war bond campaign's participants feature prominently in my appraisal. Instead, my aim is to assess and critique the rhetorical appeals contained within the Treasury's public messages while simultaneously scrutinizing the behind-the-scenes activities of the practitioners. This approach merges text and context by examining private, archival documents to reveal the means by which the propagandists created their propaganda.[47] To reflect Aristotle's definition of rhetoric, this approach investigates the manner in which the war bond strategists found their means of persuasion, given their contextual situation. At the same time, my perspective emphasizes the dynamic nature of the Treasury's campaign, recognizing that long-term rhetorical efforts can present, refine, and re-present their appeals in numerous guises over a period of years.[48] Thus, what emerges in this project is both a dynamic interpretation and a rhetorical judgment, a hybrid product that lies at the intersection of rhetorical theory, historiography, and propaganda studies.[49]

The central aim of this book, therefore, is to examine both the private and public aspects of the Treasury's war bond publicity as a rhetorical exercise in propaganda production. Based on an analysis of primary documents in the National Archives and the Franklin D. Roosevelt Presidential Library, I seek to show how the Roosevelt administration depicted the war effort to the American people in the seven war bond drives and the postwar Victory Loan Drive. Of course, the dynamic nature of the conflict meant that the administration's propaganda efforts had to change in response to—or in anticipation of—the changing wartime context. Thus, I also seek to show how the strategic dimensions of this propaganda effort evolved over the course of the war, adapting to its international and domestic exigencies.

As one might expect, the war bond propagandists' public messages took advantage of most of the existing media outlets of the time, allowing the creation of their propaganda in both verbal and visual forms. For this reason, my rhetorical analysis of the Treasury's appeals focuses on a wide variety of textual formats. In some cases, for instance, I focus on verbal discourse describing the enemy, in other cases on visual metaphors equating war bonds with weapons, and in still other cases on artifacts that combine the verbal and the visual.[50]

Each of these cases, as I argue, formed one part of an overall effort by the Roosevelt administration to fashion a particular audience during the war. According to Edwin Black, discourse inevitably exerts "the pull of an ideology" on its audience. Such discourse reveals not only much about its producer but also about the "model of what the rhetor would have his real auditor become."[51] Following Black's perspective, the Treasury's verbal and visual strategies worked in combination throughout the war effort, dynamically seeking to fashion a public marked by devotion both to bond sales and to the war effort in general.

Remarkably, that public appeared to accept the Treasury's propaganda efforts with little suspicion—despite the home front's inherent mistrust of the official information agencies. Oddly enough, even the retired ambassador Gerard—who nearly thirty years earlier had warned that the Kaiser's propaganda might be duping the American public—was himself a prolific supporter of the war bond program.[52] This ironic scenario may have been due in part to the program's nature as a rhetorical hybrid. In one sense, the top-down character of the operation highlighted its nature as a long-term public campaign, defined as "purposive attempts to inform, persuade, or motivate behavior changes in a relatively well-defined and large audience . . . by means of organized communication activities involving mass media."[53] Typically, the structured nature of such planned campaigns features "assigned roles, organizational charts, chiefs of staff, schedules of operations, specific goals, and known end-points."[54] As is evident from even a quick glance at its archived organizational charts, opinion poll results, media schedules, and so on, the Treasury's war bond program did at times resemble the highly structured approach of a public communication campaign.

In another sense, however, the bond operation exhibited unrefined qualities typical of social movements. Charles J. Stewart, Craig Allen Smith, and Robert E. Denton Jr., for instance, argue that such movements "must change as circumstances change, rarely maintain tight control over memberships, and often alter and add to goals as they proceed."[55] The Treasury's consistent concern about public morale echoes Herbert W. Simons' suggestion that "an energized membership is the strength of any movement and its *esprit de corps* is essential to goal implementation."[56] Indeed, the Treasury's frequent adaptation to the public's dynamic moods during the war partly reflects the dictum that "social movements never proceed in orderly step-by-step fashion."[57]

At first, the tight structure of organized public campaigns and the loose adaptability of social movements seem incompatible. But the Treasury's hybrid bond operation shared both of these characteristics. This internal tension between structure and adaptability is reminiscent of the military's simultaneous use of *strategy* (structured planning for battle) and *tactics* (adaptation to events within the battle). In fact, an understanding of the war bond program as a quasi-military operation explains its nature as a structured campaign that freely adapted to the ever-changing context of the war and its target audience.[58] It also offers a possible explanation for the public's evident trust of the bond program's messages: despite its government sponsorship, here was an organization with an ad hoc approach and an urgent nature to match its grass-roots ethos.

From the perspective of military psychology, moreover, the strategies of campaigns and the activities of social movements share even more similarities. Traditionally, the top-down structure of a military operation is the classic example of an organized campaign. However, since World War I, the chaos of the modern battlefield has "rendered combatants passive and stripped officers and men alike of that 'offensive spirit.'"[59] Contemporary soldiers, then, must experience battle in a series of psychological stages, much like members of social movements do. According to Anthony Kellett, soldiers first undergo periods in which their superiors instill the products of "training" and "cohesion."[60] These preparations are meant to strengthen soldiers for combat situations, where they face three more psychological stages: "apprehensive enthusiasm," "resignation," and a "terminal period."[61] Social movements, to be sure, exhibit similar stages, including "genesis," "social unrest," "enthusiastic mobilization," "maintenance," and "termination."[62]

My perspective in this book, then, is to view the Treasury's "national defense effort"[63] as a militarized propaganda campaign. Unlike its etymological link with religious practices, propaganda in U.S. history was originally associated with times of war.[64] As a result of this historical relationship with war efforts, it makes sense that propaganda campaigns—particularly those begun in the midst of national mobilization—would adopt what Paul A. Chilton calls "the warfare script," complete with militarized language to match.[65] Consequently, one can understand the Treasury's bond campaign as a rhetorical effort, whether conscious or unconscious, to socialize the American public to support the war effort financially and patriotically in a manner echoing the strategies used to condition the military's soldiers for war. This mobilization of the Treasury's propaganda effort helped fashion a military perspective that constructed a dehumanized enemy. At war's end, this mind-set also helped transform the traumatic experience of the conflict into a perfecting myth, ultimately socializing the American public for the return of peace.

As might be expected, the strategies that emerged from this militarized mind-set changed through the stages of the propaganda campaign's development. More specifically, at each militarized stage, the Treasury adapted its approach by changing its visual and verbal depictions of the American people, U.S. soldiers, and their enemies. In the prewar *training* stage, the bond program worked to connect its new bonds with the burgeoning defense effort. In *cohesion,* the Treasury attempted to use the public's rage over Pearl Harbor to unify the home front. With its first bond drive, the Treasury initiated a stage of *apprehensive enthusiasm* by developing a conflation between civilians and soldiers. Once *resignation* set in, however, the bond strategists began to stress the ironic incongruities in this civilian-soldier conflation. Finally, with the war nearing its end, the Treasury negotiated the program's *terminal period* by transforming these civilians-turned-soldiers back into civilians, while simultaneously crafting a perfecting myth that justified the bloodshed of the war and affirmed the nation's transcendent Americanism.

The balance of this book explores these stages in detail. In chapter 1 I review the history of war bonds in the United States, focusing on how previous campaigns affected the direction of Morgenthau's bond drives and how the gradual approach of World War II militarized the Treasury's operations through stages of training and cohesion. Chapter 2 examines the stage of apprehensive enthusiasm in the three drives of late 1942 and throughout 1943. In chapter 3 I analyze the Treasury's struggle with the stage of resignation in its three 1944 drives. Chapter 4 explores the final two 1945 drives—the Mighty Seventh and the postwar Victory Loan Drive—by tracing their relationship to the terminal period of the Treasury's campaign. Finally, chapter 5 assesses the implications of the militarized propaganda campaign, ultimately concluding that while the Treasury's appeals aimed to fashion a spirit of national unity, they also fostered several troubling legacies.

I A HISTORY OF BONDS TO 1942

The Path to Training and Cohesion

A Stamp's a bullet, A bond's a gun.
Buy them both till the War is won.
—U.S. Treasury Department Booklet

From the minute the war broke out, I would buy a bond at payday. I felt that by saving the money through the government I wouldn't spend it, and at the same time they would have my money to use for the war effort.
—William Pefley, Navy Yard Worker

The summer of 1940 presented the Roosevelt administration with a frustrating set of challenges. In the European war, the Allies were losing their struggle against the German blitzkrieg. Late June brought the fall of France, giving Hitler unchallenged access to the Atlantic Ocean and its sea-lanes. In July the Royal Air Force found itself in increasingly desperate dogfights with the German Luftwaffe over British soil. By August London was under siege, and British leaders were anxiously appealing to the United States for more help.[1]

In the United States the unfolding drama of the European war formed the backdrop for a series of domestic problems. One important dispute being hashed out in the White House centered around the best way to present war news to the public. As worried advisers noted, even the severity of Allied losses had not significantly changed American public opinion on the war.[2] Interventionists urged the president to establish an official propaganda agency.[3] But Roosevelt was mindful of CPI's excesses during the Great War, and he recognized that many Americans remembered them well, too.[4]

Another significant problem was grounded in war finance. With recovery from the Depression still incomplete, the financial costs of another total war could potentially cripple the economy. Roosevelt and Winston Churchill's destroyers-for-bases arrangement, completed in September 1940, only made the economic situation more difficult.[5] How would the country pay for its growing involvement in the war? Some of Roosevelt's assistants suggested raising the money through comprehensive taxes and coercive savings programs. Such programs, they argued, would help ensure the quick flow of money to the war effort. But Treasury Secretary Henry F. Morgenthau Jr. saw more benefits in persuading people to provide voluntary financial contributions to support the war. The propaganda involved in that effort, he felt, would inevitably improve sagging public morale.[6]

These frustrating deliberations over war news and war finance continued to plague the Roosevelt administration for much of the conflict. In this chapter I argue that the Treasury's war bond program was both an important factor in these controversies as well as a benefactor of them. As the European war intensified, the nation's rapid mobilization on scores of fronts was exemplified by the militarized development of the defense bond propaganda campaign.[7] Thus, the war situation in 1940 not only highlighted the growing controversies over war news and war finance but also prompted Secretary Morgenthau to begin mobilizing what would become the Treasury Department's war bond machine.

In this chapter I focus on understanding how the Treasury's war bond campaign was formed. Morgenthau's Depression-era and World War II bond programs in their various guises developed in reaction to the Treasury's World War I bond campaign, as a result of Morgenthau's creative ideas, and in the context of America's struggle to mobilize. Moreover, the war bond program adapted to the dilemmas inherent in war news and war finance. In explicating these ideas, I explore war bonds prior to 1935, the "baby bonds" approach from 1935 to 1941, and the defense and war bond program as it developed in 1941 and 1942. The evolution of the bond program in the earliest stages of World War II evidences how the Treasury's military mind-set produced a discourse reflective of the psychological stages of training and cohesion. Such material provides a foundation for understanding the war bond drives of 1942–45, the centerpiece of this book.

Pre-1935 War Bonds

After Congress declared war in 1917, Treasury Secretary William G. McAdoo immediately began to research the methods of war finance established by his Civil War predecessor, Salmon P. Chase. McAdoo found that soon after Fort Sumter fell, Chase began a program of bond sales designed to help fund the Union's understaffed and ill-equipped forces. While Chase managed to force major banking interests to loan significant money to the war effort, he also appealed directly to the public for financial support.[8] Previous U.S. attempts at war finance had vacillated between war taxes and borrowing either from the wealthy or from other countries. Chase diverged from this tradition by attempting to create "a general distribution of the debt into the hands of the greatest number of holders."[9] To facilitate sales to this large target audience, Chase hired financier Jay Cooke as a deputy in charge of bond subscriptions.

Unfortunately for Chase's Treasury, the concept of individualized bonds was unfamiliar to Americans. As chief salesperson in the "National Loan," Cooke found himself explaining that bonds were simply government-issued certificates, purchased as temporary loans to the U.S. government. The bottom line, as Cooke suggested to thousands of potential investors, was that bond purchasers would gain a return on the initial investment once the bond reached maturity.[10] In this manner, Cooke actively solicited rich investors to buy the new product, using advertisements in local newspapers to broaden his appeals. However, since the bonds were negotiable (i.e., their value fluctuated with the market), many Union investors lost money when economic growth declined after the war.[11]

Some fifty years later, McAdoo found himself studying the Civil War bond efforts with a critical eye. He accepted the financial failures of Chase's loans as a natural result of a fluctuating market. But he found fault with Chase's program because it attempted to garner public support for bond sales by focusing on financial arguments. The dearth of overt patriotic appeals, McAdoo felt, limited Chase's revenues. As McAdoo later wrote, "Chase did not attempt to capitalize on the emotion of the people, yet it was there and he might have put it to use."[12]

McAdoo's World War I Treasury Department thus engineered four Liberty Loan drives and a postwar Victory Loan drive, all grounded in patriotic appeals. These efforts represented intense sales periods during which the Treasury blanketed the country with bond publicity that appealed to "patriotic rather than commercial motives."[13] In the First Loan, for example, a popular poster featured a feminine Liberty proclaiming, "You buy a Liberty Bond, lest I perish."[14] As McAdoo remembered more than ten years later, "our unpaid helpers . . . went to work with a patriotic fever that still thrills me with admiration when I think of it."[15]

The nationalistic flavor of McAdoo's Liberty Loan publicity was influenced, in part, by the new practice of propaganda. Indeed, the bond campaign had a strong connection with President Wilson's propaganda agency, the Committee on Public Information (CPI). From a philosophical perspective, both organizations viewed their propaganda efforts as quasi-military campaigns. Each group borrowed heavily from the language of warfare, transforming their organizational work into mobilization efforts and their propaganda blitzes into finely tuned military campaigns. CPI's leader, George Creel, characterized his mission as a "fight for the *minds* of men." "The battle-line," he wrote, "ran through every home in every country."[16] McAdoo was just as candid about the Treasury's "financial front," which exhibited "the same qualities of discipline, self-sacrifice, and devotion that characterized those who served in the trenches."[17] Both propaganda efforts, in other words, produced campaigns with a patriotic outlook and distinct military philosophy.

The two organizations had more pragmatic connections as well. CPI's "Four Minute Men," for instance, offered government-sponsored public speakers who supported the war effort. According to Thomas A. Hollihan, they "were especially useful in the Liberty Bond drives."[18] Furthermore, Stephen Vaughn points out that "nearly every war poster in support of [the Liberty Loan] bond drives was the work of the CPI."[19]

Because Americans were not yet alerted to the possibility that their leaders were using propagandistic appeals, the connection between CPI and Treasury was not hidden by the U.S. government. Indeed, unlike later presidents, Wilson was not forced to choose between calling his various publicity efforts information or propaganda. Thus, McAdoo's campaign evidenced little of the public tension that would appear in the postwar years, when Americans became more suspicious of propaganda practiced by the U.S. government.

Despite its CPI connection, however, McAdoo's patriotic bond campaign remained unconvincing for many of its recipients. Many found the Treasury's jingoistic messages less than reassuring and remained "uncomfortable converting a significant portion of their savings or earnings into what was to them a new and uncertain form of investment."[20] In fact, McAdoo's program derived its $21.5 billion in sales largely from banks and other financial groups that ignored the patriotic appeals and sought only investment opportunities.[21] While significant bond sales allowed McAdoo to claim that the public was voluntarily supporting the war, the true impact was inflationary, as the spending power of the people remained in competition for ever-scarcer home front products. To make matters worse, McAdoo followed Chase's lead by making his war bonds negotiable; thousands who risked their money on Liberty Loans found that they were a losing gamble.[22]

The World War I bond campaign's relative ineffectiveness was also evident in its gradual shift from voluntary appeals to outright coercion. The forcible atmosphere, recalled several of Roosevelt's aides years later, resulted in such tremendous pressure that children were bullied into buying bonds at school, and adults who could not (or would not) buy bonds often found their homes or barns painted yellow.[23] As Charles W. Smith argues, newspaper editorials condemning the brutal behavior were "little solace to the day laborers who were forced to buy bonds, the Oklahoman who had his car seized and sold . . . [or to] the eighty-four-year-old man who was forced to buy forty-five dollars worth of bonds to avoid being [labeled] a slacker."[24] Lawrence R. Samuel points out that "fear of being publicly shamed even drove many Americans to take out bank loans to purchase Liberty Bonds."[25]

The ultimate effect of World War I's loan drives, then, was to produce a disappointing number of sales, many of them the result of force and fear. In this respect, McAdoo's struggle to sell bonds foreshadowed the dilemma between coercion and voluntarism that Morgenthau's World War II bond programs would face. The fact that the Liberty Bond program was remembered not for its patriotic, voluntary nature but for the bullying tactics of its proponents suggests the salience of this dilemma. Still, some of McAdoo's war bond ideas would remain influential in later Treasury efforts.

Baby Bonds, 1935–1941

Fifteen years after McAdoo's Victory Loan ended, the Great Depression presented the Treasury with a financial situation just as challenging as financing war had been. The new Secretary of the Treasury, Henry F. Morgenthau Jr., again turned to public bonds as a means of enlisting citizens in the U.S. government's struggle. In March, 1935, the Roosevelt administration introduced several expensive federal initiatives designed to reduce unemployment.[26] Morgenthau proposed to help pay for the initiatives by allowing the U.S. government to borrow money through an inexpensively tailored savings bond program. While previous U.S. bond offerings had generally targeted financial institutions, Morgenthau's proposal offered bonds in denominations so low they would be attractive to average Americans. As John Morton Blum reports, Morgenthau believed that "the more people owning government securities . . . the greater would be the interest of Americans in the affairs of the government, in its strength, and in its credit."[27]

Morgenthau's innovation was to sell the new bonds as nonnegotiable securities that offered a fixed, rather than flexible, return. At the time, widespread banking failures, as well as the memory of

Roosevelt's National Banking Holiday, significantly decreased the public's willingness to undertake financial risks.[28] Presumably, thought Morgenthau, citizens would be attracted to federal notes that sold at only 75 percent of their face value, yet were guaranteed by the federal government to be redeemable after a ten-year maturity period at their full value. Moreover, he proposed that if the new bonds were refundable at any time, the risk factor would seem very low. Thus, although the bond investment did have an absolute profit limit, it had the virtue of a federal guarantee behind it and a money-back option. Combined with the variety of denominations available, Morgenthau hoped that these innovations would attract even the most skeptical members of the public.

Beginning on March 1, 1935, the Treasury offered the new bonds in Series A, B, C, and D. The administration described the new bonds as "a Share in America."[29] Although the advertising budget for the new program was minimal, the bonds quickly became well-known to the general public. The smallest denominations even earned the affectionate nickname "baby bonds." Only post offices and Federal Reserve Banks sold the new notes, yet in their six-year existence, total sales accounted for $3.9 billion.[30]

Initial sales were so encouraging that in 1936 Morgenthau commissioned a Division of Savings Bonds within the Treasury Department.[31] The bond organizations of Secretary Chase and Secretary McAdoo had been dismantled after the Civil War and World War I, respectively. The 1936 establishment of the Division of Savings Bonds, therefore, was the first time the Treasury created such an office during peacetime. Although it has endured dramatic changes over the years, this organization still exists as the Bureau of the Public Debt.

To head the novel organization, Morgenthau appointed Eugene W. Sloan, a sales and marketing executive from Saint Louis. Under Sloan's direction, the division compiled a mailing list for an "aggressive direct-mail campaign," sending out 125,000 advertisements per month.[32] The initial appeals, recalled Sloan, portrayed "the 'Girl with the Flag' trademark," an image that appeared in "posters, magazine ads, car cards and point-of-sale material."[33] By 1937 the Treasury even hired several advertising agencies to promote baby bonds to the public.[34]

From 1935 to early 1941, these promotions helped sell more than 19 million baby bonds. Although most Americans were still struggling to recover from the Depression, a wide cross section of the country purchased the bonds. From the Treasury's perspective, the successful sales created "a picture of national prudence and purpose and patriotism, virtues that Morgenthau esteemed."[35] Perhaps more importantly, the Depression-era baby bond program was instrumental in increasing public confidence in the U.S. government's solvency, setting the stage for the much larger defense bonds campaign of 1941 and 1942.

Defense and War Bonds, 1941–1942

In the years following the baby bonds' introduction, growing tensions in Europe began to attract the Roosevelt administration's attention. By the summer of 1940, stunning German advances against Denmark, Norway, Belgium, the Netherlands, and France brought renewed urgency to the administration's discreet preparations for possible U.S. involvement in the war. With recovery from the Depression still incomplete, one of the most urgent discussions in the White House centered around the issue of war finance. This discussion continued into the early years of American involvement in the war.

Shifting to Defense Bonds

The White House deliberations over war finance in the summer of 1940 quickly revealed tension between advisers who supported coercive financial policies and those who backed a voluntary approach. Those in favor of enforced financial measures were influenced by British economist John Maynard Keynes, who had just published his monograph *How to Pay for the War.* Keynes was well-known for his advocacy of macroeconomic controls; in this new book he suggested a way for wartime governments to reach the "equilibrium between the spending power in people's pockets and what can be released for their consumption."[36] His conclusion was that the administration needed to institute tax increases and enforced savings programs. Without these steps, he argued, the nation risked significant inflation, as war workers' increased spending power competed for increasingly scarce or rationed products.

Following Keynes's lead, many of Roosevelt's advisers actively favored a system of war taxes combined with compulsory savings. Two of the most influential figures who shared Keynes's views were Marriner Eccles, head of the Federal Reserve Board, and Harold Smith, Roosevelt's budget director. Each was aware of the financial achievements of Morgenthau's baby bond sales campaign, but they correctly pointed out how much more a robust defense program would cost. They argued that the alternative of temporarily requiring workers to forfeit regular payroll deductions to the U.S. government would quickly raise money while simultaneously slowing inflation by reducing the public's ability to spend extra cash on scarce products.[37]

Morgenthau disagreed with such coercive measures. "I am against anything that is compulsory in this country," he told reporters. "It is just exactly what we don't want."[38] Instead, the secretary preferred a system of voluntary loans, paid for by Americans out of their patriotic support for national defense. If structured similarly to his successful baby bond program, Morgenthau thought, the voluntary loan system would present significant advantages over Keynesian-style coercion. From a financial perspective, he felt that such voluntarism could raise just as much money as compulsory policies, while maintaining the good will of both Congress and the American public.[39]

However, neither Congress nor the American public were ready for battle in the summer of 1940. Despite a growing sentiment for the Allies in the wake of the Battle of Britain, much of the country continued to resist American involvement in the war. Isolationist sentiment had remained strong in the United States after World War I, and it grew into a strident anti-interventionist movement throughout 1940. One of the most respected voices decrying American intervention was the Committee to Defend America First, which was established in September 1940 even as the Luftwaffe bombed London. Among the well-known personalities of the so-called America First Committee were former Wisconsin governor Philip LaFollette, actress Lillian Gish, and Theodore Roosevelt's daughter Alice Roosevelt Longworth. By late summer, the organization boasted 750 local chapters and ten thousand acting members.[40]

To many in the Roosevelt administration, the anti-interventionist philosophy exemplified by America First was ill-informed and even dangerous. Addressing White House concerns that the public was either indifferent to the war situation or actively against American involvement, some of Roosevelt's confidantes began to press him to establish a domestic propaganda program. Britain's struggle to survive Hitler's increasingly massive bombings in the late summer intensified the discussions. As Richard W. Steele describes them, these deliberations focused on the creation of "a national morale (or propaganda) agency with wide-ranging powers to combat isolationism."[41] But despite Roosevelt's sincere desire to encourage public support for militarization, he continued to be wary of repeating President Wilson's mistakes in the Great War.

Roosevelt's ambivalence lay both in his desire for the powerful effects of an organized propaganda effort and in his fear that the public would recognize those efforts as propaganda. Two insistent groups of advisers urged Roosevelt to take their side of the dilemma. One group, led by Lowell Mellett, was opposed to any form of U.S. government propaganda, even if labeled an "information" agency.[42] The other group was led by Roosevelt's most influential confidante, Harry Hopkins. This group advocated a strategy termed "propaganda of the act," which Steele describes as "a straightforward propaganda effort loosely coordinated by the administration and carried out at the local level." The advantage of this approach was the administration's indirect involvement, keeping Roosevelt "relatively safe from the hostile criticism a propaganda agency might attract."[43]

In typical fashion, the president made a show of listening to both sides, but his drawn-out indecision frustrated the rival groups. As a longtime Roosevelt friend, Morgenthau was very aware of the president's indecision. The secretary agreed with many others in the White House that France's utter defeat was due to "a failure of national will" in the face of Nazi propaganda.[44] As Secretary of the Interior Harold Ickes said to Morgenthau privately, "this morale stuff . . . is of tremendous importance." "You know," he continued, "that that's what licked France and Belgium and all the rest, that it wasn't the armies of the Germans, it is Goebbel's [*sic*] propaganda." Worst of all, confided Ickes, "we're doing nothing to meet it."[45] Morgenthau shared Ickes's frustration, feeling in particular that the isolationists were indirectly creating a similar situation in the United States. Moreover, he felt that those who decried government-sponsored propaganda were in effect entrenching the isolationist viewpoint. Thus, as Roosevelt continued to vacillate on the issue, Morgenthau decided that the Treasury would have to play a role in the situation.

In the fall of 1940, then, Morgenthau began planning a national defense bond program that would unite the nonnegotiable attractiveness of the baby bonds with the patriotic appeal of McAdoo's Liberty Bonds in the Great War. Such a program would give him a chance to demonstrate that voluntarism would be more effective than financial coercion. Simultaneously, the program's sales publicity would present an alternative to an official propaganda arm by offering the administration a significant, if unorthodox, opportunity to present its views on the war. Both Morgenthau and Roosevelt later agreed that the Treasury's efforts could be the best way to "make the country war-minded."[46] As the secretary lamented privately, "there just isn't any other vehicle" to raise the necessary funds and public support for the war.[47]

Despite the initial optimism of Morgenthau's ideas, however, there were several barriers to the establishment of a national defense bond program. Congress had previously set a debt limit of $4 billion on the Treasury, effectively restraining the administration's authority to raise the amount of money a war demanded. The same legislation stipulated that all Treasury securities must mature within five years of purchase, meaning that Morgenthau could rely only on short-term financial offerings. Furthermore, even though the nation was beginning the gradual and expensive process of rearmament, with the upcoming presidential campaign, looking eager for war was too great a risk.[48]

Roosevelt's healthy margin of victory in the 1940 election, however, was widely interpreted to be a general approval of the administration's now-obvious dislike of German and Japanese aggression.[49] With four more years as a comfort margin, asking the new Congress to approve a higher debt ceiling seemed safe. On February 12, 1941, Morgenthau appeared before the Senate Finance Committee and outlined his vision of a defense bond program. He emphasized to the worried panel that unlike McAdoo's World War I efforts, his new program would not use "high-pressure salesmanship or coercive propaganda."[50] Instead, he told a House committee, the Treasury wished to sell "securities of a character which should facilitate and promote thrift and savings. . . . I can think of no other single way," he continued, "in which so many people can become partners of their Government in facing this emergency. It is the purpose of the Treasury to raise money for national defense by methods which strengthen the national morale."[51] As American and British military representatives began a two-month meeting in Washington to discuss how U.S. entry into the war might proceed, and as German submarine warfare in the Atlantic reached new heights, Congress approved the Treasury's proposal for a $65 billion debt limit in mid-February, 1941.[52]

Meanwhile, Morgenthau's attention was being drawn to Britain's deteriorating financial condition. The flow of arms across the Atlantic was endangered when Britain began to exhaust its dollar and gold reserves. By mid-December, 1940, Churchill had little to offer Roosevelt in exchange for military supplies and arms. With the election safely behind him, though, Roosevelt felt he now had some breathing room. On December 17, he publicly proposed leasing munitions to the British, using the now-famous analogy of a neighbor's house fire.[53] He asked Morgenthau to draft a bill making such an arrangement acceptable under American law.[54] On January 10,

1941, lend-lease was introduced into Congress as House Bill 1776. After two months of partisan debate, Morgenthau's bill made it to Roosevelt's desk, and the president signed it into law on March 11. Although the new law was a great political victory for FDR, it increased the immediate costs of war for the United States by earmarking much of the country's expensive war production for what amounted to cost-free use by Allied nations.

Fortunately for the administration, the bond program that would ultimately help pay for much of the lend-lease expense was mobilizing even as Congress debated the merits and dangers of H.R. 1776. In early January, 1941, Morgenthau asked Peter H. Odegard, an Amherst College political scientist specializing in propaganda studies, to draw up a list of objectives for the defense bond program.[55] Morgenthau's interest in Odegard's thinking stemmed from the 1938 book *American Politics: A Study in Political Dynamics*. In this work, Odegard and coauthor E. Allen Helms examined the relationship between political actors, public opinion, and pressure groups. Of particular interest to Morgenthau were the chapters covering "the engineering of consent," in which Odegard and Helms analyzed several uses of "the fine art of propaganda." In great detail, the authors described the use of press releases, identification symbols, emotional appeals, and polling data. Using these and other strategies, they argued, a seasoned propagandist could create "a gigantic symphony" of persuasion.[56]

Although Odegard's book criticized Roosevelt's 1936 campaign style, the scholar's knowledge of propaganda techniques and personal support of the New Deal made him a logical adviser for the Treasury. Soon after Odegard accepted Morgenthau's offer to study the Treasury's options for a defense bond program, Amherst granted him leave to join the new effort in Washington on a semipermanent basis. Before long, he would become the program's visionary; his counsel shaped the campaign in long-lasting ways.[57]

In his initial study of the proposed program, Odegard quickly agreed with Morgenthau that the proposed bonds should build on the success of the baby bonds (Series A, B, C, and D). Now to be called "defense" bonds, the newer notes would represent three new series (E, F, and G); Series E would target the individual citizen-investor.[58] Like the baby bonds, the new bond sold for as little as $18.75 and matured in ten years, at which time the U.S. government paid the bondholder $25. Larger denominations of $50, $100, $500, and $1,000 were also available. All the defense bonds were nonnegotiable, a feature that Odegard hoped would ease fears that a postwar depression could once again make U.S. government bonds a poor investment.

To maximize sales, Odegard suggested that the bonds be sold at banks, post offices, and other financial institutions across the country. For those who found it difficult to invest even $18.75, the plan also called for a series of ten-cent savings stamps. The stamps would accumulate in Treasury-approved stamp albums until they totaled enough for a bond purchase.[59] Finally, Odegard envisioned an ongoing propaganda campaign that would encourage private investors to purchase defense bonds on a regular basis. Like Morgenthau, he saw in such bond propaganda an opportunity to affect domestic morale. In an early memo, he suggested that "the success of our Savings campaign will depend in the final analysis upon the extent to which we can get the American people to believe in themselves."[60]

Fearing unfavorable comparisons with the World War I war bond program, Morgenthau and Odegard took pains to suggest that the developing campaign would avoid McAdoo's mistakes. The secretary told journalists covering the developing organization that the new bond campaign "would try to profit from [the] experience of the Liberty Loans and War Savings campaigns of the last war."[61] True to Morgenthau's word, the Treasury exhaustively researched McAdoo's bond propaganda. While they found merit in some of McAdoo's ideas, both Morgenthau and Odegard were troubled by the coercive tactics used in the Liberty Loan efforts, and they resolved that their own campaign "would be devoid of high-pressure methods or flag-waving of any sort."[62]

An important part of this low-key approach was an initial reluctance to renew the World War I pattern of repeated drives. The intensive study of the Liberty Drives led Treasury staffers to conclude that "there should be no 'drive' psychology, no hysteria, and no devices to honor purchasers that would stigmatize non purchasers."[63] If the Treasury could saturate the nation in defense bond appeals, they believed, the public would respond. The writer of an anonymous Treasury memorandum later agreed, pointing out that "instead of fixing financial quotas for communities and industries, as was done in . . . World War [I], the only kind of quota we now want is to get the largest possible number of people to subscribe."[64]

With such lofty goals in mind, Morgenthau and Odegard ultimately settled on a comprehensive selling program designed to accomplish three specific objectives. First, the bonds would raise money for the war effort. Second, significant sales would—along with the inevitable war taxes—decrease the amount of available spending money in the economy, which would combat inflation. Finally, the selling program would increase popular support of the war by allowing the average home front citizen to participate in the struggle.

It was this last goal that most intrigued Morgenthau. After all, to most Americans, the ongoing European conflict remained only stark headlines from another continent.[65] But Morgenthau and Odegard were convinced that the defense bonds could act as a way to mobilize a badly divided nation in the looming face of war. Ironically, Roosevelt had planted the seeds for such a civilian mobilization some years before. In the first one hundred days of his initial term, the president recast the struggle against the Depression as a virtual war. One of the aims of his "inauguration-day call to arms," it seems, had been to construct a "great army" that would fight the Depression on a vast economic battlefield.[66]

As the United States gradually drew nearer to entering a real-world war some years later, however, Roosevelt seemed hesitant to inaugurate a propaganda organ that might officially call such a home front army into being. Throughout the first half of 1941, he continued to delay his decision on an official propaganda agency. Although Roosevelt finally established an Office of Civilian Defense (OCD) in May 1941, he failed to give the agency a clear mission.[67] Thus, whether it was by circumstance or by design, the president was already relying on Morgenthau's bond program to mobilize public attention on the war. As David Brinkley argues, the president hoped that the new war bonds "would give the public a sense of involvement in a war . . . so distant many Americans had difficulty at times remembering it was there at all."[68]

Odegard advised Morgenthau that using bond publicity to achieve such public unity would require an optimistic emphasis. In pursuit of an optimistic campaign theme, Odegard suggested that the Treasury's propaganda would need to focus on "*plus* symbols." Such appeals, he argued, "must find repeated and insistent expression in . . . copy for the radio, the press, motion pictures, and every other avenue of communication and expression."[69] Building on his academic research into propaganda, he provided examples of such themes, including "America," "Battleship," "Work," "Protect," "Home," and "Freedom."[70] "Never lose sight," he wrote, "of the things we are called on to defend: the Bill of Rights, our standard of living, our homes and families." The Treasury's propaganda, he concluded, "ought to be general enough for a wide variety of particularizations and yet concrete enough to avoid being an 'oblong blur.'"[71]

An important part of Odegard's proposed focus was the selection of an official defense bond symbol. In his quest for a "distinctly American" image to represent the program, he considered and rejected the Statue of Liberty, the U.S. Capitol, the Washington Monument, and Mount Rushmore.[72] Fellow propaganda expert Harold D. Lasswell recommended that Odegard consider the use of four arrows to tie into Roosevelt's four freedoms. Since three arrows had been the symbol used by the democratic Weimar Republic, Lasswell felt that the symbol would be inspirational to the masses of Germans who privately despised Hitler.[73] Odegard, uncertain that the bond program's symbol would have much effect on foreign populations, rejected Lasswell's idea.

Finally, Odegard decided to adopt Daniel Chester French's sculpture of the Minute Man as the Treasury program's official symbol. The image, he argued, was well-known and distinctly American.[74] The choice thus provided the bond program's proponents with a universal, populist image. As Sloan recalled, the new symbol "could be threaded through all of our publicity," quickly identifying the product as defense bonds and stamps.[75] Months later, Odegard wrote that "posters featuring the *Minute Man* proved to be so popular that it was almost impossible to keep up with the demands for them."[76]

The selection of the Minute Man as the Treasury campaign's central symbol marked an important philosophical choice. It was an image that recalled the American Revolution's sudden transformation of plowshares into swords, and civilians into soldiers. Despite the apt symbolism, however, Odegard decided to make a few changes to the image. Indeed, the bond program's adaptation of the sculpture showed just how militarized its propaganda campaign would be.

The original sculpture in Concord, Massachusetts, illustrates the tension between times of peace and times of war as the Minute Man holds in his right hand a musket while his left hand rests on the handle of a plow (see fig. 1.1). In contrast, the Treasury's new insignia tellingly featured the *Minute Man* sculpture at an angle that made the musket much more visible, leaving the plow slightly obscured behind the citizen-soldier (see fig. 1.2). From this perspective, the Treasury's version of the *Minute Man* was unmistakably a direct reflection of the nation's increasingly rapid mobilization. Although Pearl Harbor was still more than eight months away, large portions of the nation were already preparing for war.[77] As evidenced by the Minute Man image, the Treasury's war preparations reflected the mind-set of a military operation from its inception. Morgenthau's

1.1 The original *Minute Man* sculpture, by Daniel Chester French. Note the artist's emphasis on both the plow and the musket, suggesting the citizen-soldier's potential for transformation. Photograph by Carol Krauss, published by permission of the Town of Concord, Mass.

1.2 The original insignia of the Treasury's World War II bond program, featuring the *Minute Man* sculpture at an angle obscuring its plow and highlighting its musket. Courtesy Franklin D. Roosevelt Library.

bond program, in other words, was also beginning to mobilize for war.[78]

As early as the spring of 1941, then, the program that would ultimately sell billions of bonds to Americans had a firm philosophical foundation. Like the World War I effort, the new bond division would produce a patriotic operation with a distinct military flair. Yet unlike McAdoo's jingoistic and coercive efforts to wrest money from the public, Morgenthau's Treasury understood that its challenges were only partly financial. By selling the idea of national unity and pride to Americans, they sought to raise desperately needed money and at the same time stimulate public support for the coming war. It was "a kind of campaign," wrote Odegard, "peculiarly adapted to the democratic pattern of American life, simultaneously exploiting and extolling American traditions and institutions."[79]

The Defense Bond Program as a Training Phase

With its philosophical direction established, the Treasury was ready to organize the bond program's public debut. The dramatic public opening planned by Odegard would usher in the propaganda campaign's equivalent of a militarized training phase. With this initial step in mobilizing the public, the Treasury began its attempt to "replace civil with military attitudes" in its target audience. The nationwide introduction of the bond program's mission simultaneously began another aim of the training phase, the process of propagating "the values, sentiments, and attitudes" of the Treasury program.[80] With its public unveiling, then, the propaganda campaign was in effect kicking off the psychological equivalent of a national boot camp. In this intensive training period, the Treasury's ubiquitous publicity would be attempting to prepare the public for its militarized role in the coming battle.

To organize the final preparations before the program's public unveiling, Morgenthau summoned several other workers to the operation. One of them was Assistant Treasury Secretary Harold Graves, Morgenthau's most trusted staffer. Graves emerged as the primary organizer of the initial bond program, and his logistical abilities helped the bond division mobilize quickly.[81] On March 19, 1941, Morgenthau officially established the Defense Savings Staff (DSS), and by mid-April, the new group already had forty people on its staff.[82]

Working furiously, the staff soon gained momentum. DSS recruited state directors and personnel, wrote and printed ad copy, and designed and produced the new bonds. In the Radio Section,

Vince Callahan formulated a publicity campaign that called not only for five to ten bond announcements per day on all stations nationwide, but also for fifteen-minute and half-hour bond programs. Callahan recruited New York advertising agencies to help write copy. Once DSS approved the radio campaign, it asked stations across the country if they would air the announcements. As Callahan later noted, it would soon become "the biggest radio announcement campaign in the history of radio."[83]

By late April all was ready, and on the evening of April 30, 1941, Morgenthau and Roosevelt appeared on national network radio to kick off the new campaign. Marking the occasion, Morgenthau told the nation that now, "in every state and county, city and town in America—it will be possible for everyone—literally everyone—to have a chance in the National Defense effort." "Why does your government want the savings of the people?" he asked. Because, he continued, "your government wants to give every one of you a chance to have a financial stake in American Democracy . . . an opportunity to contribute toward the defense of that democracy and the right to say to yourself, 'I am doing something to help.'"[84]

Only one day after Morgenthau's dramatic pronouncement, the American public found itself buying millions of defense bonds. Bolstered by $100 million in sales on the first day, the Treasury was soon convinced that it was possible to divert 10 percent of the public's income into bonds.[85] Through the summer and fall of 1941, the Treasury continuously emphasized its 10 percent goal. Morgenthau's war bond workers reached out to schoolchildren, city residents, factory workers, and farm families. In support of the campaign, Morgenthau asked Irving Berlin to write a song for the defense bond program. "Any Bonds Today?" quickly became a popular tune and soon emerged as the theme song for the *Treasury Hour*, a weekly radio show begun in July 1941.[86] The Treasury's propaganda in this and other initial venues featured its militarized perspective, especially with its adaptation of James Montgomery Flagg's well-known World War I recruitment poster depicting a craggy Uncle Sam pointing at the viewer, asking "will YOU?"[87] Meanwhile, as Morgenthau's group continued to mobilize workers throughout the country, the central war bond staff in Washington swelled to more than 250 workers.[88]

Thus, although the Japanese attack on Pearl Harbor would not happen for another seven months, the Treasury's financial preparations for war were already well under way. As Hitler's Panzers began their surprise invasion of the Soviet Union on June 22, 1941, the recognizably patriotic Minute Man image was nearly everywhere, already featured on 30 million stamp albums and 2 million stickers, promoted by 150,000 newspaper carriers and sold from more than 250,000 sales outlets.[89] The early defense bonds also had their own poster, featuring the Minute Man and alternating slogans: "For Defense," "America on Guard," "Buy a Share in America," and "Four Freedoms Forever."[90] By mid-July an unidentified advertising executive remarked that "no promotional campaign, commercial, governmental or Goebbels', has ever spread its basic message so broadly, so quickly."[91]

The Treasury's efforts in this initial training phase, of course, occurred in the larger context of the nation's psychological mobilization for war. Interventionist sentiment grew throughout 1941 as those sympathetic to Britain and those horrified by Hitler's actions rallied to support a war movement. After August, when Roosevelt and Churchill met secretly, off the coast of Newfoundland, most Americans began to realize that the nation's involvement in war was imminent.[92] From a psychological perspective, then, large segments of the public were preparing themselves for direct involvement in the war.

From the Treasury's viewpoint, this psychological preparation for war was an important outgrowth of the bond campaign's sales efforts. Yet the success of this initial training phase appeared to be mixed because the public's mental preparation for war still seemed incomplete. On the positive side, 97 percent of the public had heard of defense bonds.[93] The Bureau of Engraving and Printing was producing two hundred thousand bonds per day.[94] Citizens had already purchased more than $2 billion in bonds.[95] And, each day, the public was targeted with the Treasury's ubiquitous propaganda, ever emphasizing "the spectacular achievements of the American people . . . the virtues of their institutions . . . [and] the advantages of their way of life over that which prevails in totalitarian countries."[96] Evidently, if the Treasury was training the public to accept its militarized philosophy, it was having some effect.

On the negative side, however, one poll suggested that only 12 percent of Americans had actually purchased defense bonds or stamps. Only 12 percent more had made any plans to purchase bonds in the future.[97] Moreover, most sales to date had been made to larger investors—such as banks and other financial institutions—and not the wage earners the Treasury most wanted to win over.[98] Worst of all from Morgenthau's standpoint, the public remained largely divided in its opinions on the war. Thus, while the Treasury's training phase seemingly captured the public's attention, the home front's psychological mobilization was still incomplete. Evidently the Treasury's propaganda campaign needed what James Darsey calls a "catalytic event" to push it into the next stage of its militarized development.[99] That event occurred on December 7, 1941.

The Transition to War Bonds and the Struggle for Cohesion

The day after Pearl Harbor, sales of defense bonds increased immediately. In Saint Louis, for example, bond purchases rose 121 percent in one week, and 358 firms in the city adopted the payroll deduction plan for buying bonds.[100] New York City's demand for bonds jumped 800 percent, and in Los Angeles—a city fearing an imminent Japanese attack—bond sales increased by 1400 percent.[101] Morgenthau called the increased sales "extremely satisfactory," but also directed the bond staff to develop "a much more intensified selling campaign."[102]

From a military psychology perspective, this intensified selling campaign signaled that the Treasury's mobilization efforts were now beyond an initial training phase and into a cohesion phase. Here the bond strategists were using the Treasury's bond machine to foster a sense of esprit de corps among home front Americans, hoping that the public would come together in support of the war effort. They were simultaneously working to create "enthusiasm, devotion, and strong regard for the honor" of a militarized America.[103]

Some of the enthusiasm for this militarization emerged in the swift demise of the label "defense" bonds. Although the change was not official until June, the public soon began using the term "war" bonds to refer to the Treasury's products. The Defense Savings Staff quickly underwent a similar change.[104] The new War Savings Staff hurriedly attempted to capitalize on the fervor created by Pearl Harbor by distributing 20 million copies of a pamphlet called "Our America." To Morgenthau's chagrin, however, some weeks later, "only 17 percent of those interviewed remembered having seen 'Our America,'" and "nearly two-thirds read less than half of it."[105] Indeed, aware that rationing would inevitably arrive, many spent January purchasing the groceries and supplies that were most likely to become scarce in the coming months, quickly reducing bond sale gains.[106] To make matters worse, the U.S. military was hardly ready to fight on a global level. The United States was girding itself for serious warfare, but the process was slow and the distractions were many.

From the Treasury's perspective, some of these distractions took the form of other promotional campaigns that sprang from the necessities of the new war. As many as sixty-two government campaigns urged citizens to take action on the home front.[107] Alongside bond posters, for example, were banners for rubber conservation, victory gardens, scrap metal drives, rationing, armed forces recruitment, and women-in-the-workforce. The bond sales program, however, was easily the largest and "most pervasive" of these campaigns.[108] One internal Treasury study found that more war bond posters were displayed in storefronts than were posters for all other U.S. government campaigns combined.[109] With its massive workforce, obvious government approval, and ubiquitous publicity, the sheer size of the project inevitably helped it stand out against the many competing distractions of the war.

One of the Treasury's early approaches in this project was a national pledge campaign. Hoping to reverse slowing bond sales in the face of rationing, some 10 million volunteers spent March and April, 1942, canvassing the nation's households with pledge cards in which citizens promised to purchase bonds each payday.[110] Other representatives visited factories and plants, trying to persuade workers to agree to divert at least 10 percent of their paycheck directly into bond purchases.[111] In a sense, these volunteers were trying to spread the Treasury's militarized message in support of national cohesion. As Morgenthau exhorted such volunteers in a January meeting, "total wars are peoples' wars; and in this total war that has spread around the globe, the battlefront now reaches into every factory and every home."[112]

The personal touch of the canvassers, the Treasury staff hoped, would add an individual appeal to the virtues of bond buying. The *Handbook for Canvassers* suggested that "the campaign is based on faith in Americans—faith that our citizens are eager for a chance to help defend our freedom."[113] The president himself told Morgenthau: "I want a sign in everybody's window not just saying, 'I bought a War Bond,' but that 'I buy a War Bond every month.'"[114] And Morgenthau instructed his campaigners "to demonstrate that the method of . . . voluntary response . . . is not only the American way, but is also the most efficient way to enlist the billions of dollars upon which our final and certain triumph will depend."[115]

Yet because the proponents of compulsory savings were renewing their criticism of the Treasury's voluntary sales program, Morgenthau also sought outside help for the localized canvassing strategy. For instance, advertisements in the Treasury's pledge campaign became the first task of the newly formed War Advertising Council.[116] Similarly, the initial projects of the War Writers' Board were primarily Treasury assignments.[117] Morgenthau also enlisted the support of Claude Wickard, the secretary of agriculture, as well as William Green and Philip Murray, the heads of the AFL and the CIO. Since all three were known to oppose compulsory savings plans, their support of the pledge campaign was natural.[118]

By late April, 1942, however, the bond program was again under attack by influential politicians and newspapers to give way to a compulsory loan program. As Henry C. Murphy puts it, "the government deficit was increasing rapidly, inflationary pressures were strong, and the Treasury was under great pressure to 'do something' about its savings bond sales program or else adopt more drastic techniques."[119] Thus, when Morgenthau assigned each state a war bond quota for May, June, and July, the Treasury's increasing desperation was becoming evident.[120] The pledge campaign's personal touch was not working well enough.

War Savings Staff in Crisis

Clearly, the Treasury's attempts to foster national cohesion were in some respects flawed. True, millions were buying war bonds, at least occasionally. But the realities and distractions of the material war created an atmosphere in which it was difficult to prepare the public for the challenges that the war would soon present. As George H. Roeder notes, it was nearly impossible "to maintain the intensity of popular feeling created by the Japanese attack. . . . Americans, protected by two oceans and the country's seemingly endless natural resources, were not really fighting a total war."[121]

One of the few bright spots for the Treasury in the summer of 1942 was the release of its *Victory War Comics,* produced in cooperation with the Family Comics corporation. Filled with scenes of familiar characters buying war bonds—including Blondie, Li'l Abner, the Green Hornet, Joe Palooka, and Superman—the comic book had two initial printings of 250,000 each and proved to be quite popular.[122] Even though its primary targets were more likely to purchase a ten-cent war stamp than a twenty-five-dollar war bond, the Treasury was pleased with the publicity. As Thomas H. Lane, one of the Treasury's publicity managers, said, "the cartoons . . . are one of the outstanding features of the whole War Bond campaign. They are done by the best people in America, get an excellent pick-up, and of course, command wide reading."[123]

Despite such isolated successes, however, the Treasury was finding it increasingly difficult to foster national cohesion with its "sporadic and infrequent" propaganda.[124] Aside from Odegard's Minute

Man symbol, the Treasury's campaign lacked a unifying focus. Odegard himself privately told pollster Hadley Cantril that he was exasperated at "the rather helter-skelter character of our own promotional activities."[125] In the field, frustration was beginning to produce "overzealous" attempts to coerce bond purchases; there were also indications that the canvassers were missing significant numbers of households.[126] Beyond that, struggles were developing within Treasury over the content of advertisements. As Lane, the publicity manager, said, "some people thought we should lean heavily on patriotic appeal, others on self-interest, others thought primarily of inflation, but they were all guesses and estimates: no one really knew or had any scientific data."[127]

This sort of confusion was also evident in the president's continuing struggle over the use of an official government propaganda program. The nation's entrance into the war led to even more intense cries for an effective propaganda agency. Bowing to pressure, Roosevelt created the Office of Facts and Figures (OFF) under Archibald MacLeish. The new organization was to succeed the floundering OCD. Yet Roosevelt gave the new agency a confusing mandate and little access to the Oval Office—the same flaws that helped destroy OCD. Moreover, upon Roosevelt's declaration of war, the military made it clear to OFF that it would allow little substantive information to be released. By February 1942, OFF had lost what little public confidence it possessed.[128]

The resulting information vacuum did little to inspire the public. As Robert Sherwood (eventual head of OWI's overseas branch) remembered it, the mess "seemed to boil down to three bitter complaints: first, that there was too much information; second, that there wasn't enough of it; and third, that in any event it was too confusing and inconsistent."[129] After much indecision, the president finally attempted to address the issue in June 1942, by creating the Office of War Information (OWI). However, in typical fashion, he limited the agency's real power in several ways, including the assignment of "a number of potentially conflicting functions."[130]

Meanwhile, the Treasury was facing its own problems. Sales continued to fall below projections through the spring and summer of 1942, signaling further disruptions in the cohesion stage. Simultaneously, the outflow of Treasury funds for the war effort reached $100 million per day in April, and $200 million per day by the end of the year.[131] To make matters worse, Morgenthau publicly promised to achieve $1 billion per month in bond sales.[132] Although Roosevelt still supported the Treasury's voluntary system in private, he made it clear that unless the bond operation improved its sales, forced savings could result. As the president said in a cabinet meeting in July, "Henry has promised to raise $1,000,000,000 a month and he's got his neck out. . . . [L]et him hang himself if he wants to or else . . . his head goes caput!"[133] As a consequence of this embarrassing scene, and of growing public criticism, Morgenthau began to doubt that he could rely on pledges and quotas to accomplish the Treasury's financial, economic, and morale goals.

The pressure on Morgenthau increased as the summer passed. To some, it was becoming clear that the Treasury's pledge campaigns were failing to sell the war effectively. Pollsters pointed out that almost one-third of the country still did not know what the U.S. was fighting for.[134] *Reader's Digest* agreed, noting that "[t]he American people are holding back. . . . [T]here is no difference of opinion among them as to winning the war; but to get them aroused to win . . . requires a higher standard."[135] From a financial perspective, the news was also getting worse. War expenses so outpaced Treasury income that in early October 1942, the war bond effort nearly ran out of operational funds.[136]

As one of the few policy makers who continued to support the war bond program, Morgenthau felt increasingly besieged. On August 6, 1942, Wayne Coy—the acting director of the Bureau of the Budget—told the president that "there is a growing unanimity of opinion, both in and out of Congress, that adoption of compulsory saving will soon become necessary."[137] Roosevelt privately asked the Treasury secretary, "Henry, now that your War Bonds are not going so well, what are you going to do about it?"[138] On September 1, Morgenthau informed his confidantes that the country had "enough money in the Treasury to last . . . from fourteen to seventeen days, which is not enough." He then told his assistant Harold Graves that he was reluctantly considering a shift away from bonds and into compulsory savings.[139]

Thus, as American participation in the war neared its first anniversary, the continuing crises surrounding war news and war finance appeared increasingly insoluble. Neither Roosevelt's propaganda agencies nor the Treasury seemed to be reaching the public with the U.S. government's viewpoint on the war. Similarly, Morgenthau was slowly losing his battle for a continued voluntary system of war finance. From the context of military psychology, the Treasury was finished with its initial training period but continued to struggle in its cohesion phase. Evidently, it was time for the Treasury's bond sales operation to try a different approach.

Morgenthau's new approach turned out to be a shift to periodic bond drives. Although Odegard strongly opposed the change, the secretary's commitment to fighting Keynesian-style forced savings was too strong.[140] Both Morgenthau and Odegard were keenly aware that the Treasury would be echoing McAdoo's reviled World War I Liberty Loans. But the Treasury staff was devoted to its roles in voluntarism and in domestic propaganda. They wanted the war bond effort to become, in Samuel's words, "the central rallying point for the war on the home front."[141] As U.S. forces increasingly entered the battlefield in late 1942 and 1943, the Treasury's new drive system was well situated to shift into a militarized phase of apprehensive enthusiasm. It remained to be seen, however, whether the move to intensive bond drives—a decision that would shape the bond sales effort until December 1945—would truly help the Treasury "build national morale and to 'sell' the war as a whole."[142]

2 WAR BOND DRIVES IN 1942 AND 1943

Developing Apprehensive Enthusiasm

There was a time when our advertising . . . was simply a constant dinning of the phrase, "Buy More Bonds," "Buy More Bonds." This was like saying "Eat more bread," and after a while people began to wonder *why* they should eat more bread.
—"Basic Copy Policy," 1943 Memorandum

A half-filled [war bond stamp] album is like a half-equipped soldier.
—*Minute Man,* Dec. 1, 1942

The turning point of World War II occurred in 1942. On the battlefield, the Allies slowly began to move from a defensive posture to an offensive position. At Midway Island in June, the U.S. Navy successfully ambushed the Japanese fleet, and the balance of power in the Pacific changed dramatically. In late October, Allied forces opened the Battle of El Alamein, forcing Germany's North African forces to retreat for the first time. And in late November, nine Soviet armies surrounded Hitler's forces near Stalingrad. Although the Axis powers would continue to offer fierce resistance, these epic struggles foreshadowed the ultimate outcome of the war.[1]

The Treasury's war bond program also faced a turning point in 1942. The post–Pearl Harbor bond-purchasing frenzy soon gave way to an escalating gulf between the Treasury's efforts to convince Americans to purchase bonds and the public's will to comply. Simultaneously, the financial costs of the war began to outpace the Treasury's apparent ability to raise money. As a result, Treasury Secretary Henry F. Morgenthau Jr. and his war bond staff increasingly found themselves fighting off proponents of compulsory savings plans.

Late in 1942, however, a series of events transpired that pushed the bond program into another, more productive phase. The three war bond drives that occurred in the next twelve months demonstrated the Treasury's growing understanding of its rhetorical power. From the perspective of social movement theory, the Treasury campaign's shift to a drive system again served as a "catalytic event," which ushered in a new stage, one analogous to a movement's "enthusiastic mobilization."[2] Here the cause becomes marked by "optimism" and "an air of excitement and inevitability." In their attempts "to meet changing circumstances," leaders seek "to raise the consciousness level of 'the people.'"[3]

According to military psychologists, soldiers face a similar stage as they arrive in a combat zone. While the initial training and cohesion phases have strengthened them for battle, the approach of actual combat produces a stage of "apprehensive enthusiasm." In this mental stage, soldiers are at once excited about their new surroundings and fearful of the coming danger. Thus, as he describes this psychological state, Peter Watson suggests that soldiers who are new to the battlefield optimistically intend "to get this little war over with."[4]

In this chapter, I argue that with its introduction of a drive system, the Treasury's militarized propaganda campaign entered a period of domestic excitement that was analogous to the combat soldier's stage of apprehensive enthusiasm. In its initial war bond drives in 1942 and 1943, the Treasury propagandized the American public, strategically conflating the worlds of soldiers and civilians while simultaneously creating a rhetorical enemy. By pitting wholesome images of Americans against an inchoate enemy, the Treasury reinforced the virtues of the Allied cause, ultimately reinforcing the Roosevelt administration's vision of the war. Accordingly, I contextualize the emergence and development of the first three war bond drives, from December 1942, through the end of 1943. I then examine the Treasury's conflation of soldiers and civilians as well as its vague depictions of the enemy. Finally, I summarize the implications of the Treasury's strategic approach in the 1942–43 war loans.

The First Three Bond Drives in Context

The lowest point for the Treasury's war bond program arrived in September, 1942. In addition to less-than-expected sales and continuing attacks by proponents of compulsory savings, a Victory Tax was enacted by Congress, effective January 1, 1943. Frustrated that his pet program appeared to be faltering, Morgenthau seriously considered giving up the fight for voluntarism. In early September, he told reporters that the new Victory Tax would not be enough to save the Treasury's war bond program. "That means forced savings," he said. "Let's call it by the ugliest name; we might as well."[5]

Morgenthau's statement produced a quick reaction from the war bond organization. The Treasury received dozens of phone calls, letters, and telegrams from its state leaders, administrators, and other workers offering to resign "if the Secretary's statement stands."[6] Some of the field staffers felt that the operation "might as well close up if that is the way the Treasury . . . [feels] about it."[7] Evidently, the Treasury's rank-and-file bond workers were willing to pressure the administration to save the voluntary system on which they had labored so hard, even if it meant threatening to quit immediately. As Jarvis M. Morse described it, the situation created a "grave danger that the organization charged with carrying on the voluntary program would disintegrate."[8]

The sudden backlash was an unpleasant surprise to the Treasury's critics. Even those most in favor of eliminating voluntarism understood that establishing a forced savings system would take months of hearings and arguments. In the meantime, the sudden collapse of the war bond program would immediately affect both the country's capacity for controlling inflation and its ability to wage war.[9] Elated by this turn of events, Morgenthau consulted with his staff about the best way to reassure the disgruntled bond workers.[10] On September 11, 1942, he clarified his views in a radio broadcast (later published in the bond program's national newsletter, the *Minute Man*): "The impression seems to have spread that I regard the voluntary War Bond program as a 'failure.' This is not only a distortion of anything I have said on the subject but it is also an injustice to the . . . devoted volunteers in all parts of the country who are working night and day to enlist the nation's savings for the war. . . . To our hundreds of thousands of War Bond volunteers, I should like to say that the nation is counting on them more than ever to carry on the magnificent work in which they are so unselfishly engaged."[11]

Meanwhile, Morgenthau continued to receive support from the president, who had his own reasons for wanting the bond program to survive. Vocal members of Congress had been suspicious of the Office of War Information (OWI) since its June inception, viewing it as Roosevelt's personal publicity machine.[12] Already the hostile Congress was in the process of eliminating funding for the Civilian Conservation Corps, the Farm Security Administration, the National Youth Administration, and the Works Progress Administration. Although much was said about cutting costs for the war effort, Polenberg argues that these were primarily political moves.[13] Thus, when the anti–New Deal alliance of conservative Republicans and southern Democrats gained strength in the 1942 November elections, OWI's domestic activities came under renewed attack. Unwilling to fight a costly political battle over OWI's future, Roosevelt suspected that his official propaganda agency's days were numbered.[14]

With OWI's domestic propaganda operations in doubt, the administration's desire to keep encouraging a war mentality in the public seemed to rely increasingly on the war bond campaign's survival. This view was widely held by those familiar with the Treasury's propaganda planning. For instance, the executives in the War Advertising Council (WAC)—whose numerous war bond advertisements made the Treasury its most important account during the war—believed that the bond machine was in reality the administration's primary effort "to mold and shape the attitudes of all the American people."[15]

Meanwhile, many of the Treasury's strategists felt that the bond program's survival depended largely on OWI's elimination. The bond staff viewed Roosevelt's latest information agency as an impediment to the Treasury's work in portraying the war to the public. Vincent Callahan, the bond program's radio chief, recalled that "when OWI came in[to] the picture, it looked for a time as if we might disband. They were hindering us right and left."[16] Thomas H. Lane similarly viewed OWI's assistance as interference, writing that he was "unable to think of a single major contribution that OWI had made to the advertising of War Bonds."[17]

Evidently, the Treasury had grown accustomed to its largely solitary propaganda mission. In August, 1942, however, OWI established the quasi-independent Bureau of Campaigns to help other U.S. government agencies coordinate their publicity.[18] Ken Dyke, the new bureau's supervisor, sought to establish a partnership with the War Savings Staff (WSS). Before long, the Treasury developed a tentative working relationship with the new office, which was a positive sign for the bond staff. Although at first there was little collaboration between OWI and the Treasury, the bond campaign's new lease on life produced a growing partnership in the coming months.[19]

Another optimistic sign for the bond staff was the Treasury's rapidly developing relationship with the advertising organizations represented by WAC. Organized not long after Pearl Harbor, WAC was a loose confederation of advertising companies that "served as a private vehicle for public information and persuasion."[20] Its member agencies assisted various U.S. government programs by creating ad copy, organizing campaigns, and finding free media outlets for the advertisements. In a unique arrangement, the Treasury agreed not to disallow tax write-offs for advertising expenses in return for WAC's support during the war.[21] Not surprisingly, a 1942 *Advertising Age* article claimed that "both local and national advertisers have been generous in devoting space and time to bond themes."[22] Indeed, one unidentified bond staffer wrote that "for reasons of psychology, momentum and prestige, the choice account of the lot was

Treasury. One or two big agencies which missed the boat on this in the beginning spent a good part of the war kicking themselves for it later."[23] As WAC's most demanding client, WSS thus obtained the free services of several of the country's top advertising companies, including Young and Rubicam. However, by meeting with its advertising experts "at regular and frequent intervals," the war bond strategists ensured that Treasury maintained controlling interest in its propaganda campaign.[24]

After September's low point, then, Morgenthau was increasingly confident that his voluntary system would survive. Well aware that the campaign still needed a dramatic change, however, he arranged to test market a small bond drive in mid-October, 1942. Held in Vineland, New Jersey, the test drive quickly "resulted in an overwhelming rise in incremental bond sales."[25] The results were successful enough for Morgenthau to overrule his primary strategist, Peter H. Odegard, who was uneasy about a return to the World War I–style of periodic drives. From the secretary's perspective, the propaganda generated in a national drive could reenergize the field staff who were so demoralized by the campaign's near demise in September. Perhaps more importantly, Morgenthau hoped that the drive's intensity would produce a heightened level of war enthusiasm in the public. Armed with pledges of support from both OWI and WAC, Morgenthau announced in early November that the Treasury would hold the first nationwide bond drive of the war. Soon called the Victory Fund Drive, this nationwide effort would last from November 16, 1942, through the end of the year.[26]

Responsibility for the drive was actually split between WSS and the Victory Fund Committee (VFC). Morgenthau had established this organization in June 1942, giving it responsibility for the more expensive F and G bonds.[27] The group's workers were recruited from financial institutions, and Morgenthau hoped that their experience in securities would make them effective in promoting bonds to wealthy investors.[28] Moreover, the secretary felt that the move left his central Treasury organization "free to concentrate on the 'E' bonds, on payroll savings, and on related matters."[29] Thus, although the change created an unexpected rivalry between the two groups, WSS used the Victory Fund Drive to focus on increasing the number of people enrolled in the payroll savings program, which automatically contributed 10 percent of a worker's pay to the Treasury every payday.[30]

The Victory Fund Drive was the first of what would become a total of eight drives during the war period. Compared to later drives, this first effort was surprisingly simple.[31] But the concentrated propaganda seemed to touch a chord in the American psyche, as sales increased sharply during the drive. Morgenthau initially set $9 billion as the drive's ambitious goal.[32] On Pearl Harbor's first anniversary (with its one-day slogan, "Let's Give the Japanese Something to Remember on Pearl Harbor Day"), the number of Americans holding at least one bond exceeded 50 million, more than 35 percent of the population.[33] By the end of the drive, the public surpassed Morgenthau's goal by amassing $13 billion in bond sales. While the total in the lower-denomination E series bonds was not as high as this number suggested, WSS met its primary objective by securing 30 million new payroll savings workers.[34] Indeed, the Treasury's bond drive seemed to energize the public to a significant degree, providing the much-needed push into a stage of apprehensive enthusiasm.

After this initial drive, an internal Treasury study posited that the use of periodic war loans would maximize bond publicity, while allowing time between drives for bond officials to review previous efforts and to calibrate new ones.[35] Accordingly, early 1943 found WSS analyzing the success of the Victory Fund Drive and beginning plans for another effort. The staff had reason to be optimistic. The burdens of public censorship and rationing, for example, were being eased by the war economy's increasing contributions to the average person's income. Additionally, the momentum of the war seemed to be turning slowly toward the Allies. Roosevelt and Churchill met at Casablanca in January 1943, agreeing that the next step in the war was to invade the Italian peninsula. Despite the optimistic outlook, however, Morgenthau was wary of the inflationary dangers posed by the nation's increasing access to extra money. Moreover, the huge financial drain of the war effort meant that a new drive would be necessary no later than the spring.[36]

The friction between VFC and WSS presented a significant obstacle to preparations for another war loan drive. After Morgenthau announced that the second drive would be held from April 12 to May 1, 1943, he asked two banking representatives from VFC to sit in on the Treasury's WSS meetings. His goal was to consolidate the two organizations.[37] Unfortunately, each side felt threatened by the possible move, forcing Morgenthau to delay the merger for more than a week. His temporary compromise, announced on March 2, 1943, was to have both groups loosely organized under the title "War Finance Committee." Although each side found the solution workable in the short term, the delay had a significant impact on the Treasury's ability to create visual appeals for the coming drive.[38]

Despite the infighting and reorganization, however, the Second War Loan was on. Morgenthau wanted Americans to buy $13 billion in war bonds during the drive. The public continued to find the Treasury's drive-based appeals compelling, confirming that the war bond propaganda campaign was in a stage of apprehensive enthusiasm. Total sales in the drive topped $18.5 billion—90 percent of the overall results from World War I's five drives *combined.* Calling it "America's Greatest War Loan," Morgenthau proudly wrote later in May that the American people "will go to the very limit of their capacity if only they understand the urgency of the situation."[39]

But after the successful second loan, the internal Treasury power struggles continued. Convinced by his advisers that the tension would become even more counterproductive before long, Morgenthau decided to restructure the entire bond effort. In June, 1943, he announced the details of a sweeping reorganization. The head administrator, Harold Graves, who helped with the bond program's prewar planning, was reassigned to the Bureau of Internal Revenue. Aware that Odegard—who was becoming more and more frustrated with the drive mentality—was planning to return to Amherst on the eve of the drive, Morgenthau enlarged the original bond sales organization and made Ted R. Gamble, the Treasury program's charismatic field organizer, its national director.[40] In effect, Morgenthau's restructuring favored WSS, eliminating the rival VFC and giving its responsibilities to Gamble. Now called the War Finance Division (WFD), the enlarged organization would be the final version of the Treasury's war bond machine.[41]

Unfortunately, the logistics of the merger were a significant challenge for the newly appointed Gamble. To make matters worse, the two groups needed to overcome what Morse calls a "heritage of rancor, jealousy and open conflict hanging like a cloud."[42] Thus, it took Gamble much of the summer of 1943 to complete the consolidation. Some critics claimed that the merger was accomplished too haphazardly, but the fast-approaching deadline to launch the Third War Loan gave Gamble little room for a leisurely transition. As a result of the lack of adequate preparation time for the drive, promotional materials for the Third War Loan were again much less sophisticated than Morgenthau wanted.[43] In spite of these constraints, though, the supply of compelling visual images for this drive increased significantly.

The Third War Loan was fortunate in that the long-awaited invasion of Italy on the eve of the drive helped set the tone for a successful effort. Appropriately enough, the drive's slogan was "Back the Attack." From September 9 to October 2, 1943, this slogan and its supporting propaganda emerged in 100 million lines of newspaper advertising space, 48,000 billboards, and 1 million store window displays.[44] The ever-present Treasury appeals in the Third War Loan were a fitting sign of the propaganda campaign's dramatically increased popularity and effectiveness. Ultimately, this final bond drive of 1943 managed to raise $18.9 billion—nearly $4 billion more than the Treasury had hoped for.[45]

By the end of 1943 the Treasury was able to look back on an eventful series of haphazard bond drives with great satisfaction. Despite some degree of internal tension, Treasury's research suggested that the drives had themselves become a major motivation for citizens to purchase war bonds.[46] Indeed, the war loans of 1942–43 managed to achieve a significant level of financial success. This accomplishment was even more impressive considering that it emerged from propaganda appeals that were often hastily crafted and whose images were sporadic and rushed. Although Odegard was now back at Amherst, his leadership in the preparation for the drive system evidently helped push the bond propaganda effort into a militarized stage of apprehensive enthusiasm. In this psychological stage the Treasury's militarized approach seemingly sought to transform home front civilians into soldiers.

Crafting Apprehensive Enthusiasm in the 1942–1943 Appeals

The Treasury's predrive efforts could be described in terms of military psychology as an initial training phase followed by a challenging cohesion phase. In the material war, American soldiers, few of whom were yet in battle or even overseas, were experiencing roughly similar stages throughout much of 1942.[47] This prolonged military inaction facilitated worrisome effects on the public's war focus. Not surprisingly, as long as U.S. soldiers remained away from the battlefield, many Americans—once over the initial shock of Pearl Harbor—were struggling to take the war seriously.

By the end of 1942, however, American forces were increasingly engaging the enemy on the battlefield. In his discussion of a soldier's psychological development in wartime, Watson points out that upon arrival in a combat zone, new troops typically enter a stage of apprehensive enthusiasm. In this period of adjustment, soldiers are normally fearful of their new surroundings and the inherent dangers of a combat zone. Still, in facing these fears, soldiers often display a simultaneous eagerness to get the job done.[48] Thus, although the psychological stress of impending combat was palpable near the end of 1942, American soldiers were finding that an intense approach to their job was an important means of reducing that stress.

Meanwhile, as America's GIs were dealing with the strain of moving into combat zones, the Treasury was strategizing better ways to connect Americans psychologically to the war effort. Up to this point, decreasing sales suggested that the Treasury's propaganda was faltering. But the basic problem was not strictly financial; it was also rhetorical. To use Edwin Black's perspective, in the Treasury's predrive propaganda, the department had an unfortunate image of its audience, one that was aimless and disorganized.[49] No wonder, then, that the public was not making its quotas; the Treasury's inconsistent propaganda presented a poor model on which American citizens could base their buying behavior. To find what Odegard called "the phantom public," the Treasury needed to take a different rhetorical approach.[50]

The shift to a bond drive approach in late 1942 helped galvanize the public. In place of Treasury's previous chaotic and disorganized propaganda, Morgenthau now insisted on a "synchronized" approach that would "tie everything together."[51] Where earlier war bond efforts often had difficulty uniting and motivating a buying audience, the dramatic introduction of an organized drive philosophy immediately helped usher in a militarized atmosphere of urgency and efficiency. As one of the Treasury's December, 1942, posters advised Americans, "make your own declaration of war."[52] Ironically, the events of Pearl Harbor were already one year old, but only now was the Treasury explicitly telling the public that it was time to fight.

Thus, just as American GIs were experiencing psychological states of fear and eagerness, so too was the Treasury's discourse fostering a psychological stage of apprehensive enthusiasm in the American public. In short, the Treasury's new drive approach offered home front Americans a militarized outlet for their own vicarious war involvement. Again in Black's perspective, the Treasury's drives helped marshal a new national buying audience, shifting the bond program into another, highly productive stage.

This stage of apprehensive enthusiasm was marked by two complementary strategies. The first conflated the worlds of civilian and soldier. The second crafted images of the enemy, images that remained vague and elusive throughout the first three war loans. Both strategies helped create the illusion that the domestic public could in fact join the war effort in a militarized sense. In the end, each strategy also helped develop constructions of the U.S. public,

U.S. soldiers, and the enemy—all inherent components of military campaigns.

The Conflation of the American People and U.S. Soldiers

The Treasury's initial strategy in its 1942–43 propaganda capitalized on the increasingly intense nature of the material war. In most cases, Americans were very interested in the developing battles, particularly in places where active duty family members and acquaintances were said to be stationed. The Treasury's resourceful approach was to take advantage of this interest as the American role in the war escalated. In what Odegard called "a period of intensification," the Treasury used its propaganda to place individual Americans metaphorically into the combat boots of the soldiers they were so anxious about.[53]

The Treasury's conflation of civilians and soldiers emerged from a systematic conceptual metaphor. George Lakoff and Mark Johnson explain that while traditional theorists treat metaphors as isolated stylistic devices, a theory of conceptual metaphors locates systematic structures in language that play "a central role in defining our everyday realities."[54] They begin by explaining that human cognition relies heavily on its ability to create conceptual domains, such as the concept of ARGUMENT (capitalized to differentiate it from the *word* "argument"). Lakoff and Johnson point out that by uniting two such conceptual domains (e.g., ARGUMENT and WAR), language users can cause others to understand the target domain (ARGUMENT) in ways structured by the source domain (WAR). Thus, in the conceptual metaphor "ARGUMENT IS WAR," one sees the target in terms of the source, that is, *arguments in terms of war.* In uniting two well-developed concepts, such metaphors can produce scores of unique linguistic expressions, each emerging from and based on the original conceptual metaphor (e.g., "I *demolished* his argument;" "your claims are *indefensible;*" and "he *shot down* all my arguments").[55] As Lakoff and Johnson explain, "It is not that arguments are a subspecies of war. Arguments and wars are different kinds of things—verbal discourse and armed conflict—and the actions performed are different kinds of actions. But [the conceptual domain] ARGUMENT is partially structured, understood, performed, and talked about in terms of [the conceptual domain] WAR. The concept is metaphorically structured, the activity is metaphorically structured, and, consequently, the language is metaphorically structured."[56]

In its first three bond drives, the Treasury developed a similar conceptual metaphor, CIVILIANS ARE SOLDIERS. This metaphoric merging of two normally separate conceptual domains developed in a series of persuasive parallels between the domestic front and the battlefront. Most important in these parallels was the equation of the soldier's weapon (often a rifle; sometimes a tank, a pistol, or a plane) on the one hand, with the civilian's weapon (a war bond) on the other. In this metaphoric equation, soldiers used weapons to assure victory; civilians used bonds for the same ends. To make the connection between home front and battlefront even more complete, bonds were further depicted as the literal means for the public to supply weaponry for the military. Thus, the Treasury's propaganda portrayed bonds as the necessary and at times sufficient way for civilians to transform into soldiers.[57]

This conflation of civilians and soldiers emerged quite clearly in the Victory Fund Drive of late 1942. Reflecting the fact that most American soldiers were not yet even overseas, much of the drive's propaganda primarily depicted scenes of home life, including celebrations of Thanksgiving, Christmas, and New Year's. Yet there were signs that this domestic scene was militarizing for battle. One of the drive's ads, for example, depicted a young soldier in a heroic pose. Although his sober expression suggested that he could see a distant battle, readers who followed his line of sight found that only the ad's main caption was visible: "Make Your Dollars FIGHT WITH HIM!"[58] Another ad claimed that "You're the next best thing to a soldier when you *buy War Bonds*."[59] An ad that focused on bonds as investments reminded readers that bond purchases can "[m]ake your dollars fighters."[60] And an ad that simply depicted a drawing of a wind-rippled American flag described the ownership role of home front citizens in the struggle: "Your Flag . . *Your* Fight . . *Your* Future!"[61] Such appeals began the conflation of CIVILIANS and SOLDIERS. When you become "the next best thing to a soldier," for example, the two concepts are already merging. When the public's dollars are fighting, and when it is "*your* fight," the conflation is even more complete.

The Second War Loan of April 1943 further developed the conflation between civilian and soldier by making more vivid the connection between individual bond purchases and the military supplies those purchases would supposedly enable. At its simplest, this tactic meant that bond literature directly equated a bond sale or a community's set of bond sales with the acquisition of specific military supplies or hardware. Of course, the promise that a specific war bond transaction would go toward a specific weapon or to a specific unit was almost always false. Yet this unspoken truth did not stop the

Treasury from making such suggestions in its propaganda, nor did it, apparently, stop some bond purchasers from believing the fiction.[62]

One important aspect of the Second War Loan's attempt to link war bonds and battlefield supplies emerged from the Women's Section of WSS. Established in June, 1942, the Women's Section had by early 1943 developed into a nationwide network, and during the second drive it offered one of its largest efforts, called "Outfitting the Outfit." This intensive campaign set bond sales targets for its constituent organizations in every state, and then encouraged each group to translate their target "in terms of complete outfits for platoons, companies and regiments." In Idaho, for example, "the statewide women's goal was set at $300,000, and every county and town translated it into terms of outfitting battalions, companies, and platoons," while women's groups in Wyoming spent the Second War Loan successfully equipping "1,354 soldiers (28 platoons) at a cost of $200,000." While such purchases actually went directly into the Treasury's war chest to be spent in the most expedient manner, most participants seemed to enjoy the idea that their money was going to a specific purchase, since "the promotion brought [an] enthusiastic response from coast to coast" in "towns large and small" and "states near and far."[63]

The Treasury's national publicity during the second drive also worked hard to reinforce the suggestion that the war bonds were in fact matériel for the nation's fighting forces. In one feature released to newspapers, for instance, the Treasury described what a bond purchaser might in fact be obtaining for the battlefield: "The Bond you buy today or tomorrow or next week may help buy the operating table upon which many lives will be saved by Navy or Army surgeons."[64] A Treasury news release further explained that from the $13 billion to be raised during the drive "may come a giant warship costing $97,000,000 or a bean pot, costing 29 cents. Somewhere in between, your money . . . fits in."[65] Privately, the Treasury advised its sales force to focus on emotional messages in establishing this connection. "It is important," advised the staff, "to dramatize the personal part they can play in the coming offensives against the Axis when they buy an extra War Bond. . . . [T]ell them . . . even though you are not able to leave your workbench, desk, or farm—you can still drill holes in a Mitsubishi Zero with your extra dollars."[66] Here the Treasury's conflation of civilians and soldiers developed a deeper connection between bonds and weapons. The concept SOLDIER necessarily carries with it images of weaponry. If SOLDIER is used to structure CIVILIAN, then CIVILIAN naturally develops a corresponding need for weaponry. The Treasury's propaganda thus supplied the appropriate link between the conflated concepts; the civilian's weapon became the war bond.

By the time of the Third War Loan in September, 1943, the strategy of conflating civilians and soldiers was well established in the bond program's propaganda. As in the first two bond drives, the Treasury found value in depicting civilians as a kind of soldier, and bonds as both the civilians' weapon as well as their actual means of equipping the military. Not surprisingly, the drive continued to stress the direct relationship between the efforts of those on the battlefront and those on the home front. Oddly enough, some of the Third War Loan's pervasive messages in this vein were delivered by a growing army of children. The Schools at War program, organized by the war bond program's Education Section, had been mobilizing schools nationwide to enlist children of all ages not only as purchasers of bond stamps, but as door-to-door bond sales representatives.[67] In part, this strategy relied on the children's natural ability to parry potential sales resistance. As one student reported, "My dad didn't have the heart to turn the children down. He bought extra Bonds that he wouldn't have otherwise."[68] By the time of the Third War Loan, however, the young salespeople were being advised by the Treasury to embellish the role of their bonds in the war effort by telling potential purchasers "We . . . are backing them up—will you help?"[69] Such appeals—delivered by young children on doorsteps across the country—offered a novel way to portray the connection between home front and battlefront and thereby increase bond sales.

The Third War Loan, then, offered increasingly creative and dramatic ways to conflate civilians and soldiers. The drive's internal campaign book said that the loan would "test the mettle of every American in the land. Each person . . . must march side by side with those who are privileged to do the actual fighting . . . and hold to it as zealously as our fighting men will hold to their invasion timetable."[70] A published ad offered a similar tone, exclaiming that "[t]he big drive is on! Not only on every battlefront—but on the home front, too. As the tempo of the war increases . . . as our fighting forces go all-out for INVASION, we folks back home must mobilize in their support."[71] Tellingly, this ad's main text was a military command: "Forward March—America!"[72] Such appeals made further connections between the world of civilians and the world of soldiers. Indeed, as the ad's use of the phrase "home front" itself suggests, the Treasury wanted civilians to explicitly envision themselves as fighting in their theater of the war.

2.1 Montage of fight scenes in the Third War Loan. Note the two civilians (*upper left*). They are holding war bonds in essentially the same position as the soldier's weapon. Courtesy Franklin D. Roosevelt Library.

The Third War Loan's visual appeals made the connection between civilian and soldier even more explicit. Of the three scenes depicted on the cover of the Treasury's advertising proof book for the drive, for example, one seemed unlikely to occur in real life (see Figure 2.1).[73] At the top left a soldier runs, rifle at the ready, mouth open in a battle cry. Slightly behind the soldier and flanking him, a woman and a man stride purposefully in the same direction. Significantly, the civilians both hold a piece of paper (presumably a war bond, though the drawing does not complete this detail) in essentially the same position as the soldier is holding his rifle.

At first glance, the two civilians are clearly out of place, surrounded as they are with depictions of war and violence. In addition to the man and the woman holding their bonds, the Treasury's image portrays dive bombers in action and an invasion scene complete with infantry, planes, a tank, and explosions. Even the text in the middle of the page references violence, proclaiming, "Here's your AMMUNITION to back the attack."[74]

Yet the civilians' very presence in this image made it perhaps the most telling depiction in the Treasury's propaganda up to this point in the war. Paul Messaris describes such scenes as montages, complex images in which an unexpected visual contrast might "stimulate the viewer's mind toward the creation of a new meaning, a synthesis of the meanings of the two conflicting images."[75] Messaris concludes that the power of such images comes directly from their startling juxtaposition.[76] Thus, while it is true that civilians and soldiers would seem to exist in entirely different worlds, in this image the Treasury featured the two civilians *behind* the charging soldier (i.e., their role was to "back the attack"), using dramatic juxtaposition to merge those two worlds.

In part, this visual conflation served to confirm the Treasury's already-established verbal link between the home front and the battlefront. Even though the scene was unrealistic in a literal sense, it operated as a visual metaphor to show that just as American soldiers were charging forward in the attack, so too were American civilians. Similarly, while the soldier was using a rifle as his powerful weapon to help defeat the enemy, the civilians could see themselves using a different weapon—the war bond. The bonds, then, were the link between the seemingly out-of-place civilians and the various war scenes in the montage. Since each of the scenes featured an image of battle, the civilians—armed with their war bonds—were acting in their role as soldiers, rushing to fight the coming battle along with the military.[77]

The use of such a complex image emphasizes how strongly the Treasury's propagandists saw the connection between the concept of CIVILIANS and the concept of SOLDIERS. "To a greater extent than ever before," explained the Treasury's internal newsletter, "Home Front met its twin brother, War Front, under the impetus of the [third] Drive."[78] The metaphorical effect of casting civilians at home as participants in the fight was evident in the drive's appeals: for bond buyers to become participants in the war was to transform their actions into those of a militarized force. Thus, while a soldier was seemingly rushing at the enemy, the civilian was likewise striding at the enemy metaphorically. While the battlefront featured sacrifices of life and limb to reach victory, the home front exhibited sacrifices of money and time to reach victory. And while a soldier might throw a grenade, a civilian might buy a bond, a financial weapon just as potent as the soldier's grenade. Such a massive conflation was consistent with Odegard's views on propaganda. In their 1938 work, Odegard and E. Allen Helms wrote that effective political propaganda uses "symbols of *identification, expectation, and demand*."[79] The Treasury's metaphoric conflation seemingly sought to turn civilians into soldiers, while the implications of the metaphor created an expectation, and even a demand that the public do their part to complete the militaristic ritual.

In the end, the bond program's metaphoric conflation in 1942 and 1943 represented strategies typically associated with the development of a military unit's apprehensive enthusiasm. Like the soldiers on the battlefront, the soldiers on the home front were depicted as being on the verge of actual combat, fostering a mood of suspense, fear, and motivation. As Paul A. Chilton explains, these sorts of "inferences take place in the metaphorical domain, but they can be mapped back into the pragmatic domain of political, social, or military action."[80] In the case of the American public, the primary application of their metaphorical conflation with soldiers, of course, was the increased purchase of bonds to do their part in the battle against an inchoate enemy.

Imagining the Enemy

The Treasury's second strategy during the first three war loan drives complemented the civilian-soldier conflation. Here the war bond discourse reflected the stage of apprehensive enthusiasm through its portrayal of an approaching enemy. For U.S. military leaders, a key to battlefield motivation is to overwhelm soldiers with discourse inspiring both "religious devotion to American ideals" and "hatred of the enemy."[81] Assuming that the Treasury's militarized propaganda reflected a similar mind-set, it makes sense that the bond strategists would have urged the public to feel similarly threatened by the enemy's approach.

Historically, propaganda that relies on the fear of an antagonist emerges from a venerable American tradition of depicting enemy images. J. Michael Hogan and L. Glen Williams, for example, note the development of enemy depictions even before the United States established its independence. They contend that as the rift with Britain grew, many colonists broadened their definition of the enemy to include those who supported the crown, even if they were fellow colonists.[82] Gregory Sieminski adds that the colonists' propaganda often depicted the demonized British enemy as savages, thus borrowing from popular contemporary perceptions of the native population.[83] Ronald H. Carpenter traces the development of such enemy images in later periods of the nation's history. Using the frontier myth as an organizing principle, he argues that revolutionary-derived images of Native Americans as savages evolved as the growing nation involved itself in other conflicts. Thus, he concludes, the nation's enemies in the Mexican American War and in World War I found themselves cast as the same sorts of "savages" recalled in popular imagination.[84]

The strategic use of these "images of savagery" is of particular interest to Robert L. Ivie. "Throughout American history," he comments, "the enemy is portrayed as a savage, i.e., as an aggressor, driven by irrational desires for conquest, who is seeking to subjugate others by force of arms."[85] These three qualities—aggression, irrationality, and force—emerge as the primary decivilizing elements in America's verbal discourse about the enemy. Ivie's research finds such dehumanizing discourse surrounding the War of 1812, the Mexican American War, World War II, the Cold War (including Korea and Vietnam), and even the post-9/11 war on terror.[86] In each conflict, the "image of the adversary as Satan's surrogate presents to the nation a perfect antagonist whose sacrifice justifies the breach of peace as it promises to eliminate the source of trouble."[87] Ivie thus concludes that an important part of America's rhetorical heritage is a genre of dehumanizing discourse that justifies warfare by depicting nations as enemies and their leaders as villains.

As participants in this American rhetorical heritage, Treasury strategists were well aware of the norms set by their predecessors. Odegard's 1938 analysis of American political strategies, in fact, described the strategic process of demonizing the opposition and their "snares, pitfalls, and betrayals."[88] Despite this awareness, the Treasury was initially hesitant to depict the enemy in anything but the vaguest terms. Just before the first war bond drive, Odegard advised the Treasury's copywriters to avoid describing the Axis with such phrases as "'Military maniacs,' 'Blood-thirsty scoundrels,' 'cutthroats,' and other rabble-rousing terms." The reason, he continued, was that "the public is wary of attempts to put Hallowe'en villain-masks on such 'ordinary' people as Hitler, etc.; even genuine documented atrocity tales smack to them of propaganda."[89]

In accordance with Odegard's private guidelines, the enemies in the Treasury's propaganda were initially rather vague; they were still shadows and not the inhuman creatures they would become in 1944's bond drives, after Odegard had returned to Amherst. But following Shawn J. Parry-Giles's suggestion that militarized propaganda is inherently confrontational, it is not surprising that the enemy's menacing presence still lurked in the background of the early drives' propaganda.[90] Indeed, the appeals in the first three drives managed to suggest that the enemy was just over the horizon, its dangerous proximity threatening international soldiers and domestic soldiers alike. Although the Treasury's audience could not yet see the enemy, it could sense the fear and tension of American soldiers, who were often depicted in this early propaganda as physically advancing into unsecured enemy territory. The Treasury's developing sense of apprehensive enthusiasm throughout the first three bond drives, then, was in effect a means of facilitating a similar sense of fear and tension in home front soldiers.

In the initial Victory Fund Drive, the enemy's presence was unmistakable. One ad, detailing the costs of a new antiaircraft gun, provided a compelling description of battle against enemy planes, narrating the gun's destructive work as it "roars into action and hurls its shell skyward into the belly of a Jap Zero or Nazi Messerschmidt."[91] A similar ad asked bond buyers to sponsor demolition bombs, which were "so important in razing Nazi war plants, interrupting railroad transportation and other war objectives."[92] And one of the drive's visual images depicted two tanks cresting a hill, rushing off to attack the enemy, while a nearby image showed several soldiers, weapons at the ready, looking intently into the distance.[93] Although in each of these appeals the enemy was unseen, the threat was as close as the gunsights used by American soldiers and as tangible as the battle smoke rising over the tanks as they engaged the enemy just beyond the viewers' sight. Indeed, the enemy's absence from the visual frame may have made its looming presence even more threatening. Isabel Cristina Pinedo points out that "what lurks outside the frame" inevitably produces "uncertainty about what one is seeing." "This uncertainty," she continues, both "generates suspense and stimulates the desire to know more."[94] For a domestic audience still uncertain of the war's outcome, the simultaneous fear and captivation generated by such an inchoate enemy

2.2 The main theme poster of the Second War Loan, suggesting a readiness to charge into combat. Courtesy Franklin D. Roosevelt Library.

could have been a powerful ingredient in the building stage of apprehensive enthusiasm.

By April 1943, the material outlook of the war was more positive for the Allies. However, while the Axis appeared to be losing momentum, the possibility that Allied forces would seize the opportunity was still uncertain. The Second War Loan's propaganda accordingly shifted to depictions of the war's turning point, meaning that the nation's soldiers were seen as taking the battle to the enemy. The drive's appeals thus consistently portrayed American forces, in the president's words, as "carrying the war into enemy territory."[95] The Treasury's propaganda reflected this shift by increasing the dramatic impact of the enemy's still-unvisualized presence.

Initially, some aspects of the second drive's literature depicted the military advance into enemy territory. One Treasury-generated speech, for instance, advised listeners that "the war is entering a new phase. The armies of the United States and the United Nations are preparing for the great offensive. . . . We are beginning to attack . . . and it always costs more, in men and blood and money, to attack than to defend."[96] A Treasury news release agreed, pointing out that "[o]ur army divisions will soon be moving against the continent to liberate the Nazi slaves. . . . War costs increase all along the line as the Yanks go on the offensive. . . . Now they are in the Tunisian desert. Tomorrow they may be battering the citadel of Europe . . . by direct assault."[97] One of the few images of the drive—its theme picture—displayed this offensive shift more subtly. A soldier in full combat gear holds his rifle and crouches in a stance suggesting his readiness to charge forward toward the enemy (see fig. 2.2).[98] This soldier, much like the ones described above, was clearly emblematic of the war's turning point.

Of course, as these American soldiers advanced into the battlefield, the enemy's presence became more menacing to the observing public. One Treasury appeal suggested that "our enemies are using their full, terrible strength and squeezing out more sinews of war from the poor bodies of their victims. We too must exert our full strength. . . . [I]f we should lose this war our enemies will use us as they have used the people of Poland, Holland, Norway."[99] A Treasury-generated speech provided a graphic illustration of the enemy's brutality and how war bonds were the best weapon with which to fight:

> In a moment, your torpedo . . . the torpedo which your War Bond dollars bought, will smash home against the side of that Japanese cruiser. A moment after that there will be an explosion. Another threat to our fighting men . . . perhaps your son or brother . . . has been sent to the bottom. If you had failed to buy the War Bonds which you have bought . . . and are buying . . . perhaps there would have been no torpedo. Then that Jap cruiser might have steamed unmolested off some beach where our

> fighting men were camped. Soon that Jap cruiser might have sent battery after battery of death and destruction against your brothers or your sons.[100]

In both these examples the enemy's brutality had increased noticeably. While the Treasury was not yet ready to depict the enemy visually, it clearly cast the enemy's actions and character as more perfidious than in earlier portrayals. The propaganda campaign was gradually creating what Cynthia A. Freeland calls "an atmosphere of mysterious, implied evil." Such an atmosphere increased the likelihood that the public would "feel puny in relation to a force" that was "vague, alien, or evil."[101] The consequent fear of the enemy further reflected strategies commonly espoused in the stage of apprehensive enthusiasm. Much like the fearful soldiers on the battlefront, the Treasury's propaganda campaign was working to fashion a sense of anxiety and tension on the home front. Thus, as the Treasury-generated speech concluded, "our enemies are not on the verge of defeat. Far from it. They are ruthless and powerful. Our victory is not assured."[102]

In the summer of 1943 the Treasury prepared for the Third War Loan by consolidating its efforts into a unified bond organization under the direction of Ted Gamble. Simultaneously, the military concentrated its attention on preparing for the all-out invasion of the Italian peninsula. It was only a partial coincidence that the invasion began just before the bond drive; throughout the summer it was rumored that the attack was imminent.[103] Still, the "invasion" theme in the drive's propaganda quickly took literal form on the battlefield, giving extra impetus to the Treasury's appeals. Indeed, the polling data that emerged from the drive's "Back the Attack" theme suggested that most people purchased bonds in order to help soldiers in battle.[104] By adapting its propaganda to its audience in this way, Treasury brought the enemy even closer to the American public, continually linking bond purchases to both the invasion's success and the enemy's defeat. As Odegard suggested in his brainstorming records for the drive, the Treasury needed to connect "3rd War Loan bond buying with the invasion of Europe . . . with [the] thought that to help make the invasion successful . . . we must also make sacrifices here at home, to buy bonds."[105]

The stark images of the Third War Loan reinforced Odegard's prescription to emphasize the invasion. This was the first drive to have a significant battery of visual images; throughout the effort the Treasury used them to present realistic depictions of an invading army and its soldiers. One of the drive's posters, for instance, featured a lifelike drawing of a beach assault, with infantrymen climbing out of the water, bayonets ready for action. In the foreground the poster featured a close-up of a soldier on the beach. In impressive detail, viewers could see his helmet netting, chin strap device, and elements of his uniform. The dramatic text of the ad reinforced the vividness of the image: "They're fighting harder than ever—are you buying MORE WAR BONDS than ever?"[106] Aside from contributing to its civilian-soldier conflation here (one of the background GIs in the image was even beckoning for more to join in the fight), the Treasury was also linking the purchase of bonds to the growing ferocity of the war. What probably drew the most attention in the poster, however, was the soldier's facial expression, eyes glaring toward the enemy (off to the viewer's left), teeth bared in a full battle cry. As before, the enemy did not actually appear in the poster. Yet as Barbie Zelizer demonstrates, an intent offstage gaze like the one in this poster actually invites the viewer "to attend to what was being witnessed even if it was not shown."[107] Thus, in such images the Treasury was linking the enemy's looming threat with the need for greater bond purchases. In the process, it was seemingly facilitating a sense of apprehensive enthusiasm by attempting to increase the public's sense of tension and fear in the face of the enemy's proximity.

To further underscore the enemy's approach, the third drive's propaganda also featured some of the first U.S. government–approved depictions of wounded Americans. One Treasury newspaper ad, for example, showed a soldier lying on the ground with two medics making him comfortable by adjusting his head and feet. The soldier's face and clothes were bloody (though no wound was actually shown), and his hands were clenched in agony.[108] Another ad reinforced the urgency of such imagery. It featured a group of soldiers running toward enemy territory, bayonets at the ready. "YOU CAN'T FAIL THEM NOW!" added the text in large bold type, "your dear ones—sons, husband, sweetheart, father, brothers, relatives and friends—are . . . engaged in those bloody battles where the scythe of the Grim Reaper flashes in every volley of the guns. The 3rd War Loan of 15 billion dollars *must* pay for the equipment . . . our boys need so desperately."[109] By beginning to feature imagery of injured American soldiers—and by verbally acknowledging the deaths that awaited many of them—the Treasury's propaganda was offering concrete evidence of the enemy's presence and aggressiveness, thereby fostering the mood of apprehensive enthusiasm.

2.3 Third War Loan poster depicting the suffering of a vulnerable civilian, promoting the idea of further sacrifices on the home front. Courtesy National Archives.

A final way the third drive highlighted the enemy's brutality was by portraying the suffering of civilians. One of the starkest posters of the drive visually depicts the aftermath of a countryside bombing raid, apparently in the European theater (see fig. 2.3). In the background is a bombed-out home, smoke still rising from the rubble. In the foreground a grief-stricken peasant stares forlornly into the middle distance.[110] While the poster portrayed a grim acceptance of tragedy, its central message was the peasant's vulnerability and helplessness. This message was in fact the Treasury's first attempt of the war to reprise a classic war appeal: the enemy's threat to women and children. As Sieminski points out, one of the most visceral justifications for war in American history has been the figurative threat that savages are about to assault or rape a feminine victim.[111] Whether that victim is a feminized Liberty, a nation, or literal humans, the American impulse to protect or seek vengeance in such situations is a common motive in war propaganda.[112] Moreover, since this particular image showed a bombed-out *home* to those on the home front, it offered a compelling sense of identification to its viewers. The poster thus sold bonds by comparing the sacrifices of war theater victims with the sacrifices of home front Americans. Simultaneously, it sold bonds by underlining the enemy's savagery in attacking those archetypal figures perceived as most vulnerable to the ravages of war.[113]

Even while remaining offstage, then, the enemy played an important role in the Treasury's first three bond drives. As U.S. soldiers moved from boot camp to the battlefield, so too did the enemy's presence grow nearer in war bond propaganda. Moreover, with each drive the enemy's degree of savagery increased, starting with an unseen and distant threat and culminating in a barbarous, faceless entity that injured and even killed soldiers and civilians alike. Although Odegard advised the Treasury's strategists to avoid obvious demonization tactics, the bond propaganda of 1942–43 nevertheless created a menacing, if still invisible, enemy presence in the war effort. Inevitably, this strategy of imagining the enemy complemented the Treasury's initial civilian-soldier conflation by encouraging the home front to identify both with their soldiers' aggressive actions and their fear of the enemy; in short, the Treasury's early drive propaganda was emblematic of the strategies associated with apprehensive enthusiasm.

Implications of the War Bond Drive Appeals, 1942–1943

The dramatic cutbacks in OWI's domestic activity some months before the Third War Loan meant that the Treasury's war bond machine was the Roosevelt administration's most important remaining source of domestic propaganda. Due in part, perhaps, to this official vacuum, the Treasury's appeals seemed to be increasingly successful in reaching the American public. Considered from a financial perspective, the bond organization overcame numerous internal struggles to surpass its $36 billion goal across the first three drives by more than $14 billion.

Considered from a morale perspective, however, the bond propaganda seemed to have been even more successful. The Treasury's Likert surveys following the Third War Loan showed that "the strongest motivation" for the millions of bond purchasers was "a deep sense of personal involvement in the war."[114] For this reason, the Treasury itself gradually became convinced that the volume of civilian war bond purchases was, at any given point, an accurate barometer of public morale. Although the relationship was probably much less causal than the Treasury's pollsters claimed, the war bond staff's thinking was clear. If bond purchases were increasing, they reasoned, then public unity and support for the war must also be increasing. And the way to heighten bond sales, they argued, was to give the home front a personal taste of the war.

In rhetorically constructing this personal sense of war involvement, the Treasury's 1942–43 propaganda worked to fashion what Black might term a "buying audience" through two complementary strategies.[115] The first approach was to conflate the world of the civilian and the world of the soldier. Encouraged by the U.S. government itself, home front Americans could envision themselves in terms of the heroic and dauntless warriors who were so bravely defending the nation. If this conflation were successful, the American public would be participating in the war as home front soldiers—and equipped with potent war bonds as weapons. Ultimately, then, they would be better prepared to face adversity for the war effort. As Michael Osborn suggests, "what we are determines what we shall do, or at least what we shall attempt."[116] In terms of the Treasury's militarized mind-set, the metaphoric connection between CIVILIAN and SOLDIER thus framed an attempt to fashion millions of civilians into the buying audience so desired by the war bond strategists.

The Treasury's second strategy then facilitated an approaching enemy that was a threat to both combat soldiers on the battlefield and to civilians-*cum*-soldiers on the home front. Anthony D. Smith points out that "the propagandist's aim is the construction of favourable self-images and negative enemy stereotypes."[117] In the process of creating such an agonistic contrast, the Treasury inevitably made the worthiness of the American cause seem much greater. Moreover, by selling civilians on the idea that they were in solidarity with America's brave, stolid soldiers, the Treasury simultaneously sought to prepare the public to see the nation's enemies as a menacing threat. Although the Treasury's propaganda presented an invisible enemy in the first three drives, the threat posed by this implied adversary may have been the most practical and effective means of gaining the public's attention. Indeed, the images put the American public on notice that the enemy was nearly at their back door.

In this manner, the Treasury's war bond propaganda seemingly worked to militarize the American public in 1942–43. Just as U.S. soldiers were arriving on battlefields in a mental state of apprehensive enthusiasm, so too was the Treasury constructing an American public prepared for its part in the battle. From the perspective of military psychology, the Treasury was using its propaganda not only to help galvanize public war spirit but also to prepare the home front for the horrific battles to come. Ironically, however, the tedium of the prolonged war effort would soon facilitate a stage of resignation in the bond program's discourse. It is no surprise, then, to find that in its mission to recapture the attention of an increasingly frustrated audience, the Treasury's stark 1944 appeals would quickly surpass the propaganda of 1942–43 in terms of their power, brutality, and savagery.

3 WAR BOND DRIVES IN 1944

Struggling with Resignation

Even without final figures, one indisputable fact emerges: as the tempo of war increases, Americans have come to accept periodic War Loan Drives as the democratic way of meeting the urgency of war financing.
—*Minute Man,* March 1, 1944

The very fact that you are free to lend according to the dictates of your conscience, that no stormtrooper comes swaggering into your kitchen to demand your money . . . adds the more weight to your responsibility.
—Henry F. Morgenthau Jr.

In November 1943, Roosevelt, Churchill, and Stalin met together for the first time at the Teheran Conference. Although some disagreements arose about the next steps in the war, it was clear to the participants that "there was now no doubt the Allies were winning."[1] This sentiment was already shared by most Americans on the home front, due in part to the president's persistent attention to morale. According to Richard W. Steele, the Roosevelt administration continuously emphasized a positive outlook in the war's early years, ultimately fashioning "a latent public faith in victory."[2]

Yet the assurance of eventual victory was little solace for an American public that was growing weary of the war effort. As the "wave of patriotic emotion passed, as sacrifices became more demanding, [and] as the danger of invasion disappeared and victory grew more certain," the more elusive that victory seemed to become.[3] Looking back, even *Life* reported that "all . . . most people could say about the conflict was, 'When will it end?'"[4] Paul Fussell explains that "as the war went on and . . . casualties [became] more numerous," it was natural that "formulations of purpose or meaning" were beginning to wear thin.[5]

Once haunted by the possibility of public defeatism after Pearl Harbor, the Roosevelt administration began to fear that the prolonged war effort "might induce complacency, or worse still, a peace movement."[6] In the Treasury, the war bond program was concerned that "too many Americans are inclined to see victory as already assured."[7] The bond strategists began to worry that before long, the home front would lose its psychological motivation to purchase war bonds. After all, if the public was frustrated with the tedium of war, how soon would notions of sacrifice turn into despondency?

The Treasury's growing dilemma over public frustration in late 1943 would be familiar to veterans of many persuasive campaigns. Social movements, for example, typically find that the stage of enthusiastic mobilization is impossible to sustain as "fatigue, fears of anarchy, and boredom inevitably set in."[8] Such movements pass into a maintenance phase in which leaders no longer try to convert the masses but instead struggle to keep the waning membership from losing the faith. In response to this psychological malaise, social movement leaders often search "desperately for a triggering or catalytic event to return the cause to the enthusiastic mobilization stage."[9]

Campaigns targeted at battlefield soldiers and based in military psychology inevitably face a similar motivational challenge. Once the novelty of being in-theater wears thin, the psychological stage of apprehensive enthusiasm quickly begins to wane. The onset of combat, injuries, and deaths of comrades, and the challenge of facing a committed enemy all hasten the abandonment of any notions of fun or excitement.[10] Soldiers thus enter a psychological period that Peter Watson calls "resignation," in which they become "chronically depressed" and must struggle against the tedium of war.[11] Yet such soldiers are frequently motivated to fight when presented with fear-inducing situations in which their self-preservation is at stake. Much like the jaded members of social movements in decline, these soldiers require increasingly forceful imperatives to goad them into the behavior their superiors demand.[12]

The American public's growing frustration with the war near the end of 1943 presented a comparable challenge for the war bond propagandists. Not surprisingly, the Treasury's militarized campaign soon began to reflect the characteristics of a resignation phase. In targeting a home front audience that was seemingly losing its sense of war unity, the war bond strategists felt that they needed to adopt increasingly strident propaganda. Much like battlefield discourse aimed at motivating exhausted troops, the Treasury's 1944 propaganda was soon presenting graphic and disturbing appeals to the American public.

This stark new approach marked a distinct shift away from the "positive" direction projected by Peter H. Odegard as he was planning the Treasury operation in 1941. However, Odegard was no longer offering day-to-day guidance to the war bond program. In the absence of his moderating influence, the Treasury's propagandists adopted the startling new approach, as graphic as it was untested.

After the experience of three war bond drives, however, the remaining bond strategists felt that they were up to the challenge. A two-day Treasury conference in November heightened the staff's resolve that the fervor of 1944's drives would eclipse earlier efforts.[13] The recently completed Third War Loan, while large in its own right, was seen as an important opportunity for the Treasury to study its methods and to perfect its results. Robert Coyne, the campaign's assistant national director, wrote that polls taken during the third drive "would be of immense value in correcting weaknesses and emphasizing strong points."[14] Thus, as the Treasury celebrated its successes of 1942 and 1943, it was simultaneously girding its propaganda machine to meet the greater challenges presented by its target audience in 1944.[15]

In this chapter, I examine how the bond strategists responded to the challenge of the public's war weariness in the propaganda of the Treasury's fourth, fifth, and sixth drives. I argue that the Treasury's 1944 propaganda campaign developed a militarized reaction to spiraling signs of public discontentment. Much like military commanders trying to motivate battle-weary soldiers to fight on, the bond strategists filled their domestic propaganda campaign with increasingly aggressive appeals aimed at provoking Americans into renewed enthusiasm for the war. I contend, however, that in retrospect the Treasury's potent propaganda in this resignation phase was problematic because it offered more humanized images of the German enemy in contrast to fostering racist depictions of the Japanese people. This divergence, I suggest, may have helped normalize the dehumanization of the Japanese enemy, ultimately creating an atmosphere in which the complete annihilation of that enemy could be considered logical. To support these arguments, I first contextualize the background of the three drives, then analyze both the growing use of incongruity in the Treasury's civilian-soldier conflation and the development of the two divergent enemies. I conclude by summarizing the implications of the Treasury's strategic approach to its 1944 exigencies.

The 1944 Bond Drives in Context

The War Finance Division originally considered holding four war bond drives in 1944. The financial success of the 1942–43 efforts suggested that the public would be able to accept a heightened number of war loans. But Secretary Henry F. Morgenthau Jr. recognized that the possibility of President Roosevelt's fourth candidacy in the fall election might become a hindrance to sales. Specifically, he feared that running a bond drive just before the election would encourage Republicans to sabotage the effort in an attempt to embarrass the administration.[16] He ultimately decided, then, to hold three war loans in 1944, two well before the election and the other just after it.

The three 1944 drives benefited from two important lessons developed in the Third War Loan. First, in an attempt to systematize its third drive propaganda across various media, the bond operation worked on a campaign book that cataloged its appeals. The book appeared too late in the drive to have any organizational impact, however, so staffers immediately began to work on one for the fourth drive.[17] That campaign book—and subsequent versions in the fifth and sixth drives—became an important organizational tool for the Treasury's staffers. A related lesson emerged from the occasional use of inflammatory propaganda in the third bond drive, such as the depiction of American casualties. The public's acceptance of such appeals convinced the Treasury that "the only way to sell more bonds—indeed to speed the entire war effort—was to get the facts of the war to the American people honestly and brutally . . . [and] without gloves on."[18]

An internal Office of War Information appraisal of the Third War Loan reinforced this perception by emphasizing the success of stark portrayals from the field. "The strongest appeal in making people buy bonds [is] the casualty lists," the report pointed out. "It may be the wrong appeal—but it works." The report elaborated that "many people have become inured to campaigns and posters, newsreels and radio, except those newsreels that carried direct appeals from wounded service men and those 'hate' pictures that showed American war dead. Everyone seems to agree that the latter are the strongest appeal and make the people so mad they dig down deep." In support of this claim, the report relayed the scene in a "small county seat" where a local storefront devoted its window display to photographs of the county's "men and women in the armed services, including those already killed and those wounded." "Many a citizen lingered" in front of the display, said the report, "and then crossed the street to the postoffice [*sic*] to buy a bond."[19]

The Treasury's increased desire for such upsetting home front propaganda was developing at the same time Roosevelt's advisers were warning him about the emerging "shallowness of morale and the fragility of public unity."[20] Approached by Morgenthau about the erosion of enthusiasm, Roosevelt agreed to order army and navy censors to release more information and images from the fronts, including material previously held back as inappropriate for public consumption.[21] The result was a sudden increase in public exposure to information on Allied losses, stories of enemy atrocities, and images "once considered taboo."[22] While some of the new information and pictures were released too late for inclusion in the fourth drive's propaganda campaign, newspaper ads for the drive managed to include several images of American prisoners of war, injured soldiers, battlefield deaths, and military gravestones.

The unprecedented propaganda, not surprisingly, gave the Fourth War Loan an intense start. The drive opened on January 18, 1944, with the Treasury hoping to produce $14 billion in bond sales. By the end of the effort on February 18, one of every four billboards in the country carried a Fourth War Loan message, and more than one thousand magazines published at least one page of Treasury-generated copy for the drive.[23] This "more intense and more direct" propaganda helped produce a $16.7 billion total; E bond sales purchased by average Americans represented a 48 percent increase over those in the Third War Loan.[24] As Treasury put it, the drive "gave all [the] signs of being more firmly implanted in the public's consciousness than any before it."[25]

In achieving its success, the drive in some ways recycled earlier efforts. Morgenthau, for instance, wanted to use the slogan "Back the Attack" again, while his War Advertising Council copywriters wanted to use something new. Ted R. Gamble, the program's national director, proposed an acceptable compromise—"Let's All Back the Attack"—but the resemblance to the earlier slogan was unmistakable.[26] New for the fourth drive, on the other hand, was a shield proclaiming "we bought extra war bonds: 4th War Loan." It was intended to be displayed in home windows next to service flags, showing that both a family member and the family's money were in the service of the war effort.[27] As a result of the drive's ubiquitous propaganda, the Fourth War Loan shield "overnight became by far the most advertised and promoted trade mark in history."[28]

Yet the drive likewise displayed some telling signs that a frustrated resignation period was settling in. In an eighteen-city comparison of Fourth War Loan displays, only two cities produced creative exhibits. The other sixteen, reports George H. Roeder, "did not come up to the standards set by their annual Christmas decorations."[29] Moreover, one-third of the "we bought extra" shields awarded by the bond program were never displayed by their winners, despite the massive promotion.[30] And although the drive's emphasis was on increasing personal participation in the war, polls taken in its aftermath revealed that 66 percent of respondents felt that Americans were no longer taking the war seriously enough.[31]

The public's evident frustration was in part fed by an increasing awareness of the frightful costs of the war. The publication of journalist Robert Sherrod's *Tarawa,* for instance, vividly brought to the home front the atrocities of combat. Sherrod's candid book described the November, 1943, capture of Tarawa Atoll by U.S. Marines, a gruesome three-day battle in which American forces "lost more men than were lost in the six-month battle for Guadalcanal."[32] "His account," relates Paul Fussell, did "full justice to the inescapable horrors," of battle, concluding that "there is no easy way to win a war; there is no panacea which will prevent men from being killed."[33] With U.S. government officials predicting that 1944 would produce a 300 percent increase in American casualties, it was little wonder that the war-weary public was finding it difficult to maintain a fighting spirit.[34]

Gamble hoped that some of the public's frustration would dissipate in the buildup to D-day. Indeed, by April 3, 1944, when the Treasury announced the upcoming Fifth War Loan, most Americans were already beginning to anticipate the cross-channel invasion of German-controlled Europe.[35] With the fifth drive set for June 12 to July 8, the Treasury was well aware that its efforts could coincide with the long-awaited attack. "Within twelve hours" of the D-day news, the *Minute Man* told its sales force, "Washington headquarters will have mailed to newspapers all over the country six full-page mats of Invasion ads."[36] These preparations were prudent, since the June 6 invasion in fact began one week before the drive officially started.

The Fifth War Loan thus took place at a critical point, as the tempo of the war increased dramatically. Armed with its twice-recycled slogan, "Back the Attack—Buy More than Before," the drive opened with a goal of $16 billion in sales—the highest of all eight drives. The Treasury also developed an insignia device for the effort. Adorned with the Minute Man silhouette and the letter *V,* the insignia represented both the drive's name and the ubiquitous wartime symbol for "victory."[37] As Eisenhower and his invasion force struggled to gain ground in and around Normandy, the Treasury placed its insignia wherever it could find space, including "milk bottle collars, match book covers, envelope stickers, blotters, [and] laundry boxes."[38] By the drive's end, Allied forces were advancing deep into France, soon closing in on Paris. Americans on the home front echoed this success by exceeding the Treasury's goal by 29 percent, netting $20.6 billion in bond sales.[39]

After the final results of the effort were in, Morgenthau congratulated Gamble on the "smashing success" of the Fifth War Loan. "The timing and the result," he wrote, "made a fitting salute to our boys as they broke through the German lines."[40] The secretary did not mention that only 1 percent of respondents in a Treasury survey were able to correctly identify the official slogan for the drive.[41] Worse, sales of E bonds—those targeting the average investor—had actually declined compared to the Fourth War Loan.[42] And as public opinion polls indicated, 18 percent of the jaded and war-weary public were now in favor of ignoring Roosevelt's goal of unconditional German surrender, instead supporting peace talks with Hitler in order to shorten the war.[43] As the initial excitement of the invasion waned, the Treasury became increasingly concerned about the public's attitude.

The domestic angst also emerged in the acrimony of the ongoing presidential campaign. Hadley Cantril, the president's personal pollster, became concerned that Roosevelt's chances of reelection were thinning in the face of strong criticism from the Republican challenger, Thomas E. Dewey.[44] The quick pace of the Allied invasion ironically resulted in even more public attention on Dewey and his charges. "People think of Roosevelt as the man we need if there is a crisis ahead," advised Cantril. It would be helpful, he continued, to "convey the impression that the years ahead *are* critical."[45] Fortunately for Roosevelt, a crisis soon appeared when fierce fighting developed in the Philippines only three weeks before the election. The president's margin of victory over Dewey was the narrowest of his career, but it meant that his war leadership would continue.

Meanwhile, the Treasury was also alarmed by the successful Allied advances in Europe. In early October 1944, Germany's defeat seemed imminent.[46] Worried that a sudden German surrender would devastate bond sales, Morgenthau commissioned several polls to determine a course of action for the Treasury. Although the results suggested that a quick victory in Europe might not have much effect on sales after all, the bond staff decided to emphasize the Pacific theater in its propaganda as a way of reminding the weary public that the war would require continued struggle on the home front.[47]

Appropriately, for the Sixth War Loan the Treasury developed a marked emphasis on the fight against Japan. The drive opened on November 20, 1944, with a goal of $14 billion in bond sales. This time the Treasury decided against a slogan for the drive, instead choosing another insignia to represent the effort. The insignia featured a silhouetted bomb—with the words "6th War Loan" on its surface—landing on a Japanese flag.[48] Proclaiming "we're out to get Japan," Treasury workers spent the drive's twenty-seven days convincing the public that "everything costs more in the Pacific."[49] By the drive's end on December 16, the Treasury netted $21.6 billion in bond sales, eclipsing its goal by 54 percent.[50] Once again, however, E bond sales had decreased somewhat, perhaps reflecting the public's continued sense of war weariness.[51]

Ironically, however, on the day the Sixth War Loan ended, the German army proved that it still had some fight left. The Ardennes Offensive—known in the West as the Battle of the Bulge—began on December 16 and quickly put to rest any speculation of an imminent victory in Europe. The military's frustration at this turn of events was evident in its decision to place eighteen-year-old soldiers in combat units and to draft civilians over the age of twenty-six.[52] On the whole, however, 1944 was a successful year for the Allies on the battlefield. Although Berlin and Tokyo were still administering punishing counterattacks, the Axis powers were clearly running out of realistic options in the war. At the end of 1944, as Gerhard Weinberg puts it, the Axis powers found "the roof falling in and the Allies pounding on the doors."[53]

From the Treasury's perspective, though, 1944's financial successes only masked its increasingly alarmed concerns about the frustrated public. True, the Treasury's periodic war loan system now appeared to be the backbone of the administration's war finance efforts.[54] But E bond sales began to decline after the record set in the Fourth War Loan.[55] As pollster Dorwin Cartwright put it, "apparently with the success of the Allied armed forces the threat to the American way of life was receding in people's minds."[56] Gamble's assessment of the public's jaded attitude was equally disappointed. In his words, "since our homes were not attacked, there were still many Americans who did not inwardly bridge the gap between the war and the way they were living their lives." "Their patriotism," he concluded, "was latent."[57]

Much like frontline soldiers who have moved beyond their initial period of apprehensive enthusiasm, then, the Treasury viewed the American public as increasingly weary of the war effort. The public's apparent sense of frustration and the elusiveness of victory combined to make it more challenging for the U.S. government's domestic propaganda to have an impact. The Treasury's response to this challenge was to present increasingly forceful and disturbing appeals in the massive propaganda waves of the fourth, fifth, and sixth drives. As these appeals suggested, the Treasury's militarized propaganda campaign appeared to be struggling through a stage of resignation throughout 1944.

Resignation and Struggle in the 1944 Drives

As 1944 neared, the Treasury felt it was ready to unleash its biggest war drives yet. They were to be drives that would saturate the country with propaganda, selling not only bonds but also the outlook on the war that the administration wanted the public to share. At the same time, though, the public seemed to be descending into war weariness, meaning that the Treasury's well-planned drives would find a very challenging target audience because Americans were increasingly unwilling to sacrifice for the war effort. With the public's discontentment becoming a great concern of the president and his advisers, the bond strategists had ample motivation to meet the changing exigence of their target audience. Thus, the Treasury's propaganda shifted into graphic and forceful appeals appropriate to a battlefield stage of resignation.

On one level, the Treasury began to use its previous soldier-civilian conflation to point out the incongruities between the home front and the battlefront. While civilians could still understand themselves as soldiers, the Treasury was now suggesting that civilians were performing their militarized role poorly. On another level, the war bond strategists began to replace their inchoate enemy images with distinct portrayals of the adversary. These portrayals, however, presented a distinct divergence between the German enemy and the Japanese enemy. By the end of 1944—with the Treasury's focus finally restricted to Japan—the propaganda campaign descended into stark images of American war dead and a bestial enemy who would fight to the finish.

Civilians, Soldiers, and Incongruity

The key pioneer of public opinion polling in America, George Gallup, often accused the Roosevelt administration of overlooking the widespread use of polls as part of its wartime domestic agenda.[58] As J. Michael Hogan points out, such statements were to be expected from an individual whose primary goal was to popularize the widespread use of polls.[59] Not until after the war did it become clear that the various branches of Roosevelt's bureaucracy did in fact use polls with growing frequency during the war. Many of the various secretive centers of U.S. government-sponsored psychological warfare, for example, relied on the leadership of such pollsters as Rensis Likert, Elmo Roper, Hadley Cantril, and even Gallup himself.[60]

An important part of the growth in government-sponsored polling during the war emerged from the planning of the Treasury's bond drives. Polls taken during the first two bond drives, for instance, were instrumental in helping Treasury strategists refine their public sales pitches. As the Treasury soon discovered, the appropriately retooled appeals had dramatic effects on bond sales.[61] By the end of the Third War Loan, Morgenthau and his strategists were firm believers in the potency of public opinion polls. Guy Lemmon, the War Advertising Council's campaign manager for the Treasury, emphasized the bond program's growing reliance on pollsters when he recalled that "the starting point for all our work" was the "findings of the Likert consumer studies."[62]

At about the same time that the Treasury's faith in pollsters was on the rise, several public opinion polls were beginning to describe some disturbing trends. These polls—published in dozens of newspapers nationwide—suggested to policy makers that the public was becoming increasingly frustrated with the war's slow progress. When 66 percent of respondents told pollsters that the home front was no longer taking the war seriously, for example, a follow-up question indicated that nearly half who felt that way had no idea what could be done to improve morale. Worse, 80 percent of respondents worried that the greatest sacrifices of the war were still to come.[63] Given the Treasury's flourishing belief in such polls, it is no surprise that Morgenthau's strategists were increasingly concerned about the public's psychological malaise. Their strategic response in the resignation phase, however, was grounded in a classic propagandist's belief: that public opinion is not just a bottom-up tool used for reading the public mood; it can also be a top-down tool used to shape the public itself by those well-versed in propaganda technique.[64]

Plans for 1944's war loans, then, were developing just as the Treasury determined that it needed to charge its propaganda campaign with appeals that would shock the increasingly war-weary home front. Taking advantage of Roosevelt's release of previously censored material, the bond staff was soon prepared to electrify the public. The Fourth War Loan's internal campaign book, for instance, reprinted the first published picture of dead American soldiers—a grim photograph of three bodies on a New Guinea beach (see fig. 3.1). "Ask your editor to take advantage of similar news picture breaks," the Treasury advised its news outlets, "and . . . write a dramatic War Loan message about them."[65] With such an approach in mind, the Treasury was preparing to adapt to the changing nature of its audience by turning the 1944 drives into a disturbing series of graphic appeals.

3.1 First photograph of dead American soldiers released to the public. The shocking nature of such images was aimed at motivating the home front to ever greater support for the war. Courtesy Franklin D. Roosevelt Library.

The Treasury's new outlook had significant implications for its civilian-soldier conflation. In the 1942–43 drives, this conflation facilitated heightened levels of public enthusiasm for the war. While it was true that some of the Treasury's earlier imagery depicted scenes of impending battle, displays of actual violence seldom emerged. The 1944 drives, however, would soon show American soldiers engaged in life-or-death combat, injured GIs bleeding from gaping wounds, and even dead troops. These scenes would inevitably foster more tension in the civilian-soldier conflation. After all, it is far less appealing to imagine oneself as a soldier when viewing a depiction of a dying infantryman.

The Treasury's 1944 propaganda quickly took advantage of the discomfort produced by the graphic nature of its new imagery. While the Treasury's rhetoric continued to indicate that civilians should be seen as soldiers in the war effort, the bond strategists used increasingly disturbing depictions of combat, suggesting that civilians were not taking their war responsibilities seriously enough. Here the Treasury was exploiting the fact that while CIVILIANS could still be seen through the lens of SOLDIERS, the convergence of the two domains was inevitably incomplete. As George Lakoff and Mark Johnson explain, "metaphorical structuring . . . is partial, not total. If it were total, one concept would actually *be* the other, not merely be understood in terms of it."[66] Kenneth Burke agrees, adding that metaphors frequently introduce "incongruity in that the two realms are never identical."[67]

The bond strategists' shift, then, was what Burke calls "peripety," a strategic moment of reversal.[68] Where the Treasury's propaganda once conflated CIVILIANS as SOLDIERS, now it depended on that same conflation to reveal the ironic incongruities between the two domains. In this sense, Americans could still see themselves as soldiers, but increasingly as *ineffective soldiers* who were not taking up their level of responsibility in the war effort. "The strongest single appeal to buy Bonds and back the attack," explained the fourth drive's internal copy policy, "is graphic comparison of the hardships we at home are asked to undergo with what our fathers, brothers, and neighbors are enduring . . . in battle." Although "this is not a new appeal," continued the advice, establishing a stark "contrast in personal sacrifice" between soldiers and civilians would give it new power.[69] With this shift, the Treasury was adopting a strategy of ironic conflation.[70] Indeed, the Treasury's strategic use of such highlighted incongruities between international soldiers and domestic ones may have been all the more powerful because the home front was by now accustomed to flattering comparisons with their GIs.

With its January, 1944, kickoff, the Fourth War Loan immediately began to develop this strategy by following its copy guide's suggestion to "thrust home the stark, realistic picture of what is physically happening to our own men in battle . . . [using] actual examples . . . photographs . . . [and] names."[71] "When you go home tonight," proclaimed one ad, "think of a boy who never will" (see fig. 3.2) The "boy," actually a solider, lies on the ground, the contorted position of his prone body suggesting the final moments of a painful and lonely death. Clearly he will never get home alive.[72] Another ad depicted a soldier being shot on the battlefield. The ad displayed an army medal for valor, explaining that the dying GI "stopped bullets intended for *you* . . . The 4th WAR LOAN is *YOUR* opportunity to do something about it."[73] Although in retrospect these images seem relatively subdued, images of American war dead and dying were taboo until just before the drive. Such images, then, responded to the public's growing sense of frustration. By heightening the level of drama in its appeals and by hinting that the home front was not doing its part in the struggle, the Treasury's propaganda reflected more resignation-based strategies. In the process, it was adapting to the war-weary public.

Indeed, at times the Treasury's new approach seemed as anxious to contrast civilians and soldiers as its earlier propaganda was to stress their similarities. One ad presented side-by-side panels of a woman on a shopping trip and a battlefront gravestone. On the left, the woman's puzzled look signified an inner debate as she decided which on-sale outfit to purchase. On the right, the gravestone was cast in shadow and offered a solemn contrast to the woman's seemingly insignificant dilemma. The ad's text rhetorically asked the obvious question: "who is making the greatest sacrifice?" The power of such appeals, of course, was grounded in the civilian-soldier conflation, which made the gulf between the shopper and the dead soldier seem even wider.[74]

The fourth drive developed this theme even further by accusing civilians of throwing parties while soldiers were fighting and dying on their behalf. As one radio spot intoned, "The day you threw a party instead of buying a War Bond—thousands and thousands of our boys were braving Jap snipers and German artillery to make it nice and cozy for you—to give you a world where you could *have* parties anytime you wanted them. Not *one* of those boys got an invitation to your party. But that's all right. They were too *busy* to come."[75]

3.2 Fourth War Loan advertisement portraying the violent death of an American soldier. The Treasury used this and similar messages to attempt to bring the painful realities of the war home to its target audience. Courtesy National Archives.

A newspaper ad echoed this theme, suggesting that "the day you threw a party instead of buying a bond" the war continued unabated for American soldiers. To complete this logic, the ad juxtaposes a large scene of struggling sailors with a smaller image of civilians in evening dress, dancing and enjoying pleasant conversation (see fig. 3.3).[76] Much like the montage image used in the Third War

3.3 Fourth War Loan advertisement offering an ironic contrast between battlefield soldiers and a home front that has decided to throw parties instead of continuing its militarized duty. Note the text's final taunt: "Did you have a good time?" Courtesy National Archives.

Loan a few months earlier, this ad presented a direct comparison between the battlefront and the home front. Yet unlike the earlier ad, these civilians were clearly shirking their military duty. Thus, although the conflation between CIVILIANS and SOLDIERS remained, the Treasury's propaganda now emphasized the incongruities between the two domains. While this shift to an ironic conflation maintained that civilians should still be understood as soldiers, it also insisted that committed home front soldiers would fight through war weariness to get the job done.[77]

To the Treasury's chagrin, however, the unprecedented propaganda of the Fourth War Loan seemed to have only moderate impact on the public's frustration about the war's progress. A March, 1944, Gallup poll, for instance, suggested that more than half of the war-weary public believed the struggle would not end until 1946 or later.[78] In the face of such pessimism, the Treasury's strategists resolved to use "down-to-earth, hard-hitting copy that welds the Bond Drive and the coming [D-day] invasion" in its next drive. "Advertising, Press, [and] Radio," they continued, "should convey a note of desperate urgency."[79] Evidently, the Treasury hoped that its garish depictions of American casualties and deaths in the Fifth War Loan would force the public to fight through its malaise.

The fifth drive's illustrations thus portrayed American casualties in more graphic ways than ever before, again evidencing a resignation stage. "Do *you* expect to be alive by dinner time?" asked one ad. "A number of Americans will not be." The explicit drawing accompanying these harsh words featured a dead soldier, his head still bleeding. His unopened field rations lay in the dirt next to him and his helmet was on the ground, revealing on its underside a picture of his sweetheart back home. "Many more Americans will be dead before this day is ended," continued the ad. "Many more tomorrow. Many every day in the weeks to come."[80] A similar ad presented what was probably the most disturbing drawing of the war drives, an image of a dead American soldier against a spartan background of smoke, fire, and crumbling buildings (see fig. 3.4). His helmet has a bullet hole in it, and a river of blood flows down the side of his face. His eyes, however, remain open in an eerie stare, and he is evidently speaking to the viewer: "I died today . . . what did *you* do?"[81] Even though they were not photographs, such drawings reproduced a compelling sense of detail and authenticity for the viewing audience. As Paul Messaris suggests, "the essential point of an ad's image can be conveyed quite adequately through a drawing."[82] The essential point of these drawings was a realistic and dramatic presentation of the sacrifices of America's GIs in battle, as well as an explicit verbal comparison with the sacrifices of the home front.

Perhaps more effective than drawings, however, were actual photographs of American dead. Such images can take on a "dual function as carrier of truth-value and symbol."[83] With its increased access to previously censored photographs from the battlefront, the

3.4 Treasury advertisement featuring a drawing of a spectral soldier demanding that the home front reader sacrifice to buy more bonds during the Fifth War Loan. Courtesy Franklin D. Roosevelt Library.

Treasury's fifth drive took advantage of this dual function. "So you can't buy another war bond," intoned one ad. "Take a good look at this American soldier as he lies in the mud of Rendova Island in the Southwest Pacific, victim of a Jap air raid. It's not a pleasant scene, is it?"[84] The dead man in the photograph was lying face down, covered with mud, his possessions scattered around him. The knowledge that this image was of an actual soldier's corpse gave the picture a vivid element of finality. "When you are asked to buy an extra War Bond to Back the Attack," the text continued, "think of this picture of your fellow American blasted by the concussion of a Jap bomb thousands of miles from home. Then, brother, don't you think you will want to dig a little deeper to back up his comrades?"[85] The testimony of such pictures, of course, evidenced further use of ironic conflation. Here was an actual photograph of an American soldier, dead far from his homeland and loved ones. By relying on what Barbie Zelizer calls "photography's aura of realism," the war bond strategists were trying yet another way to reach the war-weary public.[86] Faced with such indisputable evidence of their soldiers' terrible sacrifices, home front soldiers would be more likely to recognize that they were not yet making the same effort or sacrifices as those on the battlefront—or so Treasury hoped.

The Fifth War Loan's propaganda found still other ways to drive home its ironic conflation. At times, the drive's appeals seemed to be taunting the public with their melodramatic descriptions of the home front's apparent shortcomings. "Thinking of buying a bond?" asked one ad. "Men are dying while you make up your mind."[87] Another ad addressed the public's potential weariness of bond drive hoopla: "Tired of lending? You don't know what being tired is!" The accompanying photograph depicted a half dozen GIs, collapsed upon their return from an exhausting tour at the front.[88] The simplest appeal in this vein accompanied the garish "I died today . . . what did *you* do?" image (fig. 3.4). "The next time you pick up your paper or listen to the radio news," advised the text, "have a conference with yourself. 'Am I doing as much as I can to help win this war? Am I matching what *I* can do with what the boys are doing over there?'" Another appeal asked "what did I do today that some mother's son should die for me tonight?" Evidently, suggested the Treasury, the answers to these questions were "no" and "not enough."[89]

In such appeals, the bond staff was clearly capitalizing on the partial incongruity between CIVILIANS and SOLDIERS. Indeed, as Burke's perspective suggests, the Treasury's new approach was emphasizing the ironic connection between the "integral motives" of "villainy" and "virtue."[90] That is, if home front civilians were truly soldiers, then they could share in the virtues of American GIs. By playing on the incongruities between the home front and the battlefront, however, the Treasury was simultaneously holding up the virtue of soldiering and the villainy of not living up to a soldier's duties. In this ironic conflation, then, the Treasury was seemingly using graphic images of its soldiers to solidify its civilian-soldier conflation and to induce guilt among the public, potentially motivating an increased commitment to the war effort.

Whether they were drawings or actual photographs, such graphic images of American war casualties in the fifth drive were an important part of what appeared to be the Treasury program's increasingly desperate resignation phase. Yet once again the shocking war bond appeals seemed to have difficulty prodding the home front back into an enthusiastic war fervor. Despite the drive's proximity to the D-day invasion, for instance, the sale of E bonds actually *declined* for the first time since the initial war loan in 1942.[91] Worse, nearly a fifth of the public now said it would consider peace talks with the Nazis in order to shorten the war effort.[92] As the initial excitement of the invasion waned, then, the Treasury's concerns about the home front's war weariness continued.

By November's Sixth War Loan, the Treasury was still trying to reach the public through realistic depictions of the war. While the drive's propaganda shifted focus to the Pacific theater, it remained quite graphic. Although "death and pain are done in France," intoned a soldier in one ad, "*here* the enemy is very much alive. . . . His bullets still are made of lead. . . . Their angry whispers still foretell of sudden death for me and others crouched in slime and mud."[93] Underlining this danger was an image that showed a series of American soldiers grimly carrying their war dead back from the battle.[94] Another image depicted American prisoners of war. Their despondent posture and wide-eyed, blank stares gave stronger meaning to the caption: "*next* year isn't soon enough for them."[95] As before, these images continued to portray American soldiers as endangered, exhausted, even killed in action. Implicit in such depictions was the Treasury's ongoing ironic conflation of its heroic battlefront soldiers and the faltering civilian soldiers on the home front.

The Sixth War Loan also featured explicit comparisons between home front and battlefront. "Our part has been easy," insisted one ad. Buying bonds, it continued, would be a way to "*prove* our thanksgiving" for the unimaginable sacrifice of those on the front lines.[96] But while the Treasury minimized the work of those on the home front, it reminded Americans that its soldiers "*can't* come back till it's over, over there!"[97] "Your country is still at war," exclaimed another ad, "are you?"[98] Yet another ad made the conflation between home front and battlefront even clearer with its photographs of exhausted soldiers recovering from battle and carrying their war dead on stretchers. "You can't afford it?" asked the text. "Neither could they!"[99] As in many of 1944's other images, these ads allowed direct comparisons between home front and battlefront. The Treasury continued to ask the public to view CIVILIANS in terms of SOLDIERS. But as Burke suggests, "the seeing of something in terms of something else . . . necessarily involves varying degrees of incongruity."[100] Thus, by emphasizing the ironic incongruities between the two domains, the bond strategists were in effect using guilt appeals to reach an audience mired in the frustrations of a long war.

The significance of the Treasury's use of this strategic incongruity becomes clearer when examined in light of the more favorable comparisons that preceded it. With its patriotic zeal, the Treasury initially attempted to portray the public as soldiers and bonds as their weapons. But increasing public war weariness as 1944 neared motivated the Treasury to shift its approach to highlighting the shortcomings of the public in comparison with its GIs on the battlefront. If, to borrow Black's perspective, the Treasury had initially worked to create an enthusiastic buying audience with its propaganda, by 1944 its propaganda was portraying a far different audience, one that was clearly falling short of its militarized duties.[101] No longer could average Americans perceive themselves as perfect soldiers in the war effort, even though they were conditioned to do so. In fact, the Treasury's new strategy played on the public's expectation of favorable comparisons by creating an unfavorable incongruity. The public was simultaneously goaded by the expectation to live up to the "perfect" duties of American soldiers and the accusation of failing to meet that expectation.[102] Thus, if the public felt an atmosphere of guilty urgency in seeking to live up to its militarized promise, that atmosphere was rooted in the increasingly shrill appeals of the bond program's resignation phase.

As the Treasury's 1944 propaganda increasingly disturbed the metaphoric bond between home front and battlefront, however, the average American purchased fewer and fewer E series bonds. Moreover, the public's frustration seemed to *increase* along with the Treasury's use of ironic conflation. The heightened drama of the Treasury's resignation propaganda, then, appeared to have trouble impacting the public, despite the shocking and disturbing appeals.

In part, the Treasury's in-your-face strategy may have backfired in the same way excessive fear appeals can lead an audience "to ignore, minimize, or deny the importance of the threat."[103] Robert L. Ivie makes a similar conclusion about Cold War "idealist" rhetoric, in which pacifists created a "self-defeating" rhetoric by blaming Americans for faults normally associated with the Soviets. This rhetoric, Ivie reports, labeled the United States "irrational, coercive, and aggressive."[104] Not surprisingly, the idealist rhetoric was ultimately rejected by its target audience as a failure.

In the same way, while the increased intensity of 1944's drives seemed to gain the target audience's attention, it also alienated them. As Odegard predicted at the beginning of the bond efforts, "although it may be possible to sell quickly a large volume of bonds by using certain high pressure procedures, the net result, however impressive financially, will be bad when measured in terms of good will and national unity."[105] The Treasury's strategic shift in its civilian-soldier conflation, then, seemed to epitomize Odegard's warning and may in fact have revealed how tenuous the connection between bond propaganda and public morale could become. Odegard's warning was tested, however, in another way in 1944—this time in the bond program's depiction of two very different enemies.

Depicting Two Divergent Enemies

As the Treasury was developing its conflation of civilians and soldiers in 1944, it was simultaneously extending its enemy imagery. Consistent with Ivie's research on decivilizing discourse, the bond propaganda continued to depict the enemy with pointed verbal accusations of aggression, irrationality, and force.[106] During the Fourth War Loan, for example, the Treasury immediately capitalized on the news of Japanese treatment of American prisoners in the Bataan Death March. Although this incident had occurred nearly two years earlier, the distribution of the information during the Fourth War Loan electrified and angered the public.[107] As the Treasury's internal newsletter described it, "with the release of the horrible story of Japanese barbarism in the Philippines came a boiling anger that was reflected in a skyward upturn of daily Bond sales. 'Avenge Bataan' drives sprouted all over the nation."[108] In accordance with Ivie's findings, such verbal strategies were an important means of continuing to demonize the enemy for public consumption. As Paul R. Pillar explains, "it is easier to raise armies, money, and morale if a conflict is viewed as a struggle between good and evil."[109] The Treasury's newsletter thus encouraged its sales force to tell the public that "*the enemy is more powerful today than at the beginning of the war.*"[110]

The primarily verbal focus of Ivie's research, however, does not completely account for the depth and direction of the Treasury's enemy depictions in 1944. Instead, Jürgen Link's perspective offers an account of the verbal *and* visually based depictions in the Treasury's propaganda. Link argues that humans have the capacity to characterize two different sorts of enemies.[111] The first kind is typically personified as a devil playing poker, chess, or some other game with rules. This enemy has various evil characteristics, but his personification indicates that he is at least aware of the rules and can have some sense of responsibility.[112] Although this nemesis is undeniably a mortal enemy, he does have some important humanlike qualities and therefore negotiation with him is possible.

The second kind of enemy is "symbolically assigned to . . . chaos." These are enemies who—at least as humans depict them—"cannot be symbolic partners or even opponents; they are excluded from the start as co-players and are incapable of following the rules of the game."[113] They are, in short, savage creatures or monsters, and negotiation with them by definition is impossible. In propaganda, Link suggests, such enemies often become "germs, cancer cells, or swarms of vermin."[114] These dehumanizing images help produce a not-so-subtle attitude toward this type of enemy. To those viewing such propaganda, this enemy does not deserve to be treated as human. Instead, it logically invites annihilation or extermination.

The Treasury's 1944 propaganda campaign gradually portrayed both types of enemy, especially in its use of demonizing imagery. The German enemy, as presented in the Treasury's propaganda, was undeniably evil. While Hitler and his Nazi soldiers appeared to present a significant threat to Americans, however, they remained essentially human. Thus, they became "devils vested with human traits"—though vicious, unethical, and dangerous, they were still presumably rational and thus aware of the "rules" of war.[115] The Japanese enemy, in contrast, was depicted as a series of despicable, brutish beasts. In the Treasury's propaganda, Japanese soldiers eventually developed into racist caricatures without evident morals, precepts, or even a sense of humanity. In Link's words, they became "part of a peril that lacks subjectivity, that is not even human."[116] This depiction of the dehumanized Japanese enemy was a strategic choice, characteristic of the Treasury's resignation phase. Unfortunately, it may also have helped usher in an atmosphere of public opinion in which the use of the most extreme forms of warfare against Japan could seem reasonable, even expected.[117]

In the Fourth War Loan, the Treasury's strategists set the stage for these dichotomous images by keeping the enemy generally out of sight while simultaneously increasing its threatening nature.[118] The primary poster of the drive depicted an American soldier who diverged from earlier images in two ways (see fig. 3.5). The soldier was among the first in Treasury propaganda to actually deploy his weapon—in this case a grenade. Although the grenade is still in his throwing hand, his stance indicates that he is about to hurl it at the enemy, giving the poster an effect of incipient motion. A second difference was that this soldier—again for one of the first times in a bond drive appeal—faces away from the onlooker in a partial rear view, throwing his grenade in the same direction the viewer is looking. Such stances are significant because "there is a suggestion of an interaction with someone whom we do not see."[119] Here, of course, it was the enemy soldiers who were clearly just out of view, and the soldier was one moment away from opening fire on them. To underline this impression, the poster's text tells viewers to "[l]et 'em have it," implying that the purchase of a bond would make its mark on the battlefield.[120] The positioning of the grenade in relation to the poster's text offered a similar—though more subtle—message: "buy [grenades] extra bonds."

The fourth drive's appeals depicted the approach of the enemy in other ways. A billboard for the drive, for instance, gave the viewer a "subjective shot," which offers "the visual experience of seeing the world through someone else's point of view."[121] In this image, the audience saw through a submarine's periscope, viewing a sinking Japanese ship that had just been hit by the submarine's torpedo. Although the only indication of affiliation was the ship's Japanese flag, the viewing civilian-*cum*-soldier was clearly assumed to be supportive of this strike on unseen sailors, as the ad's text exclaimed, "let's all back the attack!"[122] Another image depicted an out-of-sight enemy attacking Americans. Here, alarmed American sailors were shown atop a ship that was being bombed. The lethal bombs plunging into the side of the ship, the image implied, resulted from the enemy's perfidy.[123] Such images, though presenting an anonymous adversary, remained powerful reminders to the public that there was a dangerous enemy who was ready to engage American forces with potentially lethal power. Indeed, by showing the direct effects of the enemy's proximity, this image subverted "rationality by reversing cause and effect."[124] In other words, by showing the results of the enemy's attack without showing the enemy itself, the drawing fostered what J. P. Telotte calls "a chilling suspense" in its viewers.[125] Moreover, by intoning, "while your $100 nestled in the bank," the image not only reinforced its civilian-soldier conflation, it also implied that the home front soldiers' financial selfishness was playing a part in the enemy's attack. Such appeals exemplified the

Fig. 3.5 Primary poster for the Fourth War Loan. The image implies that the enemy is just outside the frame, within throwing distance of a live grenade. Note the positioning of the grenade between "buy" and "extra bonds." Courtesy National Archives.

Fourth War Loan's resignation-based efforts to reinvigorate its target audience.

In the Treasury's Fifth War Loan, the strategic portrayal of the enemy began to develop a close-up focus. Almost immediately, the depiction of Germans and Japanese diverged. In the radio broadcast launching the drive, for instance, the Treasury offered an extended comparison of "the words of our enemies" with "statements of free men from many lands."[126] As reprinted in the Treasury's booklet, *These Are Their Words on Freedom and Tyranny,* however, the only enemies given voice were the "devil's brood"—Hitler, Goebbels, and other Nazis.[127] The Japanese, in contrast, were not even accorded an opportunity to express themselves, even in the sort of hate-filled venom the booklet assigned to Hitler. Following Link's perspective, here was an immediate signal that one enemy was allowed "subject status," while "those representing external chaos" were not.[128]

The imagery of the fifth drive followed a similar pattern. Nazi soldiers made one of their initial appearances in an ad featuring an Allied dive bomber (see fig. 3.6). For the first time, the Treasury showed an American attack from the enemy's perspective. This time the American combatant remains faceless. The Germans, on the other hand, are quite visible, either writhing in pain from the attack or running in fear.[129] In another image, an American infantryman was shown plunging his bayonet into the torso of a German soldier. Although the victim was holding a knife in stabbing position, his face was a mask of mortal pain.[130] All these German soldiers were being accorded subject status; despite their threatening appearance, they were clearly humanized, implying a rational "sense of responsibility."[131] Although they represented intimidating figures, their appearance was distinguishable from American soldiers primarily by their uniform.

Compared with its depiction of humanized German soldiers, the Treasury's portrayal of the Japanese enemy in the fifth drive quickly developed a *dehumanized* focus. Incongruously, the text accompanying the ad in which the German soldier suffered a bayonet wound demeaned not the Nazis but their Pacific ally. The ad's text began, "'That's the way I like to see them,' said Gen. MacArthur when he saw the rows of dead Japs in the Admiralty Islands." The text then emphasized the alleged barbarity of the Japanese, arguing that "in this war—the costliest, cruelest war of all time—our boys must fight with savage fury. Kill or be killed!"[132] Another ad supplied a Japanese image to these textual sentiments, showing an American soldier using his rifle stock to force a Japanese soldier to the ground

3.6 Fifth War Loan advertisement showing German soldiers under attack from an anonymous American pilot. This view of the enemy suggests that he is menacing, but not dehumanized. Courtesy National Archives.

(see fig. 3.7).[133] The hairless victim has a primitive expression and is depicted almost entirely upside down. This brutal look and subservient posture, combined with the righteous anger on the face of the American soldier, underlined the Treasury's increasingly dehumanized image of the Japanese. In comparison with the German

3.7 Treasury advertisement for the Fifth War Loan, portraying a righteous U.S. Marine killing a dehumanized Japanese enemy. Note the victim's clawlike right hand (*bottom center*). Courtesy National Archives.

soldiers—and their resemblance to depictions of American GIs—the Japanese enemy was already being portrayed as more savage, even brutish. With such irrational enemies, says Link, "dialogue . . . would be symbolically absurd."[134]

One ad for the drive allowed a direct comparison of the two enemies in the Treasury's propaganda.[135] It was a cartoon, showing a giant hand labeled "5th War Loan" pushing Hitler and Tojo (i.e., Japanese war minister Tojo Hideki) from a cliff. Hitler appeared in caricature, but was clearly human; his expression was one of bemused worry. Tojo's depiction, in contrast, showed signs of racist imagery. His eyes, for instance, were shown behind large spectacles, giving him an ignorant, oblivious air. Furthermore, the drawing represented him with only two teeth, which protruded obscenely from his mouth. His overall appearance made him look quite inhuman, even animal-like. While the ad invited viewers to use bond purchases in the fifth drive to push both "Hitler and Tojo into oblivion," it was clear that the divergence between the European enemy and the Asian enemy was growing in the Treasury's depictions.

By November 1944, it looked to many observers as if the Germans were about to surrender, so it is not surprising that in Sixth War Loan depictions the Nazi enemy disappeared almost entirely. Indeed, the drive's propaganda effectively relocated the battlefield to the Pacific. "Although the Germans are licked," explained one ad, "these Jap-fighters must go on . . . sweating, fighting, bleeding . . . till the last Jap has had his belly full of war—and says so."[136] Another ad exhorted: "Let's pour it on them! Let's shove the men, the ships, the guns, and the planes over there in an overwhelming, irresistible, avenging flood that will wind up this Jap business fast, once and for all!"[137] And the general poster for the drive featured a sweating American GI, his teeth bared, looking angrily at an image of the Japanese islands. The ad's text read simply, "Next!"[138] To even the most oblivious reader, such powerful images and words made it clear that the fight had moved to the Pacific.

Meanwhile, the Japanese enemy was becoming more and more of a dangerous creature in the Treasury's propaganda. "From the start," intoned the sixth drive's internal handbook to its national sales force, "the Jap has been a cruel, treacherous foe. He has inflicted on us the worst defeats in our military history . . . the bitterest medicine this nation ever had to swallow. Without dragging in atrocity stories, we should be able to capitalize on the hostility the American people feel."[139] But as some of the appeals in the sixth drive demonstrated, the Treasury was quite willing to use atrocity tales and anything else it could find to dehumanize the Japanese enemy. The Sixth War Loan cry "there's more to remember than Pearl Harbor!" for instance, continued to dramatize the atrocities of the Bataan incident nearly a year after its news became public.[140]

In fact, the Treasury's public depictions of the Japanese enemy in this last drive of 1944 often emerged as potent images of dehumanization, images that have not lost their power to shock, even some sixty years later. One appeal, for instance, cried, "Help stamp out this snake-in-the-grass" (see fig. 3.8). Here, a gigantic shoe marked "6th War Loan" is about to stomp on a serpent with the hissing, monstrous face of a Japanese soldier, complete with fangs. As the image's text emphasizes: "slimy, treacherous, tough—that's the kind of enemy we've got to lick in the Pacific."[141] A similar ad suggested that viewers should "strangle this octopus" as it showed Uncle Sam's hands doing exactly that to a tentacled creature—which was portrayed with an ugly caricature of a Japanese face, spectacles, buck teeth, and a pointed tongue.

In addition to stomping and strangling, the Treasury's propaganda recommended other extreme forms of violence as appropriate for the Japanese enemy. One ad shouted, "They Stabbed Us in the Back; Let's Give It to Them Face to Face." The accompanying full-page image was a realistic, detailed drawing of a GI using a flamethrower to incinerate a nearby Japanese soldier, who was depicted upside down and flying backward through the air even as the vivid flames consumed him. The ad's caption justified this personal violence by asking, "Remember that bloody Sunday when the Japs stabbed us in the back? Remember those dark days when we had to give way on half a dozen fronts in the Pacific? Remember how you wished you, *personally,* could do something about it?"[142] An even more telling appeal, perhaps, described the Japanese to rural bond buyers as a sort of crop. Using this troubling comparison, one ad suggested that "our farm boys harvest Japs" while another described an armored vehicle as a "Jap harvester," in direct visual comparison with a tractor.[143] Clearly, whether they were serpents, savages, or plant life awaiting an American reaper, the Japanese enemy in these images was no longer human and seemed to deserve the worst violence possible. As a soldier in yet another ad summarized, "you can't kill too many of them for me."[144] Such appeals represented a dehumanized and troubling culmination of the Treasury's dynamic depiction of the Japanese enemy in 1944.

In its struggle against the public's perceived war weariness, then, the Treasury elevated its enemy imagery to new levels. As Link's

3.8 Sixth War Loan advertisement featuring a caricature of a dehumanized Japanese figure. In late 1944 the Treasury's propaganda began to depict the Japanese as snakes and other creatures, implying that this particular enemy deserved an especially violent death. Courtesy National Archives.

research suggests, the human mind can accommodate two very different kinds of enemy.[145] Evidence of this ability appears not only in the Treasury's verbal texts, but also in the image-based appeals of its graphic 1944 propaganda campaign. Yet in these divergent depictions of the enemy, one must question whether the Treasury in effect helped call into being an audience that in fact could see the Japanese as less than human. As Black argues, audiences "look to the discourse they are attending for cues that tell them how they are to view the world, even beyond the expressed concerns, the overt propositional sense, of the discourse."[146] The real-world implications of Black's suggestion for the Treasury's 1944 target audience are sobering. If an audience is persuaded to view an enemy as human and rational, then it may be possible to negotiate and even to make peace with that enemy in spite of his undesirable characteristics. But if an audience is persuaded to view an enemy as an irrational, inhuman savage, then such peaceful steps are much more difficult to justify.

It should not be surprising to find, then, that even after the D-day invasion and the stark propaganda of the Fifth War Loan, many Americans were still willing to negotiate with Hitler for peace. After all, the German enemy was relatively humanized, and disappeared in the Treasury's ubiquitous propaganda altogether by the end of the year. The Japanese enemy, in contrast, increased in its depicted brutality throughout the three drives. By the time the Sixth War Loan portrayed a shift in the battle to the Pacific, there was only one kind of enemy left, and it was cruel, savage, and inhuman.[147] At best, this lack of Japanese personhood meant that few Americans could quibble with the demand that Japan surrender unconditionally. After all, how does one negotiate peace with inhuman savages? At worst, such depictions could have helped create a climate in which the eventual use of firebombs and even the atomic bomb against Japanese cities could seem justified, even paramount. Ultimately, then, it is important to consider whether the sense of dramatic urgency evident in the Treasury campaign's resignation propaganda worked to exacerbate the public's tendency to support drastic action against this dehumanized Japanese enemy.

Implications of the 1944 War Bond Drive Appeals

Although the Treasury spent much of its 1944 efforts describing the Japanese and German enemy, its true adversary was the public's frustration at the war's slow progress. If the bond drives are viewed as a military operation, then Treasury may be seen as trying to motivate its battle-weary home front troops—the public—into renewed action on behalf of the Roosevelt administration. From January's Fourth War Loan to November's Sixth War Loan, the bond staff adapted its strategic approach by developing appeals characteristic of a resignation stage. These appeals contradicted Odegard's 1941 advice to the Treasury by seeking to shock the increasingly discontented public into buying bonds and into caring about the war effort once again. The stark appeals of the year's three drives were clear reminders that the Treasury was engaged in a mission much broader than a simple financial effort. But in responding to its exigency throughout 1944, the Treasury's militarized propaganda campaign arguably contained seeds of destructiveness.

In a sense, of course, the public's mood presented the bond staff with few palatable alternatives. As John Morton Blum suggests, the Treasury's increasingly stark appeals "grew naturally out of the recourse to market research as a guide to promotional content."[148] Faced with evidence of an increasingly frustrated home front audience, the Treasury's approach echoed the demands of a military leader trying to galvanize exhausted troops. But in its attempts to adapt to the public's war weariness through the use of resignation-based shock appeals, the Treasury was ultimately left with two disturbing strategies.

One strategy relied primarily not on patriotism, but on guilt. It built on the favorable conflation between home front and battlefront by pointing out the ironic incongruities between international soldiers and domestic ones. Although this approach was imbedded in the original civilian-soldier conflation, it featured heavy-handed ad copy and images that portrayed home front soldiers as shirking their militarized duties. Such an approach apparently did not positively impact public morale or bond purchases. Indeed, E bond sales decreased somewhat throughout each of the 1944 drives.[149]

The other strategy emerged as a dichotomous enemy. On the one hand appeared the villainous Germans, whose simultaneous qualities of threat and rationality corresponded with Link's devil-like enemy. On the other hand emerged a jingoistic portrayal of the Japanese enemy, which corresponded with Link's chaos-infestation enemy. Although such appeals were perhaps successful in capturing the public's attention, in retrospect they risked creating a dangerous attitude toward the Japanese people. To be sure, the Treasury's propaganda did not in any way cause the attacks on Hiroshima or Nagasaki. That the war bond appeals might have helped create a public that could applaud such extreme unconventional warfare, however, is another question.[150]

In any case, the Treasury's militarized 1944 propaganda appeared to adapt its strategies in response to the public's growing malaise. By exposing the home front to some of the most appalling images of the war, the war bond propaganda thus exemplified discourse appropriate to the battlefield's desperate resignation stage. As evidenced by both polls and bond sales, the Treasury faced significant obstacles in completing its mission. But in the end, its results were reflected in Odegard's warning to Morgenthau in the bond program's planning stages. "It would be easy to stampede the country into buying . . . by frenetic appeals to fear or by frantic beating of the patriotic tom toms," he wrote. "But if you start a campaign that way you'll hear your appeals re-echo with a hollow sound before long."[151] The end of World War II, however, was now only eight months away. Once again, the Treasury's propagandists would have to reconsider their strategic approach to depicting the administration's vision of the war to the public. This time, with the nearness of victory, the bond organization would find itself entering a terminal period in its militarized war effort.

4 THE MIGHTY SEVENTH AND THE VICTORY LOAN

The 1945 War Bond Drives as a Terminal Period

> In the past three years, more than eighty-five million Americans have invested billions of dollars in Bonds. Never before have so many people held such a direct share in a great national effort.
> —Excerpt from FDR's Last Radio Broadcast

> When you have to deal with a beast, you have to treat him as a beast.
> —Harry S. Truman

The first months of 1945 were good ones for Allied forces in the European theater. Two weeks after Germany initiated its end-of-the-year counterattack through the Ardennes Forest, its resistance withered and the rapid progress of Eisenhower's invading force into the heart of Germany continued with even greater momentum. By March 25 the expanse of the German Rhineland was free of Nazi forces. From the east, Russian forces entered Berlin on April 21. The end of April brought news of Hitler's suicide, and on May 8 the remaining German forces accepted the Allies' demand for an unconditional surrender. Not surprisingly, the sudden V-E day celebration brought thousands to Times Square, shouting, "It's over, it's over!"[1]

Still, other phases of the war effort were proceeding with more difficulty. At the Yalta Conference in early February, Churchill and Roosevelt found Stalin increasingly unwilling to give up the territory won by his Red Army in the march to Berlin.[2] In the Pacific, U.S. Marines encountered incredible hardships, casualties, and death tolls as they fought for every yard of a seemingly endless chain of islands on the way to Tokyo. One estimate suggested that victory over Japan might still be eighteen months away.[3] To make matters worse, President Roosevelt died unexpectedly on April 12, leaving the nation's war effort under the untested leadership of the new president, Harry S. Truman.

Despite these challenges, even the most pessimistic observer could not deny that the war was in its final phase. For the millions of U.S. soldiers still in combat zones, this gradual approach of victory was at once exhilarating and frustrating. Military psychologists point out that in such situations, soldiers frequently contract so-called short-timer's syndrome. This mental state produces a tendency toward diminished group identification as well as a gradual withdrawal from fellow soldiers, both of which cause feelings of guilt.[4] Much like the members of social movements, these soldiers face an inevitable psychological shift to a terminal period. In response to this concluding crisis, movement leaders often articulate a last-ditch reduction of their aims to one single issue or solution.[5] Military leaders echo this strategy by demanding that soldiers join together for one final push in the fight.[6] Both activists and soldiers, then, can face the beginning of their terminal period armed with a psychological determination to finish one last task. By initially demanding a final push from their warriors, leaders attempt to delay the ultimate transformation of the effort from a struggle marked by strategy into a memory marked by a "perfecting myth."[7]

The development of such a perfecting myth is a second part of the final transition from an organization's active campaign into its dissolution. At this point, members of social movements often "drop back into the institutions from which they came."[8] Peter Watson points out that "returning soldiers" confront a similar transition into civilian life, one marked by "psychological difficulties."[9] The challenges of such transitions are eased, however, by the creation of perfecting myths, which re-create the campaign's efforts in glowing tones. In these myths, even unpleasant actions and sacrifices emerge as "praiseworthy and heroic" deeds.[10] Ultimately, then, the creation of perfecting myths can help meet the challenge of justifying the tremendous sacrifices made for the cause.

In 1945 the Treasury's propaganda campaign was forced to negotiate similar challenges as it faced the terminal period of its militarized wartime operation. The tasks of first motivating the public for one final push, then crafting a perfecting myth, roughly corresponded to the home front's moods following V-E day and V-J day, respectively. Initially, the aftermath of Germany's surrender in early May naturally produced a national sense that at long last the war was nearly over.[11] Since Japan was fighting on, however, the propaganda of the subsequent Seventh War Loan was perfectly situated to refocus the public on one final dramatic effort. The aftermath of Japan's surrender, in contrast, soon led to a massive psychological demobilization in which, according to Lisle A. Rose, the magnitude of the sacrifices and toil of the war became more evident.[12] Thus, the postwar Victory Loan was in a good position to help create the war's perfecting myth, recasting the incredible struggles and tears of the effort into a legacy of sacred triumph.

Throughout this two-step negotiation of its terminal period, the Treasury seemingly worked to transform its home front soldiers back into civilians. Just as the U.S. government prepared the public for war, so did it prepare the public for peace, using nationalistic images and symbols to justify the public's role in the bloodshed and to reaffirm America's superiority at war's end. The difficulty of this psychological demobilization, however, was made all the more challenging because the Treasury had to balance the need for an increasingly vigilant buying audience as the war continued, with the need for a tolerant public ready to make peace after the enemy's final surrender.

In this chapter, I examine how the Treasury's propaganda campaign responded to this complex set of exigencies in the final year of the war. I show that the strategies embodied in the Treasury's Mighty Seventh and Victory Loan efforts were an integral part of the bond program's continued adaptation to both the evolving context of the war and the changing moods of its target audience. After establishing the context in which these final two drives developed, the remainder of the chapter supports my arguments in three sections. The first section examines the Treasury's transformation of its home front soldiers back into civilians. The second section explores the diminishment of the Treasury's enemy imagery. The final section traces the Treasury's creation of a perfecting myth based in images of Americanism. I conclude the chapter by summarizing the implications of the Treasury's 1945 strategies.

The 1945 Bond Drives in Context

Germany's unexpected counterattack in late December 1944, had a strong, if temporary, impact on public opinion. Even after the Allies repulsed the Ardennes Offensive, in fact, Gallup polls suggested that the percentage of Americans who felt that the German surrender was still six months or more away was suddenly up to 64 percent.[13] As the Germans fought on into 1945, it was increasingly obvious that Hitler and his inner circle were hoping that the tension among Roosevelt, Churchill, and Stalin would ultimately splinter the Allied cause long enough for Nazi forces to regain their fighting strength. Even with its back against the wall, Germany was displaying tremendous willpower in its fight to stave off defeat.

Concerned about Germany's long-term potential to wage war even after an unconditional surrender, Secretary Henry F. Morgenthau Jr. proposed a radical idea in late 1944. In effect, his so-called Morgenthau Plan recommended that the Allies strip Germany of its industry, turning it into a primarily agrarian state. As described by John Morton Blum, Morgenthau's idea made "a strong stand for the dismemberment of Germany."[14] Despite serious concerns about such an objective from other cabinet members, both Roosevelt and Churchill initially approved of the idea. Once it was leaked to the press and published, however, Roosevelt denied that he had any interest in removing Germany's industry.[15] Frustrated once again by the president's ambivalence, Morgenthau continued to lobby the White House to support his plan throughout early 1945.[16] Although these efforts would ultimately have an unforeseen impact on the leadership of the war bond program, Roosevelt's death in early April effectively settled the issue.

The futility of Morgenthau's White House struggles in early 1945 was matched by the slow progress of Allied forces in the Pacific. As kamikaze pilots began their terrifying strikes, U.S. Marine strategists concluded that it would take thousands of casualties to win back the Philippines.[17] In February, an Associated Press photographer named Joe Rosenthal captured the image of six marines raising the American flag on Iwo Jima's Mount Suribachi. While the picture quickly became a sensation on the home front (as well as a powerful image in the war bond campaign), the five-week bid for the tiny island cost twenty-five thousand American casualties.[18] Tellingly, of the six marines in the famous photograph, three never left Iwo Jima alive.[19] It was clear that Japan was determined to fight on.

Meanwhile, the Germans were nearly finished in the European theater, as February and March brought the continued destruction of the nation's heartland. While Hitler desperately fired his new V-2 rockets at London, the Allies were closing in on Berlin from the east and from the west. On Valentine's Day, the Allies firebombed Dresden, killing thirty-five thousand civilians. By early April, Germany's Army Group B was surrounded, leading to the capitulation of 320,000 troops, the "largest mass surrender of the war."[20] Roosevelt's subsequent death gave the Nazis some hope that the Allies would falter, but the attacks never stopped. As the invasion entered its final phases, "the cities of western Germany lay in rubble." Indeed, "there were not enough targets left" for the Allies to attack.[21]

The dramatic battle for Iwo Jima and the final push to Berlin were occurring as the Treasury's propagandists were making plans for the Mighty Seventh war bond drive. As usual, Treasury was worrying about the public's mood. Clearly, V-E day would occur very soon, meaning that the short-timer's syndrome characteristic of a soldier's terminal period would likely affect the public. But despite Germany's surrender—and Roosevelt's sudden death—the Treasury's primary aim was to focus Americans on one final push. As Morgenthau said on the opening day of the drive, "We have had our period of exultation over the great victory in Europe. Now it is time for us to get back to serious business—to the business of taming and civilizing the Japanese in the East and to the business of helping to rebuild civilization in the West."[22]

In many ways, the big push of the Mighty Seventh lived up to the drive's nickname. The overall goal of $14 billion was somewhat smaller than the Fifth War Loan a year earlier, but its E bond goal of $4 billion was the highest of the war.[23] Beginning on May 14 and closing on June 30, the drive offered home front Americans the expected spectacle of publicity and promotion. As part of the drive's appeals, all seven of the nation's five-star generals and admirals signed a public letter asking for massive purchases of war bonds. At the Treasury's request, their letter appeared in various forms on the front cover of more than three thousand national magazines during the drive.[24] Amid the excitement of touring variety shows, Hollywood starlets, and captured enemy submarines, the seventh drive ultimately produced the greatest totals of the war: $26.3 billion overall and $3.97 billion in E bonds.[25] In surpassing its overall goal by 188 percent, the Mighty Seventh was another triumph for Morgenthau's bond campaign.

Morgenthau's public triumph, however, masked internal tension in the White House. Upon taking office, Truman initially said that he was dedicated to preserving all of Roosevelt's war aims.[26] Soon, however, differences emerged in the new president's views. One of the most important was on the surviving aspects of the Morgenthau Plan. Following the advice of those in the cabinet who opposed Morgenthau's ideas, Truman eventually decided that stripping Germany of its industry would present significant disadvantages to Europe's postwar economy.[27] While Morgenthau was understandably troubled by this decision, he was also upset that Truman was increasingly avoiding him, even on questions of economic policy. Before long, it was rumored that Truman was grooming a new Treasury secretary but was waiting for the conclusion of July's meeting with Churchill and Stalin to make the choice public.[28] Tensions increased throughout June until Morgenthau confronted the president in a private meeting on July 5, just before Truman was to leave for the Potsdam Conference. Aware that his outspoken opinions on Germany and other matters were gradually alienating him from the president, Morgenthau offered his resignation, which was accepted.

Truman then appointed Frederick M. Vinson—one of Morgenthau's long-time antagonists—as the new Treasury secretary.[29]

As Morgenthau prepared to move back to his New York estate in early July, the bond program was plunged into uncertainty. Without Morgenthau's continued sponsorship, some felt that the Mighty Seventh could well have been the last drive, or that the new secretary would want to appoint fresh leadership for a new campaign.[30] The uncertainty lasted until July 24, when Secretary Vinson agreed to meet with Ted R. Gamble—who was still the program's national director—to talk over the future of the bond program. Together, Gamble and Vinson agreed that despite the possibility of a Japanese surrender in the coming months, the continuing costs of the war as well as the expenses of occupation and demobilization necessitated one more drive.[31] Moreover, perhaps because Vinson was planning to reduce the scope of the bond effort after its final war loan, the new secretary made no significant changes to the bond program's staff.[32] Although the Japanese surrender would not occur for another three weeks, the war bond staff immediately dubbed its upcoming final drive the Victory Loan.[33]

Elsewhere, events were in motion that would justify this premature use of the word "victory." At Potsdam in late July, Truman casually told Stalin that the United States was nearly ready with a new weapon that might end the war quickly.[34] When Japan rejected the Potsdam Conference's renewed call for an unconditional surrender, Truman set in motion the process that would lead to the early August use of atomic weapons on Japanese cities. On August 6 much of Hiroshima was destroyed, and Nagasaki was bombed three days later. Japan sued for peace on August 14, its defeat assured. For the sailors cheering the sudden end of the war on their ships in the Pacific, says Blum, "victory is what it had all been about."[35] On the home front, people "poured into the streets" as "church bells pealed," "streetlights blazed," and "car horns sounded" to celebrate V-J day.[36] Not to be left out, the Treasury announced later in the week that "the War Bond is off the market; the Victory Bond salutes its great predecessor, and joyously takes over."[37]

The long-awaited finish of the most destructive war in history was truly a moment to celebrate for millions of Americans. With the conflict officially over, home front soldiers and battlefront soldiers turned to the final psychological transition into peace. For many Americans, this change meant not only that its GIs would be returning home but also that the home front soldiers could begin to let down their guard. The realities of demobilization, however, were not that easy. The defeat of Nazi forces in Europe, for example, strengthened the Soviet grip on Eastern Europe. Although the Soviets were technically an American ally for much of the war, few people were under the illusion that the United States and the USSR would continue to work together in peace.[38] The need to occupy both Germany and Japan also meant that America would not return to its isolationism of the 1930s. Whether they liked it or not, Americans were soon seeing that the price of their victory would become global leadership and global vigilance.[39]

Although the logistical challenge of getting millions of GIs home was important, the military was also concerned with the psychological transition to peace. As far back as August 1944, military studies began to suggest that the end of the war would "bring changes in the mental condition of troops which will present special problems to the command." In particular, leaders worried that after the initial thrill of victory, "general war weariness and revulsion against the destruction of war" would set in.[40] For their part, many soldiers were also worried, thinking about what Joanna Bourke calls the "stigma and fear attached to the combatant re-entering civilian society."[41] Not surprisingly, then, the military's research soon found that a significant number of soldiers were beginning to question the value of their victory, saying that "they 'sometimes' or 'very often' felt the war was not worth fighting."[42] The final act of the military's terminal period would prove to be quite challenging.

The American public was also negotiating psychological challenges in the transition to peace. In part, these challenges were rooted in the same doubts faced by soldiers. As Allan Nevins pointed out to his returning military audience just after the war, although "fighters of course suffer far greater perils, pains, and hardships, this does not mean that soldier and civilian attitudes are fundamentally different." Indeed, in the adjustment to peacetime, he continued, "the distinction between the home front and fighting front is partly unreal . . . in terms of basic psychology."[43] Much like battlefront soldiers, home front soldiers experienced distress and angst in the aftermath of the final victory.

A particularly important challenge in the public's psychological transition to peace was growing concern about the use of atomic weapons by the United States.[44] Lane Fenrich points out that pervasive visual documentation of the Holocaust in the months before V-E day conditioned Americans to understand that mass atrocities were caused by "evil people." The dreadful reports from witnesses in Hiroshima and Nagasaki, he suggests, subsequently forced the public to begin an uncomfortable reevaluation of America's deeds in the war.[45] The unwanted angst of America's emergent leadership role in the world and developing tensions with the Soviets made the distress even worse.[46] For many home front Americans, the joy of victory no longer seemed quite as sweet. In Geoffrey Perrett's words, "buds of doubt and revulsion were already beginning to sprout."[47] Charles C. Alexander agrees, describing Americans' "overriding uneasiness," and pointing out that "the war not only left them with the burdens of world power and leadership, but it stripped them of a great deal of their claim to moral primacy and historical uniqueness."[48]

In the midst of these uncomfortable revelations, the war bond staff was preparing its final drive. Running from October 29 to December 8, 1945, the Treasury's Victory Loan reminded the public of the 12 million men and women in the service who would be demobilized over several months. The bond drive's discourse also stressed the need for occupying forces in the Axis countries. Finally, the Treasury reminded Americans of their lost war leader, producing a two-hundred-dollar memorial victory bond imprinted with Roosevelt's image.[49] The bond program's modest goal of $11 billion for the drive acknowledged that Americans would be less focused on bonds with the war over.[50] Yet at the war loan's conclusion, public sales topped $21 billion.[51] In the words of Robert Coyne, assistant national director for the bond program, these final results were "indeed a fitting final chapter to the greatest story ever written of American civilians working together for their country and for each other."[52]

On December 8, 1945, the Victory Loan Drive ended, and with it the victory bonds became savings bonds, just as they were before 1941. On January 1, 1946, Secretary Vinson officially ordered the War Finance Division to become the U.S. Savings Bonds Division. With the War Finance Division officially demobilizing, the Treasury's militarized propaganda campaign reached the conclusion of its terminal period. Although the Treasury would be redeeming its war bonds for several decades, the end of the powerful war loan drives meant that the financial transition to peace was complete. Still, the successes of the two 1945 drives would remain an inspiration for the Treasury's postwar bond appeals. As before, these final two drives exhibited the Treasury's continuous concern for—and adaptation to—the moods of its target audience. In this way, the

Mighty Seventh and the Victory Loan Drive embodied the Treasury's negotiation of the bond program's terminal period.

Negotiating the Terminal Period in the 1945 Bond Drives

The 1945 drives emerged from a dynamic period. The German surrender and the deaths of Roosevelt, Hitler, and Mussolini made Americans much less likely to focus on the goals of the Mighty Seventh. The use of atomic weapons, Japan's surrender, and the excitement of demobilization were similarly distracting to the public in the Victory Loan. Simultaneously, there was the problem of keeping Americans committed to the war while also preparing them for peace. This section explores how the Treasury adapted its propaganda to these complex exigencies in its two final drives. In particular, I analyze the transformation of soldiers back into civilians, the disappearance of enemy imagery, and the creation of a perfecting myth grounded in Americanism. Each of these strategies played an important role throughout the bond program's terminal period, helping the public shift from a war mentality back into a psychology of peace.

Turning Soldiers Back into Civilians

In its previous drives, the Treasury's propaganda conflated soldiers and civilians, and then pointed out the ironic incongruities in that conflation. In early 1945, however, the public's mood turned once again. This time, the prospect of V-E day encouraged the home front to think of the war as nearly over. Consequently, the Treasury's civilian-soldier conflation changed accordingly. As the Treasury's pollsters pointed out, "24 percent of the population think that there will be less need for bond-buying after victory in Europe." The pollsters' recommendation, not surprisingly, was that "as the war draws to a close publicity should begin to emphasize different things."[53]

The Treasury's adaptive approach in the face of the public's changing mood was to begin the preparation of its home front soldiers (and returning veterans) for peacetime. Since before Pearl Harbor, most of the bond program's appeals had focused on transforming civilians into soldiers, or on reinforcing that transformation. With the end of the war in sight—and with the public already eager for the war to end—it was now time to produce an atmosphere of peace. Thus, as increasing numbers of battlefield soldiers returned to America, the Treasury's militarized propaganda would now reflect the psychological process of demobilization.

An important aspect of the Seventh War Loan's transformation of its soldiers into civilians was the idea that many soldiers were already returning home to their families and occupations. Asking, "How could *he* afford *this*?" one pair of ads portrayed two soldiers-*cum*-civilians.[54] The first image depicted a soldier whose battle experience had apparently left his eyes damaged, as much of his face was covered in a white blindfold. The second image showed a soldier with one amputated arm, his eyes looking longingly at the violin in his remaining hand. In terms of effectively gaining attention, both these images violated viewers' expectations by illustrating a significant difference from the familiar. In discussing the immediate attraction of such images, Paul Messaris explains that "if the discrepancy between the unfamiliar shape and some preexisting one is only partial, the mental task of fitting in the new shape becomes more complicated. As a result, such partially strange shapes can cause us to pay closer attention."[55]

Despite their attention-grabbing properties, however, the most obvious focus of these ads was on the sacrifices made by the two soldiers. In previous drives these men would have been portrayed in a battlefront hospital, or in combat, struggling to survive. What was new here was that both were depicted at home, beginning the transition into civilian life. Their wounds were professionally treated; their hair was carefully combed; and they were wearing the military's garrison outfit, complete with ties. The sight-impaired soldier was even holding a toddler—presumably his son or daughter. The subtext in these images, then, presented the idea that soldiers ultimately could make it back and would transition into life on the home front. "Every 60 seconds, one of us comes home," stated another ad. "But . . . I don't want any pats on the back, or parades. Just a chance to get fixed up."[56] In other words, although these men were coming home with battle scars, they were also resuming their former lives. For the Treasury's audience, such images warranted the assistance of soldiers in their reentry into civilian life. They also sanctioned the Seventh War Loan's final push to purchase war bonds and help all the nation's GIs come home.

The transformation of soldiers back into civilians is also evident in one of the Seventh War Loan's billboards (see fig. 4.1).[57] In this image, three men—a GI on the left, a sailor on the right, and a civilian in the middle—create a triangle, with the civilian's arms creating two of its sides by resting, buddylike, on the shoulders of his friends. The front side of the triangle is formed by the connection between the GI and the sailor, each holding a corner of the same oversized war bond. This triangle, comprised of the three men and the war bond, presents a unified solidarity that is reinforced by the group's relaxed pose and

4.1 Treasury billboard used during 1945's Seventh War Loan, showing camaraderie between home front and battlefront. Note that the war bonds complete the "bond" between the billboard's figures. Courtesy National Archives.

their friendly, direct eye gaze. The ad's caption, "the Bond between us," is at first glance a reference to the war bond uniting GI and sailor as well as a means of conflating civilians and soldiers. But the pun on "bonds" refers also to the camaraderie between the men, an idea reinforced by the civilian's arms thrown around his friends' shoulders. Clearly, these men "all belong to the same overarching category."[58] Put another way, the relaxed portrait emphasized that soldiers like the GI and the sailor would soon be coming home to interact with civilians and, ultimately, to again become citizens themselves.

To help ensure this process of transformation, the image explicitly invited viewers to participate in the group's camaraderie. The direct eye contact from all three men signified "an attempt to inspire trust."[59] Their welcoming smiles clarified that viewers were "asked to enter into a relation[ship] of social affinity" with them.[60] Playing a part in this relationship with an inanimate and yet vital role was the war bond—framed in the foreground as the central focus of the image. The Treasury's admonition to prompt the transformation of soldiers into civilians by financing the return of veterans was thus an unmistakable part of the billboard. By purchasing "the Bond between us," Americans would be following the advice of the nation's five-star generals to "speed the return of your fighting men."[61]

By October's Victory Loan Drive, the transformation of soldiers back into civilians was far beyond its early stages. The final psychological demobilization of the Treasury's terminal period was being enacted as America's GIs slowly returned home. Although the drive's images most often showed *battlefield* soldiers undergoing this transformation, the ever-present conflation between battlefront and home front suggested that the public, too, should be transforming itself back into peacetime civilians.

Initially, the Victory Loan's propaganda acknowledged the slow pace of demobilization. One Treasury image, for example, presented a close-up image of two GIs in casual uniforms, sharing the view from a ship's porthole. The first soldier was beaming and making eye contact with someone just out of sight. Clearly, he represented those military men who were just about to see their families again. His comrade's facial expression, in contrast, exhibited a wistful, long-suffering desire to get home. His heavenward eye gaze suggested that his reunion would not be soon. The image's text reinforced the need for endurance in such situations: "For some of them," the text intoned, "it may take a year."[62] Thus, the Treasury was careful to caution Americans to be patient as they waited for their GIs to come home and complete their transformation to life in America. At the same time, it stressed the high price of demobilization and the consequent need for ongoing bond sales to finance the transition from war to peace.

The Victory Loan also began to depict the actual process of transformation from soldier into civilian. One newspaper ad, for example, depicted a soldier disembarking from his troop ship, apparently just a few steps away from his return to the United States (see fig. 4.2). As with the soldiers in the porthole, this GI's combat gear is gone, replaced by a comfortable and attractive garrison uniform. Clearly, as the text proclaims, "he has done his job." The point of illustrating his disembarkation, though, was to show that he would soon be able "to reconvert for peace." The image implied that after mustering out, he would be able to return to his hometown and complete his transformation. Although he is still wearing a military uniform, the ad depicts him in the final stages of military service. Soon he—and millions of other soldiers—would be coming home to resume their civilian lives. To make this demobilization process even easier, the ad encouraged viewers to buy extra bonds in the Victory Loan by repeating the drive's primary slogan: "They Finished Their Job . . . Let's Finish Ours."[63]

In its poster adaptation of Norman Rockwell's *Homecoming G.I.*, the Victory Loan even portrayed the final transformation of soldiers back into civilians (see fig. 4.3).[64] In this well-known scene, a young soldier returning from service in the war arrives home to the stunned delight of his family, neighbors, even an excited dog. Seventeen people witness his arrival, including a shy girlfriend peeking

4.2 Victory Loan advertisement portraying a disembarking soldier in garrison uniform, symbolizing the transformation from soldier back to civilian. The Treasury encouraged citizens to buy more bonds to finish the conversion back to peacetime. Courtesy National Archives.

4.3 Treasury adaptation of Norman Rockwell's *Homecoming G.I.*, featuring a returning soldier at the moment of transformation back into the civilian world. Note the service stars in the neighborhood's windows. Courtesy National Archives.

around a corner (one person's upper torso is cut off by the "Hasten the Homecoming" headline). All the expected elements of a fitting homecoming are present in the image. Indeed, according to Derek Nelson, the poster "deserves an award for emotional symbols per square inch."[65] Despite its innocent appearance, however, the poster presented an eloquent portrayal of the soldier's transformation back into civilian life.

In fact, the strength of Rockwell's image is in its depiction of the exact moment of transformation. The boyish soldier stands in front of his home, frozen between his past and his future. There is an implied history in the picture—the soldier as a boy growing up in the neighborhood, as a teen yearning to see the world, as a young man going off to fight the enemy.[66] There are symbols of the future as well. Beyond the immediate joy of the reunion, the relative working on the roof represents future work, or prosperity. And the shy girlfriend represents a romantic interest, perhaps marriage and family. Yet in the image the young GI remains completely still, standing in front of his home while taking in the scene along with the viewer. In a sense, Rockwell was depicting him on the dividing line between his old life and his new, at the precise instant of his transformation back into the civilian world. In this frozen moment, he was both soldier (still dressed in army green) and civilian (at home with friends and family). His next step, the poster implies, would transform SOLDIER back into CIVILIAN.

The presence of the neighbors brings another level of meaning to the poster. In the small section of neighborhood visible in the image, no fewer than five windows boast service stars. In the foreground, obviously, the closest service star will soon be taken down. But the others will remain, as their soldiers are not yet home. Although some of the neighbors are smiling at the hero's imminent reunion, an element of envy and of unfulfilled expectation is also in their faces. How should they "hasten the homecoming" for their own GIs? They should "Buy Victory Bonds," of course.[67] In this way the Treasury poster united continued bond buying with the final return of America's GIs. Buy victory bonds, the Treasury was saying, and your soldiers will come home from the battle in which "all Americans fought."[68] Buy victory bonds to help the veterans "start life anew."[69] Thus, the Treasury encouraged Americans to anticipate the return of their loved ones and to purchase victory bonds to help ensure that return. In this manner, its Victory Loan propaganda sought to facilitate the final conversion of battle-weary American soldiers back into American civilians.

Throughout 1945, then, the Treasury developed one more facet in its conflation of civilians and soldiers. Where once its propaganda reflected the transition of the home front into a de facto battlefront, now it mirrored the reverse of that process by changing soldiers back into civilians. Once again the Treasury's propaganda campaign was facilitating a particular kind of audience.[70] This audience was meant to deal with the challenges of the bond program's terminal period by experiencing a final demobilization. It was a demobilization, however, that focused exclusively on soldiers, leaving the Treasury's enemy imagery largely intact.

The Disappearing Enemy

In its earlier drives, the Treasury had gradually increased the potency of its enemy depictions through the Sixth War Loan, where the Japanese enemy was dehumanized as savage and monstrous. The racism reflected in this part of the Treasury's propaganda campaign was a clear sign that the Japanese enemy was being categorized differently from the German enemy. The potential result of this divergence, in hindsight, may have been to encourage an atmosphere of public opinion in which the use of the most extreme measures against this dehumanized enemy would seem logical, even imperative.

Soon after its use of jingoistic enemy images in the Sixth War Loan, however, the Treasury's propaganda abruptly turned away from the enemy. In the Mighty Seventh's battery of literature, in fact, the word "Japs" was used sparingly.[71] The public appeals seemingly avoided the word, and the enemy was depicted in only a few of the drive's many images. Instead, the Seventh War Loan propaganda returned to scenes of battle in which the enemy was offstage—much like the Treasury's appeals before 1944. Exclaiming "They're Fighting *Two* Battles on *One* Beachhead!" for example, a newspaper ad showed another beach invasion. Although viewers could see the expected soldiers, planes, and falling bombs in the image, no enemy was apparent.[72] Similarly, in the ad, "This time—go all out!" the Treasury showed a drawing of a GI gesturing for home front soldiers to follow him, presumably to join in the battle.[73] Although flashes on the horizon indicated that desperate fighting was ongoing, it was distant, and no enemy was visible. As these and similar images suggest, the enemy largely disappeared in the Seventh War Loan's propaganda.

Thus, as the Treasury began to deal with the challenges of the bond program's terminal period, it simultaneously began to diminish its verbal and visual depictions of the enemy. Considering that the war was in its closing stages, this dramatic change in the Treasury's propaganda was an expedient choice. After all, "as surrender nears, even total wars become nontotal."[74] The Treasury's reduced enemy imagery, then, was understandable given the approach of victory.

Jonathan A. Becker's analysis of Soviet political cartoons provides some insight into this process. After exploring numerous images of the American enemy, Becker shows that there was a dramatic decline in such imagery from 1987 to 1990, so much so that he refers to the United States as "a disappearing enemy."[75] Pointing out that this disappearance took place while the USSR was attempting to open a dialogue with the United States on arms negotiations, Becker argues that the sudden change sent a positive message about Americans to the Soviet readership. As he puts it, the decline in enemy imagery was designed to reduce anxiety over the American "external threat," which for years had inspired "fear of and opposition to arms reductions agreements" among the Soviet public. In other words, the enemy "disappeared" in these cartoons because the Soviet government was preparing its people for public negotiations with a nation it habitually demonized as "an inherently aggressive enemy bent on world domination."[76]

The U.S. government found itself in a similar political situation in early 1945. On one hand, continued dehumanization of the Japanese enemy was desirable because it could keep the public committed to the ongoing Pacific battle by feeding its hunger for vengeance (a feeling still simmering from what was popularly seen as the treachery of Pearl Harbor).[77] On the other hand, with Germany almost out of the war and Japan clearly losing, there was an increasing possibility that the United States would need to make sudden peace with a people who had been portrayed in its official publications as inhuman beasts.[78] Indeed, Dennis D. Wainstock points out that around April 1945, the Japanese were finally initiating backdoor peace overtures to the United States.[79]

This situation was an important dilemma for the still-untested Truman administration. If the dehumanization stopped, public hatred of the Japanese might diminish, hurting the American public's willpower to push to the finish.[80] If the dehumanization continued unabated or even increased, trying to justify potential peace negotiations with a still-bloodthirsty enemy—which by definition could not make peace—might be difficult. Such justification would also be likely "to invite charges of betraying FDR's legacy and the memory of those who had died in what was regarded as a war of treachery."[81] The prudent policy, as evidenced by the Treasury's propaganda in the Mighty Seventh, was simply to discontinue the dehumanizing imagery and focus on other appeals, including the transformation of soldiers into civilians. This course of action even had some precedent: the German enemy disappeared from the Sixth War Loan's propaganda at exactly the same time it appeared to U.S. government officials that German forces were about to give in.

In the wake of the Japanese surrender in mid-August, however, the Truman administration's dehumanization dilemma was no longer as salient. Still, the postwar propaganda of the Victory Loan echoed the Mighty Seventh in its reluctance to revive the use of enemy imagery. Like the Mighty Seventh's appeals, this drive presented several battle scenes, all used to summarize the war's sacrifices.[82] Although no enemy was visible in these images, the nearness of battle implied an adversary's presence. The enemy's continuing role could also be inferred by the Victory Loan's numerous depictions of injured and rehabilitating GIs[83] and by the drive's primary slogan: "They Finished Their Job . . . Now Let's All Finish Ours."[84] But with peace in effect, explicitly dehumanizing the enemy was no longer necessary. One Treasury ad confirmed that "there's nothing but Peace, glorious Peace, ahead for us."[85] Perhaps because many postwar Americans were increasingly revolted over the bloodshed and toil of the war, the vanquished enemy failed to reappear in the Victory Loan's propaganda. Much like the Seventh War Loan before it, the bond program's final drive essentially ignored the enemy, ultimately focusing inward on the transformation of soldiers into civilians and on a celebration of the nation's sudden victory.

In this way, the Treasury's depictions of the enemy diminished throughout 1945. In part, this disappearance of the enemy was a natural extension of the idea that the potential for peace requires a diminished public perception of the enemy's alleged savagery.[86] But from the vantage point of some sixty postwar years, it is noteworthy that while Treasury was preparing its target audience for the transformation of soldiers into civilians, it offered no parallel discourse to transform the enemy back into a peer nation. Of course, the lack of such transformative discourse in the Treasury's propaganda is in some ways understandable given the Treasury's situation. After all, the war bond propagandists' job was to build public morale and to raise funds for the war, not to worry about the enemy's unresolved rhetorical status. Yet the Treasury's time-bound context masked an important issue—that once an enemy has been thoroughly dehumanized through official channels, discontinuing the dehumanizing propaganda is unlikely to heal public perceptions of that enemy.[87]

Thus, while aspects of the American popular media did undertake an unofficial rehumanization campaign of the former enemy nations soon after the war, the Truman administration's silence on the issue, in retrospect, is worth noting.[88]

In sum, while the Treasury halted its use of dehumanization throughout the terminal period, its propaganda allowed previous images of the bestial enemy to endure. The persistence of such dehumanizing images as the war reached its climax arguably had an impact on public opinion about the dehumanized enemy and its punishment. As Chappell points out, "characterizing the war as a battle against irrational fanatics implied that the war could not be ended on rational terms."[89] Hikins argues that the "rhetoric of unconditional surrender" helped create a linguistic trap in which the United States had little choice but to use the bombs it had created.[90] The Treasury's 1945 campaign may have contributed to this trap by never counteracting the potency of its previous dehumanizing propaganda. At the time, however, few would have noticed this rhetorical silence, in part because, near the war's end, the Treasury's domestic propaganda suddenly featured an increased reliance on nationalist images. These images helped create a perfecting myth in which depictions of American triumphalism would ultimately eclipse what some saw as the horror and toil of the war.

Americanism and the Treasury's Perfecting Myth

As the Treasury was winding down its civilian-soldier conflation and its enemy imagery throughout 1945, it simultaneously escalated its invocations of Americanism. In part, such nationalist appeals sanctioned the transformation of soldiers into civilians and the disappearance of the enemy in the Treasury's propaganda. The primary functions of the increased reliance on Americanism, however, seemed to be to warrant the final push on the home front during the Mighty Seventh and to justify the bond program's perfecting myth as it developed in the Victory Loan Drive.

The Treasury's use of such nationalist appeals suggests that they can be a powerful tool in propaganda.[91] An important assumption here is that nationalism is in fact a rhetorical creation. Paul C. Stern, for example, points out that "constructionist" views of nationalism stress "the socially created nature of nationality."[92] John Breuilly agrees that nationalism is often the result of a "manipulative" process that "promotes the interests of particular groups."[93] For propagandists, then, nationalism can be a powerful appeal in which the construction of public unity is solidified through the use of familiar national symbols. As Anthony D. Smith points out, "by the use of symbols," citizens can be "reminded of their common heritage and cultural kinship and feel strengthened and exalted by their sense of common identity."[94]

Although some historians see such appeals to nationalism as a precursor to war, Barry R. Posen argues that "nationalism is as often a consequence of conflict as it is a cause."[95] The construction of nationalist images near the end of conflict is fairly common. Because they can be used to facilitate "national histories, traditions, identities, [and] perceived interests," appeals to nationalism can be particularly useful to the propagandist attempting to unite an exhausted and guilt-laden population at war's end.[96] Indeed, in the Treasury's case, the use of nationalist images helped it negotiate the two-step process of its terminal period throughout 1945.

To be sure, the Treasury's propaganda campaign had occasionally relied on nationalist images at earlier points in its history. In 1942's Victory Fund Drive, for example, the bond program used images of Uncle Sam to prompt bond sales.[97] And the American flag was a common feature in advertisements for 1943's Third War Loan Drive.[98] Yet such images diminished after 1943, until the Sixth War Loan in late 1944 offered few, if any, nationalist appeals. The two 1945 drives, however, exhibited a surge of Americanism. Whether they were images of Uncle Sam, the American flag, the Statue of Liberty, or the late President Roosevelt, the Treasury's nationalist appeals quickly replaced earlier images of dead soldiers and dehumanized enemies.

The strategic use of such nationalist images first appeared in the Seventh War Loan in order to help warrant a final push on the home front. As this process played out in the Mighty Seventh's propaganda, the drive's context is particularly important. With the war in Europe nearing its end and the Pacific struggle moving into its closing stages, the Roosevelt (and then Truman) administration had a vital interest in motivating the public to coalesce in a climactic state of total war. Such a state would need to connect the public with its militarized duties in the most decisive way possible. Thus, the Treasury's strategists seemingly used their Mighty Seventh propaganda to unite the public under the rubric of Americanism, ultimately promoting a unified front in the climactic phase of the war effort. In this way the Treasury's propaganda campaign worked to motivate its target audience to stay focused and united for the last determined push before the conclusion of the war. As one ad put it, "Is this too much to ask of any person who says 'I am an American?' Hardly."[99]

The bond strategists established the new sense of Americanism very quickly. On May 14, 1945, the first day of the drive, a newspaper ad appeared that clearly portrayed the sense of emerging nationalism.[100] The ad showed a series of battle scenes, arranged in a winding line from top to bottom, creating a progression of images. The battle developed from individual soldiers to a flying bomber to a battleship in rough seas. The ferocity of these struggles was evident in the series of explosions surrounding each phase of the battle. At the bottom of the line, however, appeared an American flag, superimposed over one of the detonations. In part, the flag's transcendence over the explosion was reminiscent of the mythlike survival of the American flag as described in the national anthem. Indeed, the appearance of the flag near the end of the winding images indicated an "outcome" of the battle, a transcendent American triumph.[101] Moreover, a series of three war bonds were depicted over a corner of the flag, not only conflating bond purchases and Americanism but also emphasizing the importance of bond purchases to the final victory. Finally, the ad's text was superimposed over the bonds, demanding that the viewer "Pour out your might in the MIGHTY SEVENTH."[102] The ad, in other words, used images of Americanism to portray the ultimate victory, to stress the role of bonds in that victory, and finally to exhort viewers to put forth a mighty effort in the final push toward that victory.

A similar series of messages appeared in the primary poster of the Seventh War Loan, which adapted the Iwo Jima photograph into the bond campaign.[103] At first glance, of course, contemporary viewers saw the original image as static in a literal sense—it was, after all, an image frozen in time (see fig. 4.4).[104] But the picture's theme provided the undeniable suggestion of an underlying story. The scene conjured up images of the struggle that had led to this moment, the hardships endured by these anonymous marines, and the surging American forces that would follow this small unit. The angle of the flagpole, in fact, reinforced the incipient narrative by suggesting the idea of motion, or "dynamic action."[105] For viewers of the original image, all these ideas were united in a depiction of the ancient military act of planting a flag on territory newly won from the enemy. The powerful symbolism of the battle flag has been used since ancient times, both to increase the fervor of one's own combatants and to dismay the enemy.[106]

Although the photograph of the Iwo Jima flag-raising was a powerful symbol in its own right, the Treasury's appropriation of its elements into a propaganda poster strategically enriched its complex

4.4 Original photograph of the flag-raising on Iwo Jima, perhaps the war's most famous image. Note the hazy sky and its difference from the Treasury's poster adaptation in figure 4.5. Courtesy National Archives.

meanings (see fig. 4.5).[107] To begin with, the Treasury's poster stressed the fact that the marines were not planting just any flag; they were planting the American flag. In the original image, the marines' flag was only partially unfurled; although it was identifiable to viewers as the American flag, the bulk of the design was obscured. The Treasury's propagandists depicted a greater amount of the flag in their poster; compared to the familiar image, the Treasury's version of the flag was more prominent and identifiable. The bond strategists added to this alteration by transforming the slightly hazy skies in the famous shot. In the poster, the skies became dark, stormy, even threatening. By enhancing the prominence of its flag and displaying it against the backdrop of a suspenseful sky, the Treasury gave its poster a much stronger dramatic look.

To most of the poster's viewers, of course, the flag was by definition the sacred, preeminent symbol of the United States and of Americanism itself. In a sense, its presence on what was recently enemy territory was the sign of a purification of polluted land. Janice L. Edwards and Carol K. Winkler agree that the tableau signified

4.5 Seventh War Loan poster adaptation of the Iwo Jima image. Compared to the original still image (see fig. 4.4), the flag is much more visible, while in the sky dramatic storm clouds have appeared. Courtesy Franklin D. Roosevelt Library.

"a sacred effort, as the bodies strain in unified action and the hands reach heavenward in lifting the flag."[108] The low angle of the image, in which both soldiers and viewers looked up to the flag, reinforced what George H. Roeder calls its "mythological transcendence."[109] Objects viewed from a low angle occupy a higher position than the viewer and thus represent higher status and importance.[110] The Treasury's dramatically enhanced flag, then, symbolized more than a momentary triumph in a protracted battle. It told a story of Americanism overcoming great adversity and ascending over enemy territory. This story could be shared by all Americans, and indeed the poster's very sense of dramatic accomplishment and herculean effort invited viewers to project themselves into the impending victory.

More importantly, the poster implied that the job of completing the victory belonged to Americans as a group. Consider, for instance, the anonymous marines. Because their faces were obscured (in both the original image and the poster adaptation), they were a group united in action more than individual soldiers.[111] The poster's text ("Now . . All Together") reinforced this notion. So did the text of "Victory Can't Wait," a Treasury newspaper advertisement that used a silhouetted version of the Iwo Jima image. Proclaiming "Americans! Stand shoulder to shoulder in the Mighty Seventh," the Treasury used this ad in part to signify the conflation of civilians and soldiers underneath the country's most important nationalist symbol.[112] At the same time, it symbolized the unfinished business these united Americans needed to complete: the ongoing purchase of war bonds to bring the troops home.

The enhanced flag in the Treasury's Iwo Jima poster, then, had two symbolic functions. On one level, the flag was part of a "goal," a tool used by the marines (and, by extension, all Americans) to strive toward a sense of nationalist victory.[113] By projecting themselves into the struggle depicted in the poster, viewers could play a part in achieving this goal. On another level, once raised, the flag in its transcendent position would bestow that very sense of sacred Americanism on its subjects, girding them for the final push in the fight for freedom. As the Treasury demanded, "Let's Prove We're All in This Together!"[114] "No American," it continued, "can afford *not* to answer this vital call."[115]

Just over one month after the Seventh War Loan's conclusion, however, the war came to an abrupt end, and the desperate need for such a final push was gone. Instead, the postwar awareness of the struggle's overwhelming toil and sacrifice began to produce in some citizens the inevitable revulsion characteristic of demobilizing soldiers. As Martin Gilbert writes, "many, including those who vividly recall the unbridled celebrations, also remember the doubts and problems remaining; the uncertainties which did not necessarily end with the ending of the war against Japan."[116] John Fousek agrees, pointing out that "some voices in the national discussion" after V-J day questioned "both the completeness of the victory and the righteousness of the nation."[117] Thus, as the Treasury dealt with the second stage of the effort's terminal period—the psychological challenges of demobilization—it was likewise in need of a perfecting myth to help ease the transition into peace.

The Treasury's Victory Loan was an excellent vehicle to create this myth and disseminate it to the public. Indeed, an organization's terminal period is the best time to create one. With a broad perspective that encompasses all of an organization's triumphs and failures, leaders of terminating efforts can begin the process of transforming the entirety of those experiences into a myth "of absolute perfection and morality."[118] Since the Victory Loan opened nearly two months after Japan surrendered, its planners were able to account for the public's postwar mood. Yet the drive was also situated close enough to the war's conclusion that it emerged as the nation was still taking stock of the overall war experience. Thus, not long after the war, the bond program was able to once again rely on nationalist images, this time to create a perfecting myth of the war experience.[119]

In part, the Victory Loan's perfecting myth worked to justify the sacrifices of the war for a public exhibiting growing doubts about the worth of its victory. If Americans were fixating on the bloodshed and toil of the war, the Victory Loan quickly worked to subsume such negative memories by retroactively transforming the overall struggle into an epic victory of Americanism. Thus, even as the Victory Loan's propaganda served a demobilizing function for the Treasury's militarized public, it simultaneously valorized the nation's overall war effort by using the Treasury's massive publicity machine to create and disseminate a myth of nationalist triumph.

The Victory Loan's propaganda facilitated this mythic triumph in several ways. Initially, the Treasury began to create a selective history of the war. In its ad, "For the Last Time, America—Buy *Extra* Bonds!" the Treasury showed a progression of eight images that attempted to summarize the war.[120] Each image was linked with a major Allied victory as well as with one of the bond drives. The connection between victories and drives, however, was quite tenuous. The "1st War Loan" image, for instance, was linked with Pearl Harbor—which occurred *almost one year* before the initial drive did.

And the image for the sixth drive was paired with "Normandie," although in the real war, the Sixth War Loan opened long after the D-day invasion. In terms of a retrospective look at the war, this ad worked to create a selective history, awkwardly fitting the Treasury's bond drives into the scenes of America's war victories.

Significantly, the ad used this selective history to submerge any negative memories of the war. No mention was made, for example, of Allied losses, or of the atomic bombs, or of the pain and frustrations of war. Instead, the focus was on a sanitized version of America's triumph. The biggest image, predictably, was the last, reserved for the pairing of the Victory Loan and "Tokyo-Victory Parade." Instead of scenes of battle, this image showed several soldiers marching in parade formation through a Tokyo street, prominently displaying an American flag. These were the soldiers, the ad intoned, who were now returning home to "find a real place in the America they saved for all of us." With such images of Americanism, the Treasury was offering a justifiable version of the war, one that featured breathtaking victories and a triumphant nation, but little bloodshed or toil. As the text summarized, "we came through the greatest danger in our history, to our greatest victory."[121]

Another part of the Victory Loan's perfecting myth was the portrayal of Roosevelt as the war's hero. Announced just one month after the war's end, the special two-hundred-dollar Roosevelt bond quickly became an important part of the Treasury's effort to cast Roosevelt as the primary hero of the epic victory.[122] The bond's portrait of the president was predictably flattering. There was no trace of the man often described as "sickly" and "weakened" in the last months of his life.[123] This heroic Roosevelt appeared to be quite healthy, exuding an unmistakable sense of confidence, leadership, and authority. The Treasury's promotion of the bond confirmed that it was meant to valorize the fallen president, describing it as issued "IN MEMORY of the leader of the heroes who gave their lives for the victory they did not live to see."[124]

As the Treasury's words implied, the Victory Loan was suggesting that this "leader of the heroes" was also a martyr in an epic struggle.[125] One of the drive's posters reinforced this message (see fig. 4.6).[126] It features a family of five standing before a grave site. Viewers share the family's perspective as they look up at a dramatic vision of the late president, floating ghostlike above the grave marker. In the president's spectral image, viewers see a vital, healthy man. His transcendent position above the grave communicates a sense of greatness, even holiness. This impression is reinforced by the wreath

4.6 Treasury poster used during the Victory Loan. Here the fallen president reappears as a transcendent martyr, now motivating the public to purchase Victory Bonds. Courtesy Franklin D. Roosevelt Library.

on the tombstone, an ancient symbol of "the victory that martyrdom implies."[127] The poster even suggests the surpassing significance of the president's martyrdom by emphasizing the very shape of the tombstone—a large cross. In this manner, the Victory Loan propaganda helped re-create Roosevelt as a heroic martyr of the war. The choice of the former president—an obvious symbol of Americanism—thus became an important part of the Treasury's overall mythic retelling of the war.

But if Roosevelt was the primary hero and martyr of the war, the Treasury's Victory Loan propaganda campaign also transformed the American public into heroic participants in his triumph. Unlike other Treasury bonds, the front of the Roosevelt bond supplied an epigraph, taken from a radio address given two days after the attack on Pearl Harbor. Here, Roosevelt's words celebrated the role of the American people in the effort, describing "every single man, woman, and child" as a "partner" in it. The spectral poster repeats Roosevelt's words, emphasizing how Americans shouldered their "common load" during the war. Thus, while using the language of the fallen hero to emphasize the magnitude of "the most tremendous undertaking of our American history," the Treasury allowed Roosevelt's heroic status to transform postwar Americans—both civilians and soldiers—into active participants in the sacred myth.[128]

The true legacy of that triumph, however, became clear in another Victory Loan poster that depicts a large eagle in the act of spreading its wings for flight (see fig. 4.7).[129] This potent symbol of nationalism appears in intersecting rays of light, representing America in the afterglow of its righteous triumph. Much like the Iwo Jima image, the eagle's nationalist symbolism was reinforced by the poster's low angle, in which the eagle seems to be floating above the viewing audience.[130] The key feature in this poster, though, is the stack of *bonds* in the eagle's talons.

The potency of this intriguing image of nationalism existed on at least two levels. On the more obvious level, the poster suggested that the target audience see the war's end as an opportunity to buy more bonds. The caption ("Victory—now you can invest in it!") encouraged this notion by presenting an understanding of "victory" as both desirable (almost a tangible product) and future-oriented (an investment that should one day yield a profit).[131] If the postwar audience was beginning to believe that its victory was increasingly hollow, the Treasury's message was to appreciate the victory bond both for its present value and for its long-term potential. Thus, in buying "victory" bonds, the public would in a sense be investing in and thus

4.7 Victory Loan poster representing a victorious America in the aftermath of war. Note the war bonds held in the eagle's talons. Courtesy National Archives.

celebrating the innate value of the victory itself, as well as their own participation in it.

On a second level, the eagle poster was a rejection of victory as a vindictive celebration and simultaneously an endorsement of victory as a communal unification. Whittick points out that the ancient

Greek symbol for victory was "the eagle carrying the serpent in its talons."[132] Such an image represented the transcendent victory of good over evil. In this poster, the Treasury could easily have chosen to borrow the Greek symbolism to reinforce the nature of its complete triumph over the enemy it had once dehumanized as a serpent. But such a message might have fostered disenchantment with the total victory, especially since peace with the serpent, so to speak, was now in effect. Instead, the Treasury placed its war bonds in the eagle's talons. Whether it was a conscious or unconscious choice, this image implied not victory over the defeated foe, but victory built on the solidarity and sacrifice of untold bond purchasers—America's home front soldiers. In depicting a positive and validating image of nationalist victory to the millions of citizens in its target audience, the Treasury's Victory Loan campaign was thus a critical participant in the mythic process in which World War II became "the best war ever."[133]

The construction of such postwar myths, of course, is nothing new. Nationalist justifications were crafted after the Revolutionary War, the Civil War, and World War I.[134] Yet the Treasury's World War II myth was unprecedented precisely because the war it mythologized was so much more destructive than any that preceded it. While the United States undeniably played a heroic role in many areas of the war, recent scholarship has brought increasing attention to less admirable aspects of American participation in the war, including the deaths of untold numbers of noncombatants at the hands of the U.S. military.[135] The Treasury's 1945 discourse worked to create an audience worthy of the war's mythic victory.[136] But by relying on a selective history that deflected attention from America's more negative contributions to the war, the Treasury's perfecting myth ultimately helped call into being an audience less willing to consider its human fallibility and more willing, instead, to see itself as heroic and infallible.

Throughout 1945, then, the Treasury relied on nationalist images to negotiate the bond program's terminal period. In the Seventh War Loan, such images called upon Americans to coalesce for one final push in the war effort. In the postwar Victory Loan, these images helped create a perfecting myth of the war that warranted the bloodshed, expense, and sacrifice of the home front soldiers. Ultimately, the Treasury's discourse in its last two drives targeted Americans in order to help them accept and even celebrate the final victory. In the process, the bond program inevitably completed its own transition from war into peace.

4.8 1946 *Minute Man* cover featuring the sculpture's plow and minimizing its musket. As the magazine's caption stated, "the plow remains," reinforcing the return of the nation's civilian-soldiers to their peacetime duties. Courtesy Franklin D. Roosevelt Library.

Implications of the 1945 War Bond Drive Appeals

In June 1946, the cover of the bond program's newsletter, the *Minute Man,* featured a photograph of its familiar namesake, the Daniel Chester French sculpture (see fig. 4.8).[137] To many of the publication's readers, however, this particular view of the sculpture might have looked somewhat unfamiliar. From years as the war bond program's primary symbol, the Minute Man—and his musket—would be familiar to readers. But they were probably much less familiar with the sculpture's plow. The picture presented in this edition of the *Minute Man* showed the sculpture from its other side, highlighting the plow and minimizing the musket. The Treasury's point was not subtle. "It is a reminder," intoned the editor, that "at heart, he is a man of peace. . . . [W]ar or no war, yesterday, today, and tomorrow, the plow always remains."[138]

In some ways, the two contrasting faces of the Minute Man encapsulated the Treasury's 1945 propaganda campaign. In one sense, they served as a symbol of transition. By conflating civilians and soldiers within a nationalist context, the Treasury began the transformative ritual of a homecoming in which battlefield soldiers and home front soldiers alike could transform into civilians. By submerging its enemy images and then replacing them with elements of a mythic victory, the war bond strategists called forth a shift from potential revulsion at the war's excesses to an acceptance and valorization of their triumph. Thus, the Treasury's strategists adapted to 1945's dynamic exigencies with propaganda that embodied the Minute Man's transition from war to peace.

The Minute Man's two contrasting faces also served as a symbol of demobilization. The Treasury's war bond effort can be understood as a militarized propaganda campaign that experienced many of the same struggles faced by the nation's front line units. In negotiating its terminal period in 1945, the war bond program was in a sense preparing the home front army for the final transition to peace. By featuring the Minute Man's plow and deemphasizing his musket, this last issue of the *Minute Man* was, to borrow its words, being "mustered out." As millions of wartime bond purchasers were themselves turning to the possibilities of postwar life in a victorious America, they too were heeding the War Finance Division's final command to "carry on."[139]

5 ASSESSING THE TREASURY'S WAR BOND LEGACIES

Militarized Propaganda, Enemy Constructions, and the War's Perfecting Myth

Looking to the future, [the Victory Loan] helps us to cross the bridge from wartime to peacetime prosperity, and so to lay the foundation for the Thanksgivings of the future.
—Fred M. Vinson

Every war begins as one war and becomes two, that watched by civilians and that fought by soldiers.
—Gerald F. Linderman

Sixty years after America's victory at the end of World War II, the war experience remains a vibrant topic. Japanese planes continue to attack Pearl Harbor to the delight of millions of movie fans. The nation's World War II Memorial is now open on what some consider the country's most hallowed ground. Fiftieth anniversary news stories about the Korean War invariably mentioned how that struggle is overshadowed in communal memory by the larger, worldwide conflict that preceded it. Tom Brokaw's book of memories on the war quickly rose to the top of the best seller lists.[1] And the national D-day memorial was dedicated, with all the pomp and circumstance required for honoring those who, most would say, are our nation's most heroic veterans.

Clearly, the triumphant legacies of World War II live on. Despite revisionist histories that have attempted to dismantle, piece by piece, the various myths and legends of the conflict, the enduring notion of "the good war" remains, ever-resistant to critique.[2] This is not to say that our myths and legends about the war are necessarily misguided. Myths and legends are often based on at least some fundamental truths. Rather, the enduring "goodness" of the war may suggest something about ourselves, looking back all these years later. It is comforting, after all, to think that once upon a time there was no question that America acted bravely, that it saved others, that it sacrificed nobly, that it was, in fact, *good.* The historian Warren Susman neatly captures the essence of this cultural need in his phrase "uses of a usable past."[3] Particularly in an age in which the world's image of the United States has become increasingly negative, and where terrorism and fanaticism are the order of the day, it is indeed useful to think back to a time when all was well.

The problem with such comforting thoughts, however, is that they tend to diminish our capacity or desire for critical self-reflection. In the case of World War II, such critical self-reflection will only become more difficult as the years pass. We are told that veterans of the war are now dying at the rate of one thousand per day, and each passing prompts more discourse about the war's righteousness and virtue.[4] But the sobering result of these losses is that at some point no one will be left who can remember anything about World War II but that which is *reconstructed*—in movies, in scrapbooks, in stories, or, especially, in our cultural myths. As it is, the farther one recedes from the conflict, the more sacred the war's myths seem to become. As Michael C. C. Adams concludes, "the popular image of World War II is incomplete." "It is distorted," he continues, "by oversimplification and glamorization."[5] And it is this very distortion that continues to nurture our mythic legacies of the conflict—legacies that arguably restrict our ability to carefully sift through the lessons of the war and to learn more about our past, and about ourselves.

One of the key participants in the construction of these World War II legacies was the U.S. Treasury Department. The Treasury's militarized propaganda campaign was a primary source of the Roosevelt administration's domestic propaganda throughout the conflict. The Treasury's bond program provided the U.S. government with cost-free advertising that reached millions of Americans throughout the war years. Unlike the government's *official* domestic propaganda agencies, the Treasury's ubiquitous efforts did not come with the stigma of a propaganda program; for this reason they effectively sidestepped the wary public's distrust.[6] Many people who lived through the Treasury's massive campaign did not perceive its propagandistic overtones.[7]

Some sixty years later, the various roles of the Treasury's propaganda campaign in constructing the legacies of the conflict seem more visible. At the heart of the enduring image of "the good war," for example, lies a valorizing perspective of World War II very similar to the one fashioned by the Treasury's propagandists soon after the war's conclusion. Of course, the bond program was not the only participant that formed the legacies that emerged from the war. But in three areas—militarized propaganda campaigns, enemy constructions, and the war's perfecting myth—the Treasury's contributions were significant, and remain powerful.

The Legacy of the Militarized Propaganda Campaign and Its Evolution

Odd as it may seem, relatively little scholarship focuses on the World War II home front. As Geoffrey Perrett suggests, "America's domestic history appears to have jerked to a halt in 1939, then revived at breakneck speed six years later."[8] No wonder, then, that our knowledge about the U.S. government's domestic propaganda production during the war is very limited. Typical research on propaganda production during the war focuses on America's *international* efforts.[9] Even Allan M. Winkler's work on the Office of War Information (OWI)—Roosevelt's official propaganda agency—stresses the organization's internal and external struggles, ultimately implying that the collapse of its domestic branch in 1943 left a propaganda vacuum on the home front.[10]

Clearly, however, there was not a domestic propaganda vacuum during World War II, despite OWI's travails and its eventual focus on international propaganda. Instead, the Treasury's massive war bond program became the administration's unorthodox means of propagandizing the public. The campaign's propaganda production fostered a home front audience that was very aware of the Treasury's widespread messages.[11] Indeed, Lawrence R. Samuel describes "the overwhelming popularity of the bond program among essentially all sectors of the population."[12] This popularity, from the Treasury's perspective, was a central reason why the program's propagandists felt that war bond sales were an accurate barometer of public morale during the war. Although it is of course impossible to establish definitive causality between bond sales on the home front and the level of public morale, the depth of the Treasury's belief on the issue—and its reliance on countless internal polls supporting that belief—suggests that there was at least an association between the two. Samuel offers a similar assessment, suggesting that through its war bond program the Roosevelt "administration did indeed succeed in its objective to give Americans a personal stake in the war."[13]

In its quest to become the arbiter of home front morale during the war, the Treasury's propaganda reflected a militarized mind-set. The bond program's discourse worked to mobilize the public, turn bonds into weapons, dehumanize the enemy, and transform civilians into soldiers—all in a manner echoing military campaigns. With the Minute Man as its primary symbol, the bond program's language, outlook, and philosophy produced a de facto military operation that seemingly sought to transform the home front into a battlefront. This approach was apparent in the Treasury's occasional orders for citizens to "forward march!"[14] to "attack!"[15] to "carry on!"[16] and to raise their "battle flag."[17] In such discourse, Americans became much more than a collection of civilians supporting the war. Under the Treasury's guidance, the public's efforts became military sacrifices while its "ideas and emotions" became "as important to winning the war as bombs and tanks."[18] Thus, much like military leaders training soldiers for combat, the Treasury's propaganda facilitated the mobilization of the American public for its part in the war. As Peter H. Odegard wrote after the conflict, the Treasury's aim of "psychological mobilization" was critical in "sustaining the fighting spirit of the American people and promoting national unity."[19]

In the process of propagandizing the American public, the Treasury's messages exhibited the psychological stages used by military leaders in preparing soldiers for battle. By reflecting these stages, the Treasury's discourse evidenced a strategic approach that evolved as the perceived moods of the home front shifted. Thus, with its initial training stage, the Treasury worked to associate bonds with the growing defense effort. Significantly, this stage occurred before Pearl Harbor, meaning that the connection between bonds and defense was already well established before the declaration of war. Once American involvement in the conflict began, the Treasury exploited this connection in the program's cohesion stage. Here the bond strategists took advantage of the war fever emerging from the attack on Pearl Harbor by crafting the public into a unified home front army. While this stage helped affirm the bond program's voice on the home front, the distractions of wartime meant that the Treasury's initial quota approach inevitably found its target audience difficult to reach.

With the introduction of a drive approach in late 1942, the Treasury's militarized mind-set evolved into a stage of apprehensive enthusiasm. The bond drives of 1942 and 1943 worked to capitalize on the public's energy and tension by linking bond sales with the military's progress in the material war. When public frustration at the war's prolonged tedium eventually emerged, the Treasury's propaganda campaign took on the characteristics of a resignation period. The public's perceived angst in this phase fostered increasingly graphic and disturbing appeals throughout the 1944 drives. By the war's last year, the promise of victory produced propaganda reflective of a terminal period, prompting the Treasury's discourse to evolve one last time. The bond campaign adopted nationalist images to facilitate one more push from the home front and to warrant the transformation of soldiers back into civilians.

The centerpiece of this militarized propaganda campaign was the Treasury's conflation of civilians and soldiers. The initial introduction of the conflation was the rough equivalent of arrival on the battlefield, thus reflecting the stage of apprehensive enthusiasm. The eventual emergence of the psychological stage of resignation, though, required harsher appeals similar to those used to motivate war-weary troops. Consequently, the bond propaganda evidenced a strategy of ironic incongruity, maintaining the civilian-soldier conflation but emphasizing the discrepancy between the heroic soldiers on the battlefront and the less heroic soldiers on the home front. By war's end, the discourse of the Treasury's terminal period prompted one last push in the fight—then warranted a psychological demobilization from soldier back into civilian.

While the Treasury's messages were the primary source for this conflation and the mind-set it reflected, other voices reinforced the bond program's militarized perspective.[20] Perhaps due to its status as the first and largest client of the War Advertising Council (WAC), for example, the Treasury's philosophy of selling the war to the public emerged in many of WAC's other ventures. Not surprisingly, WAC's goals of "arousing the reading public, dispelling apathy, and bringing the war into the life space of the individual" bore a striking resemblance to the Treasury's aims.[21] Indeed, partly because of WAC's influence, ads for scores of commercial products during the war echoed the themes and moods of the Treasury's propaganda. Consider, for instance, the Nash-Kelvinator magazine ad entitled "For Joe and Pete and Jack and Harry," which appeared during the Fourth War Loan. Its depiction of a shell-shocked GI standing in front of dozens of battlefield graves echoed exactly the tone of the Treasury's appeals during that drive. Moreover, the ad borrowed directly from the Treasury's militarized perspective by telling its home front audience: "let's all back the attack!"[22]

This widespread dissemination of the Treasury's perspective helped form a wartime context in which the home front itself evidenced signs of militarization. Throughout the war years, the Treasury's domestic audience was told again and again about its critical role as soldiers in the conflict. This militarizing message was so pervasive that even loose change could take on strategic significance in the war effort.[23] No wonder, then, that by 1945, "the war was 'real' to all, soldier and civilian alike."[24] "In a war where civilian and military roles often overlapped," writes Michael S. Sherry, the militarized public "often felt they were . . . on the front lines."[25]

Evidence suggesting the home front's militarization also emerged in the connection between bond sales and the material war. As the program's national director, Ted R. Gamble, explained, "every time there is a serious reversal on any of the fighting fronts, there is heavier Bond buying on the home-front."[26] In fact, as Americans "backed the attack" throughout the war period, they purchased war bonds at startling rates. The home front soldiers loaned the U.S. government $185.7 billion during the war. This total made up more than half the overall cost of America's role in the entire conflict. Although bond sales fluctuated occasionally, particularly in 1944, the Treasury's private research continually suggested that there was a powerful connection between bond sales and "personal involvement" with the war's events.[27]

The Treasury's militarized perspective was even reflected in the news media, which often described the bond program in military terms. Shortly after the D-day invasion, for instance, the *Los Angeles Times* published an editorial cartoon that showed a giant hand planting an American flag onto a map of France. The arrows depicting the invading forces were labeled "bonds," while the caption "Home Front Beach Head" confirmed that as the army was fighting in Normandy, so too were the domestic soldiers fighting at home.[28] By variously describing the bond operation as "Minute Men" and as a "volunteer army of 5,000,000" that would "marshal forces" in the war effort, the popular press promulgated the Treasury's militarized outlook.[29]

The widespread nature of this militarized perspective, however, was ultimately grounded in the Treasury's own verbal and visual depictions. Treasury Secretary Henry F. Morgenthau Jr. encouraged the war bond strategists to convince bond buyers that they were "the next best thing to a soldier."[30] The Treasury's propaganda emphasized this theme continuously throughout the war, even showing direct visual analogies between civilians and GIs. Such images, as Paul Messaris points out, "are typically meant to give rise to some emotional disposition."[31] To the extent that the Treasury's depictions gave civilians a stronger emotional incentive to see themselves as active in the war, it makes sense that there were indications of a militarized public on the home front. Such a connection, in fact, evidences Edwin Black's argument that discourse can call into being a particular kind of audience, one that fashions itself in the image suggested by that discourse.[32]

If the Treasury's propaganda reflected a militarized approach, then the bond campaign itself was well situated to disseminate such a mind-set. On one count, its sheer size and depth were larger than any previous campaign.[33] On another, it was the first large-scale propaganda campaign to rely on statistical sampling, meaning that unlike earlier efforts, the Treasury could methodically study its target audience's wants, needs, and morale.[34] Finally, the Treasury's militarized campaign inundated the public at one of the most important formative moments in the nation's history. In other words, by undertaking an extensive and convincing depiction of the militarized populace at a time filled "with enormous implications for the nation's sense of itself and its place in the world," the Treasury presented a model of military effectiveness that would echo in later years.[35]

It is no surprise, then, to find that later propaganda efforts by the U.S. government developed in a manner reminiscent of military operations. In establishing support for Pres. Harry S. Truman's Campaign of Truth, for example, lobbyists used "the language of all-out warfare."[36] The cold war–era Voice of America controlled its workers in ways that reflected "military training and maneuvers."[37] And the Federal Civil Defense Administration, described by Laura McEnaney as yet another Cold War "propaganda effort," developed into "a *paramilitary* program, situated between the priorities of the defense establishment and the cultural ideals of the postwar home front."[38] Thus, although the Treasury itself no longer participated in wartime propaganda efforts, its successors in large-scale propaganda production articulated a similar mind-set.[39]

The Treasury's militarized approach may therefore have contributed to a long-term militarization of U.S. culture. Sixty years after World War II, we now live in what Patrick M. Regan calls an "armament culture." Such cultures are marked by the "maintenance of favorable public attitudes toward the military, and the subsequent extension of military-based organization into the civil sector of society."[40] This pervasive atmosphere of militarization is quite evident in contemporary America. As Diane J. Garsombke points out, for instance, business managers increasingly "take military principles as their own beliefs and make assumptions, goals, and plans for the organization based on military concepts, behaviors, myths, and language."[41] Cynthia Enloe suggests that this cultural process has similarly extended to the militarization of "toys, jobs . . . fashion, faith, [and] voting."[42]

This pervasive militarization has inevitably nurtured a mind-set in which social problems become enemies that must be attacked.

Thus, over the last several decades, the United States has fostered wars on poverty, drugs, AIDS, and crime. Waging what President Carter called "the moral equivalent of war" time and again has certainly been useful in gaining the public's attention for various causes.[43] Yet Sherry points out that cultural militarization also presents a host of disadvantages, among them "spending on useless armaments, lavish subsidies to corporations, failed or fickle military actions, [and] capricious state repression."[44] Enloe also believes that prolonged militarization produces disturbing effects. In her words, "the more militarization transforms an individual or society, the more that individual or society comes to imagine military needs and militaristic presumptions to be not only valuable but also normal."[45]

Of course, the militarized mind-set of the Treasury during World War II was not the only contributor to this ongoing legacy of cultural militarization. As Regan points out, there were signs of a growing military outlook in American culture at least as far back as 1900.[46] George Creel's Committee on Public Information and the Great War's Liberty Loan efforts evidenced a similar mind-set. Still, the powerful reach of Morgenthau's militarized depictions occurred in the midst of a war to which "Americans increasingly return" in their "search for a usable past."[47] Thus, while it is impossible to measure precisely the Treasury's role in the construction of this militarized legacy, its contributions are worth noting. To borrow Odegard's phrase, placing "America on guard" during the war helped produce a militarized culture both in the short term and in the long term.[48] As Odegard himself recognized, however, it was a culture that not only privileged soldiers but also necessitated a requisite enemy.

The Legacy of the Treasury's Enemy Constructions

Although most nations construct adversaries, the United States has historically approached this rhetorical task in rather transcendent terms. Paul Kecskemeti, for instance, shows how "wars waged in the spirit of the traditional American approach . . . are essentially crusades. The conflict is seen as one of good pitted against evil."[49] On one side of this divide is the United States, described by Philip Wander as "the manifestation of Truth, Justice, and Freedom."[50] On the other side is the enemy, which becomes "the very personification of violence and strife."[51] Robert L. Ivie argues that in the heat of wartime, this depiction of epic conflict between the virtuous America and the villainous adversary becomes quite compelling.[52] Hans Speier agrees, pointing out that in American wars "the popular image of the enemy influences both the conduct of soldiers and any popular definitions of war aims."[53]

As these various viewpoints suggest, there is fairly widespread recognition that the United States is well versed in using what Sam Keen calls "the hostile imagination."[54] Yet the *process* of enemy construction is much less familiar to us. In particular, the evolution of enemy images—from their emergence as conflicts approach to their submergence near war's end—is still obscure.

The Treasury's World War II propaganda campaign offers several insights into the evolution of enemy images during war. The Treasury's strategists relied on a rhetoric of mobilization before the war and a rhetoric of demobilization at war's end. This process paralleled a military approach, which is often grounded in the psychological stages faced by battlefield soldiers. In its adoption of "the warfare script," the Treasury's propaganda campaign depicted an enemy as a means to motivate its home front soldiers.[55] Again, this process echoed the military's process of preparing its soldiers for the kill.

The resulting evolution of the Treasury's enemy constructions featured several stages. In its earlier drives, the Treasury relied on inchoate depictions of the enemy. These images avoided portraying the adversary directly, yet they still communicated the looming danger presented by his proximity. Once the Treasury's propaganda evidenced a period of resignation, however, its enemy imagery reflected a more vivid and visual essence. When depicted, the German enemy maintained a humanized appearance in spite of its villainous presence. The Japanese enemy, in contrast, soon developed a dehumanized appearance, ultimately descending into racist images of serpents and beasts. As Jürgen Link suggests, this divergence was significant, representing the gulf between an enemy "conceded subject status" and a "'fanatical' enemy" who is denied both subjectivity and rationality, and who is thus fit only for extermination.[56]

Both sets of enemy images disappeared in the Treasury's discourse during the terminal period. In part, this disappearance was related to the approach of the Allied victory. As Kecskemeti suggests, "when a war is in its terminal stage, factors that make it more or less total are no longer dominant."[57] By eliminating its dehumanizing images of Japan, the Treasury in effect acknowledged that the end of the war was near. Simultaneously, its propaganda worked to prepare the public for negotiations with an enemy once characterized as incapable of making peace.

What was not visible in the Treasury's propaganda, however, was a means of rehumanizing the enemy at war's end. As before, this scenario followed a military pattern. After all, the purpose of dehumanization on the battlefield is to enable the GI to kill the enemy. To rehumanize the enemy once the killing is complete would be to unravel that justification, and to invite shame and self-mortification in one's own soldiers.[58] As Dave Grossman points out, military leaders prevent this scenario by attempting to convince soldiers "that their opponents are not really human but are 'inferior forms of life.'"[59] In a similar way, the Treasury's dehumanizing images served to justify the war's great sacrifices and atrocities for its home front troops. If the Treasury had retracted these images at the end of the conflict, then the natural revulsion and questioning following a war might have been much greater. Thus, instead of rehumanizing the enemy at war's end, the Treasury simply ceased its dehumanizing images and increased the level of its nationalistic appeals. Much like the military model, the bond program demobilized its soldiers, but effectively allowed its enemy imagery to endure in the imagination.

Several scholars have suggested, that the government's enemy imagery may have ultimately played a role in the divergent fates of its World War II adversaries. For the German enemy, America's dehumanizing propaganda during the war centered on the Nazi leadership, meaning that little rehumanization was needed once German soldiers surrendered.[60] As Robert MacDougall explains, "the Germans as a people did not evoke the same level of hostility as the Japanese—and the hostility that did exist focused primarily on Germany's Nazi government and the individual figure of Adolf Hitler."[61] With the dehumanized Nazi leaders dead, executed, or put on trial at Nuremberg, the citizens of Germany and Italy soon emerged from the war as sympathetic figures. Indeed, Faris R. Kirkland notes that war correspondents "Ernie Pyle and Bill Mauldin recorded how quick American soldiers were to succor Italians and Germans when they occupied their countries" after the war.[62]

The fate of the dehumanized Japanese enemy, of course, was far worse. "In contrast to the treatment of Germany and Italy," writes Christopher Thorne, America's propaganda "attacked the entire Japanese people, and not their Emperor or Prime Minister alone, as being the embodiment of evil."[63] The placement of all Japanese people in the "category of 'subhumanity,'" adds James Weingartner, "rendered normal the wholesale violation of the generally accepted rules of warfare."[64] Significantly, it was these very images of subhumanity that the Treasury never reversed. As a result, the war bond propaganda may have helped contribute to a climate on the home front in which public support for vanquishing or exterminating the dehumanized enemy could exist.

No one would argue, of course, that the Treasury's propaganda directly resulted in the use of atomic warfare. The circumstances that produced Hiroshima and Nagasaki were extremely complex. Racism, for instance, was clearly a contributing factor. Despite perceptions of the Kaiser's perfidy in the previous war, during World War II "America's white enemies were rarely described in racial or even ethnic terms."[65] The opposite was true of the Japanese people, who found themselves immersed in the same derogatory language and imagery used for centuries to dehumanize Native Americans. Lisle A. Rose argues that this racist "wartime hysteria" in which "all Japanese of whatever age or sex were barbarians" eventually turned into "the formal national creed, and it culminated in an act of nearly unimaginable monstrosity."[66] Takaki agrees, noting "the significance of race in America's history as well as in the decision to drop the bomb."[67]

Whatever its roots, the wartime construction of the Japanese enemy appears to have contributed to a troubling legacy that continued long after the conflict. The image of the inhuman Asian adversary—drawn from racist archetypes and stoked by the U.S. Treasury's powerful propaganda campaign—lived on after World War II. Following the conflict, for example, the popular press "continued to emphasize the innate and perverted violent nature of the Japanese."[68] Peter Stanley suggests that such images remain commonplace in American discourse, particularly in times of domestic unrest. In such times, he writes, American "imagery of Japan almost invariably turns toward conspiracy, insidiousness, deceit, fanaticism, regimentation, and a kind of discipline and loyalty that is somehow less than fully human."[69]

This dehumanizing legacy of the Asian enemy has not been restricted to the Japanese. MacDougall shows, for instance, that the "racial and ethnic prejudices" used to demonize Japan during World War II reemerged "after China joined the Communist world in 1949 and reassumed the mantle of America's Yellow Peril."[70] John Dower points out how quickly "Japan and China changed places" in the nation's consciousness. Once "heralded by Americans during the war for their individualism and love of democracy," he explains, the Chinese swiftly became "fanatics" and "the unthinking horde."[71]

In Korea and Vietnam these sentiments were applied to still other cultures, renewing and nurturing World War II's earlier depictions. The Korean conflict produced descriptions of "a yellow tide of faceless masses" and "cruel and nerveless sub-humans."[72] In the Vietnam conflict, American soldiers faced "the same . . . degraded enemy, now labeled 'gooks,' 'dinks,' [and] 'slopes.'"[73] These dehumanizing attitudes would not have seemed out of place in many of the Treasury's 1944 war bond ads. Indeed, such similarities moved Thorne to wonder if "American attitudes towards the Vietnamese as opponents and as a people . . . owe anything to the popular images of those other 'yellow' enemies that had been cultivated during the Pacific conflict?"[74]

In addition to their dehumanizing legacy, the Treasury's enemy constructions may also have helped produce a sense of cultural desensitization to violence and horror. In their bid to shock the public into renewed war fervor after 1943, the war bond strategists began to depict wounded soldiers, battlefield grave sites, and shell-shocked prisoners of war. The graphic nature of these images gradually increased to the point where the sight of bloody wounds and even corpses of American GIs became normalized. By the end of 1944, the public was quite used to images that were once censored as taboo.[75]

In part, the subtext of such graphic depictions was a sense of hatred toward the enemy who was responsible for all the blood and death. The Treasury's propaganda thus dutifully supplied images of the enemy to be hated. Indeed, the graphic nature of the enemy's depictions grew at roughly the same rate as the images of bloody and dying GIs. In this way, the increased dehumanization of the enemy in the Treasury's discourse was linked to the increased use of shocking and disturbing images from the battlefront. Not surprisingly, this pervasive aspect of the Treasury's enemy construction helped produce a public that was somewhat inured to war's traumatic experiences. As MacDougall suggests, "the dehumanization of the Japanese enemy in so much of popular culture desensitized the American people to the horrors of war."[76]

For the most part, this widespread desensitization was rooted in the visual aspects of the war's propaganda. Although the bond campaign's verbal discourse contributed to this trend, it was the Treasury's pervasive visual depictions of dead soldiers and bestial enemies that were the most compelling and memorable. These images were extremely successful at what Ralph K. White calls "*painting a picture*" for the public.[77] Such vivid mental pictures can "linger in the collective memory of audiences."[78] Unfortunately, prolonged public exposure to such horrifying visual images ultimately makes the atrocities of war seem more acceptable and even more natural.[79]

In the end, the desensitizing effects of the graphic bond propaganda may have contributed another aspect to the legacy of the Treasury's enemy constructions. Although these constructions began with an implied enemy, they soon evolved into depictions of a savage and bloodthirsty adversary that was never rehumanized. By World War II's end, the public was so numb to such graphic imagery of the war that even the sensational photographs of the Holocaust had much less impact than many expected.[80] Several years later, the public's desensitization was still so ingrained that media depictions from the Korean War quickly resorted to "images of destruction and American death" in order to gain attention.[81] Of course, the Treasury Department has not been the only participant in creating such a legacy of desensitization. But its pervasive and powerful enemy constructions during WWII were probably a factor in producing a domestic tolerance for atrocity and horror. Ironically, the most disturbing aspect of the war for many Americans would have been the realization that their desensitization encouraged them "to endorse actions that in peacetime would have been unthinkable."[82] This sort of realization was exactly what the Treasury's perfecting myth helped mask.

The Legacy of the Treasury's Perfecting Myth

Our collective memory of World War II has sanitized many of the conflict's more horrific aspects. For example, the Second World War produced 50 million deaths—humans killed across the globe in "bombings, shootings, bayonetings, gasings, garrotings, hangings, drownings, beatings, starvation, suffocation, radiation, fire and disease."[83] Millions more survived the war, but "with missing limbs, shattered faces, diminished mental capacity, and other permanent physical and emotional disabilities."[84] Many of the war's experiences were so horrible, suggests Paul Fussell, that soldiers uniformly believed that "the real war will never get in the books."[85]

Such unsettling aspects of the war were not fully visible immediately after V-J day in the summer of 1945. Yet home front Americans were well aware of the sacrifices, toil, and bloodshed involved in the war. For many, the use of atomic bombs against Japanese cities exacerbated the feeling of malaise and uncertainty. Soon after the attack on Nagasaki, for instance, one New Yorker wrote Truman that she was "impelled to . . . tell you how stunned and sick at heart I am over what our country has just done to Japan and her people—thousands of them innocent." "I think it is a disgrace," she continued, "that America should be involved in such a diabolical thing."[86] Rose notes that a shaken *New York Times* journalist concurred with this view, writing that "we clinched victory in the Pacific, but we sowed the whirlwind."[87]

These postwar sentiments indicate that the horrific aspects of the war were at times quite evident in the aftermath of victory. As Simon Serfaty explains, "the time of peace is a time of regret. The peacemaker relives yesterday's events so that he will not repeat the mistakes that made the present what it is." Yet paradoxically, he continues, "the time of peace is a time of hope, too."[88] This contradictory nature of war's aftermath is fertile ground for the creation of a "perfecting myth."[89] In such myths, the disturbing aspects of a campaign are deemphasized while its positive aspects are highlighted. In the case of World War II, the horrors of war soon became nearly invisible in public discourse, while the heartening and heroic aspects of America's involvement gained precedence. Indeed, this perfecting myth of the war is one of its most enduring legacies. Even sixty years later, the mythic transcendence of the conflict as "the good war" continues to resist critique.[90]

The U.S. Treasury's important contributions to this enduring legacy were twofold. Not surprisingly, the bond strategists worked to reconstruct a version of the conflict that omitted the less-than-heroic episodes of America's wartime participation. None of the bond program's postwar appeals, for instance, mentioned the mass detention of Japanese Americans during the war. Nor did any of them highlight the firebombing of Dresden, or the occasional atrocities committed by U.S. Marines in the Pacific theater, or dozens of other topics that would have jeopardized the myth's justification of the war. Tellingly, only a few Treasury ads even mentioned atomic warfare. One of these ads—a Victory Loan cartoon imitating a Ripley's "Believe It or Not" format—maintained the Treasury's mythic theme by focusing on the costs of the bomb in the context of other late-war expenses. This normalizing perspective was reinforced in the cartoon by a far-off perspective of the bomb's mushroom cloud that obscured any scenes of destruction, or suffering, or death.[91]

Of course, highlighting such negative aspects of the war would be highly unusual. The function of wartime propaganda is to valorize the institutional source, not condemn it. Yet all wars, by definition, have horrible and repugnant elements. For this reason, any version of a war that provides an essentially romantic account is, to paraphrase Kenneth Burke, selecting a particular reality while simultaneously deflecting another.[92] From the vantage point of sixty years or more, it is easier to see what the Treasury's appeals did not mention, and thus what aspects of reality were being deflected. It is these very aspects of the war that are often excluded from the nation's collective memory. As Adams points out, World War II's "myth is distorted not so much in what it says as in what it doesn't say."[93]

But while the bond campaign's perfecting myth worked to conceal some of the nation's more questionable actions from the recent past, it simultaneously valorized the nation in its victorious present. The resulting images of Americanism were grounded in the Truman administration's emphasis on "a more nationalistic statement of the war's purpose than Roosevelt generally offered."[94] As these nationalistic images emerged in the Treasury's postwar propaganda, they presented a compelling optimism in the face of the public's growing sense of disillusionment. It is true that Americans "could not evade the brute fact in August 1945 of their sudden acquisition of overwhelming global power . . . through their singular possession of atomic weaponry."[95] The nationalist images of the Treasury's perfecting myth, though, worked to celebrate, rather than mourn, this growth of American primacy.

Significantly, the Treasury's images of heroic nationalism emerged just as America was entertaining the widespread notion that "global war would transform the world for the better."[96] The Victory Loan's image of the ascendent eagle, war bonds in its talons, for example, represented a triumphant nation unchallenged at the end of history's greatest war. Just as the eagle was about to take flight, so too was the nation poised to assume its role as a superpower, fresh from a victorious struggle against the vanquished powers of evil. The Iwo Jima image reinforced this notion, visually emphasizing the nation's strength and determination in the face of adversity. Philip Gleason points out that "World War II shaped the self-understanding of Americans . . . in regard to what we now call American identity."[97] John Fousek agrees, pointing out that "the notion that 'America is the number-one nation' . . . in effect achieved its hegemony" in the immediate postwar period.[98] The Treasury's powerful propaganda thus strengthened the self-perceptions of an American public considering the nation's emerging role in the world by presenting a comforting myth of the war that was grounded in nationalist images. In this manner, the Treasury's propaganda campaign played a role in shaping the maturing sense of American identity in the postwar world.

The legacy of this constructed American identity is still evident. If the nation "emerged from World War II as a fully matured great power," it was soon "prepared to usher in a new golden age in its own image."[99] America's new identity—forged in the heat of battle and mythically perfected in the Treasury's postwar propaganda—thus served to prepare the public for a continuing role in the fight against tyranny. Indeed, as Fousek suggests, "the potency of the Cold War ideology that emerged between 1945 and 1950—an ideology that dominated U.S. public life at least until . . . 1991—derived largely from its nationalist appeal."[100]

As before, the Treasury was one of many participants in creating the legacy of the war's perfecting myth. Yet its adoption of Americanism at war's end offers a glimpse into the larger mind-set of the Truman administration at the precise moment when America's superpower status was confirmed in the postwar world. The nationalist images imbedded in the Treasury's perfecting myth provided an immediate means of submerging the war's negative aspects within a stronger narrative of American triumphalism. In the short term, such images were well situated to ease the angst of a public experiencing growing anxiety and revulsion in the war's aftermath. In the long term, those images helped produce a master narrative of the war that remains enshrined in our nation's memorials, our memory, and our movies.

The movie blockbuster *Pearl Harbor* borrowed heavily from the propaganda of World War II for its publicity. Several of its promotional posters—with the faces of its actors spliced in—were in fact faithful reproductions of war bond posters. Similarly, a recent campaign by the ZixIt Corporation (an e-mail encryption service) also adopted imagery from the U.S. Treasury's bond posters for its magazine ads. Obviously, the images in such posters no longer sell war bonds. Yet their alluring visual power still seems to resonate with consumers. Although many of these depictions of World War II were crafted by the Treasury's propagandists more than half a century ago, they continue to evidence a compelling sense of the war's drama.

This dramatic and powerful imagery emerged from a World War II propaganda venture that merged rhetorical aims and militaristic philosophy to produce a campaign "around which the vast majority of Americans rallied."[101] Morgenthau's desire to sell the war to the public and Roosevelt's inability to maintain an official propaganda agency intersected in the war bond program as early as 1941, some seven months before Pearl Harbor. By the end of the war more than four years later, the Treasury had sold billions in bonds to millions of Americans. All the while, it communicated the administration's views on the conflict to the home front through the largest propaganda campaign of the war.

There is little question, obviously, about the significant size and scope of the Treasury's propaganda operation on the home front. What remains are more philosophical questions about the morality of the war bond program and its strategies. At this point, to put it bluntly, one might ask whether Morgenthau's Treasury propaganda was noble or ignoble?

Perhaps the best answer to such a question is a mixed one. If one were to judge the war bond propaganda as morally corrupt, one could point out that it emerged from a program that set out to deceive the public by disguising its true aims, that it used disturbing and graphic images of the dead and dying to cajole its audience, that it fostered racist and jingoistic perceptions of other humans, and that it fashioned a perfecting myth that hid the horrific aspects of the war behind a mask of nationalistic imagery. In contrast, if one were to judge the war bond propaganda as essentially noble, one could point to its service in helping unify the nation in a time of peril, its role in helping defeat totalitarian regimes, and even its economic contributions, such as controlling wartime inflation and convincing Americans to conserve and to save.

Inevitably, then, one's moral assessment of the Treasury comes down to a means-ends dilemma with no clear-cut answer. Most people would probably agree that the war bond strategists felt that they were serving their country and that they were attempting to do so honorably. Their ends, particularly as Odegard outlined them in 1941, appear to have been admirable. Yet the realities of war and the complex nature of the dynamic home front audience appear to have gradually drawn the Treasury's propaganda—its means—into a moral trap. Near the end of the war, the bond program's messages were certainly not admirable, by almost any standard. For many, however, the most difficult question will remain unresolved—and this must be a question that propagandists face continually: were even these dubious means justified by the propaganda program's more admirable ends?

Clearly, the conclusions that one takes away from such a difficult dilemma are highly individual. If they emerge, however, from the context of cultural self-reflection, they offer far more than an unquestioning acceptance of World War II's myths and legends. What they offer instead is a healthy investigation into America's past and the choices that have been made in the context of war. This type of self-reflection is particularly welcome in today's society. It might be said that more recent wars have seen different approaches to propaganda than those used in World War II. Yet many of the same moral questions persist. Thus, whatever the source of modern propaganda—whether government, corporate, or institutional—an urgent awareness of the potential for moral traps is both healthy and admirable.

As for the Treasury, the bond program's successor bureau no longer engages in war-related propaganda campaigns as it did during the 1940s. Still, the powerful legacies of its World War II efforts continue to echo. Whether it is a militarized culture, a lingering sense of racism toward Asian nations, or the myth of the "good war," many aspects of the Treasury's powerful depictions still affect us today. In the end, these ongoing legacies suggest that Gerald F. Linderman's assessment of war is no longer accurate. Writing of the Civil War, he argued that "every war begins as one war and becomes two, that watched by civilians and that fought by soldiers."[102] Sixty years after World War II, it is possible to see that the greatest conflict in history has diverged from Linderman's assessment. This conflict—the one fought by Brokaw's "greatest generation"—started out as one war fought by soldiers.[103] It soon became a second war watched (and fought) by civilians. Finally, it emerged as a third war, one constructed after victory and nurtured in collective memory ever since. Ironically, it was the U.S. Treasury—through its war finance, its domestic militarization, and its perfecting myth—that ultimately played a starring role in all three wars.

NOTES

Introduction

1. James W. Gerard, *Face to Face with Kaiserism.* Quotations are from "Another Great Book by Ambassador Gerard," advertisement, *Washington Post,* Feb. 15, 1918.
2. "The Kaiser's Secret Army in America," advertisement, *Washington Post,* Dec. 1, 1917.
3. Thomas Jewett Hallowell, letter to the editor, *New York Times,* May 10, 1915.
4. J. Michael Sproule, "Social Responses to Twentieth-Century Propaganda," in *Propaganda: A Pluralistic Perspective,* ed. Ted J. Smith III, 8.
5. Thomas A. Hollihan, "Propagandizing in the Interest of War: A Rhetorical Study of the Committee on Public Information, *Southern Speech Communication Journal* 49 (1984): 241–57; Robert Jackall and Janice M. Hirota, "America's First Propaganda Ministry: The Committee on Public Information during the Great War," in *Propaganda,* ed. Robert Jackall, 137–73.
6. Lawrence R. Samuel, *Pledging Allegiance: American Identity and the Bond Drive of World War II.*
7. Jackall and Hirota, "America's First," 158.
8. Garth S. Jowett and Victoria O'Donnell, *Propaganda and Persuasion,* 3rd ed., 163.
9. James R. Mock and Cedric Larson, *Words That Won the War: The Story of the Committee on Public Information, 1917–1919,* 339.
10. Charles Gilbert, *American Financing of World War I,* 1.
11. Samuel, *Pledging Allegiance,* 5.
12. Ibid.
13. William G. McAdoo, *Crowded Years,* 374.
14. Hollihan, "Propagandizing," 247.
15. See, for example, John Dewey, "The New Paternalism," *New Republic,* Dec. 21, 1918, 216–17; Philip Gibbs, *Now It Can Be Told;* and Walter Lippmann, *Public Opinion.*
16. Harold D. Lasswell, *Propaganda Technique in World War I,* 221.
17. Jowett and O'Donnell, *Propaganda,* 104–106; Sproule, "Social Responses"; and Allan M. Winkler, *The Politics of Propaganda: The Office of War Information, 1942–1945,* 4. As Sproule suggests elsewhere, CPI's overzealous efforts to unify public opinion helped usher in an "environment of cynicism and disillusionment" throughout the 1920s and early 1930s. See his "Propaganda Studies in American Social Science: The Rise and Fall of the Critical Paradigm," *Quarterly Journal of Speech* 73 (1987): 63.
18. John Morton Blum, *V Was for Victory: Politics and American Culture during World War II,* 21–31. OWI was responsible for "white," or overt, propaganda. The Office of Strategic Services was responsible for "black," or covert, propaganda overseas. See Jordan Braverman, *To Hasten the Homecoming: How Americans Fought World War II through the Media.*

19. Blum, *V Was for Victory,* 8, 21; Richard W. Steele, "Preparing the Public for War: Efforts to Establish a National Propaganda Agency," *American Historical Review* 75 (1970): 1642.

20. Winkler, *Politics of Propaganda,* 70.

21. Braverman, *Hasten the Homecoming;* Sydney Weinberg, "What to Tell America: The Writers' Quarrel in the Office of War Information," *Journal of American History* 55 (1968): 73–89. Although OWI's funding for domestic operations had been cut significantly, it maintained operational control over some of its campaigns. Moreover, it developed a cooperative relationship with the Treasury's war bond planners through at least the summer of 1944. See "Treasury-OWI Relations (from the Inception of OWI to the Beginning of the Fifth War Loan Drive)," [1944], Box 17, Folder 5, Peter H. Odegard Papers, Franklin D. Roosevelt Presidential Library, Hyde Park, N.Y.

22. William H. Conner and Leon de Valinger Jr., *Delaware's Role in World War II: 1940–1946,* 2:144. The $350 billion estimate is in 1947 dollars. Goodwin reports a smaller overall cost of $304 billion. See Doris K. Goodwin, *No Ordinary Time: Franklin and Eleanor Roosevelt: The Home Front in World War II,* 487.

23. Dorwin P. Cartwright to Peter H. Odegard, report, 2 Aug. 1945, Box 13, Folder 2, Odegard Papers. The war bonds of World War II, incidentally, are the direct antecedents of contemporary savings bonds, in function if not in militaristic purpose. The Treasury defines a "savings bond" as "a contract showing that money has been loaned to the United States, which promises to repay it, with accrued interest, when the bond is redeemed." See Treasury Department, Office of Public Affairs, U.S. Savings Bond Division, *50 Questions and Answers on U.S. Savings Bonds,* 1.

24. Samuel, *Pledging Allegiance,* 58–64; Treasury Department, *A History of the United States Savings Bond Program,* 12–13.

25. See, for example, Jarvis M. Morse, *Paying for a World War: The United States Financing of World War II,* 92–95. While FDR verbally and interpersonally supported the Treasury's efforts, Elmer Davis, head of OWI, frequently had trouble even getting face time with the president. See Blum, *V Was for Victory,* 18–19, and Winkler, *Politics of Propaganda,* 68.

26. Blum, *V Was for Victory,* 8.

27. Treasury Department, *History,* 7.

28. John Morton Blum, *From the Morgenthau Diaries: Years of War, 1941–1945,* 17, hereafter cited as Blum, *Years of War.*

29. Franklin D. Roosevelt, *Public Papers and Addresses of Franklin D. Roosevelt,* 12:380. FDR was referring to the $15 billion goal of the Third War Loan.

30. "A Suggested Outline for a Presentation of the War Finance Program," [1941?], Box 32, Folder 3, p. 3, Odegard Papers.

31. [Peter H. Odegard], "Symbols, Symbol Specialists, and Social Control," lecture notes, [Mar., 1942], Box 3, Folder 11, Odegard Papers. There are other reports that the administration saw the bonds as propaganda devices. Morgenthau said the war bonds "gave to the average citizen a sense of the war's meaning and of the urgent nature of the national danger." See Henry F. Morgenthau Jr., *War Finance Policies: Excerpts from Three Addresses by Henry Morgenthau, Jr., Secretary of the Treasury,* 3. Blum cites an assistant secretary of the Treasury, writing that the program's "decision [was] to use *bonds* to sell the *war,* rather than vice versa" (*Years of War,* 17–18, emphasis in original). Nelson agrees that the financial purpose of the bonds was secondary to their motivational purpose: "When it came to persuading Americans to buy bonds, much of the pitch depended on patriotism. . . . [W]riters and artists, film-makers and radio broadcasters worked together for the common

purposes of not only lifting the spirits of the people . . . but also to help finance the war." See Derek Nelson, *The Posters That Won the War,* 43. See also Samuel, *Pledging Allegiance,* 14–16, and Morse, *Paying for a World War,* 105–106.

32. Blum, *Years of War,* 17–18. Here Blum points out that Morgenthau "opposed placing a bond sales booth at Rockefeller Plaza in New York because 'that's the place where they sell the most precious jewelry. . . . [T]hose aren't the kind of people I want to reach,'" 17–18.
33. Ted R. Gamble, "Of What We May Be Proud," *Minute Man,* Mar. 1, 1944, 3.
34. Judy Graves to Odegard, Oct. 13, 1942, Box 32, Folder 3, p. 3, Odegard Papers.
35. Samuel, *Pledging Allegiance,* xiii, 209. As a further example of the bond propaganda's impact, consider the Treasury's Schools at War program (closely linked to the bond drives), which "helped lay the groundwork for marketers to recognize children and teenagers as population segments with particular wants and needs, key to [the] consumer culture of the 1950s and 1960s." See Samuel, 209, and his description of the Schools at War program, 34–37.
36. David Brinkley, *Washington Goes to War,* 123.
37. Morse, *Paying for a World War,* 1.
38. For works describing the home front's various problems during the war, see Paul Fussell, *Wartime: Understanding and Behavior in the Second World War;* George Q. Flynn, *The Mess in Washington: Manpower Mobilization in World War II;* and Studs Terkel, *"The Good War": An Oral History of World War II.*
39. Morse, *Paying for a World War;* Laurence M. Olney, *War Bond Story.* The earlier drives are partial exceptions, as the Treasury was still experimenting with its approach; not until the Third War Loan (in late 1943) did the full complement of appeals come together.
40. Olney, *War Bond Story,* 84.
41. Treasury Department, *Art for Bonds: Posters from the Bureau of the Public Debt.*
42. Steele, "Preparing the Public," 1644, 1646. FDR adviser William Y. Elliott advocated domestic propaganda distributed locally yet organized, in a quasi-official manner, by the administration. He termed the strategy "propaganda of the act."
43. See, for example, Douglas Walton, "What Is Propaganda, and What Exactly Is Wrong with It?" *Public Affairs Quarterly* 11 (1997): 1–31.
44. Peter H. Odegard, "The Spirit of '76," review of *Propaganda and the American Revolution,* by Philip Davidson, *Saturday Review of Literature,* Mar. 7, 1942, 5.
45. This definition of rhetoric is borrowed from Shawn J. Parry-Giles, "'Camouflaged' Propaganda: The Truman and Eisenhower Administrations' Covert Manipulation of News," *Western Journal of Communication* 60 (1996): 162.
46. Aristotle, *Rhetoric,* 1355.
47. See Brett Silverstein, "Toward a Science of Propaganda," *Political Psychology* 8 (1987): 49–59, who argues that "propaganda analysts must use some of the methods developed by investigative journalists and historians, particularly the unearthing of quotes from diaries, correspondence and in-house memoranda," 55. See also Martin J. Medhurst, "Eisenhower and the Crusade for Freedom: The Rhetorical Origins of a Cold War Campaign," *Presidential Studies Quarterly* 27 (1997): 646–61, in which he argues that "to explicate or analyze any text, whether a single speech or a multiyear campaign, one must thoroughly understand the contexts that form the *raison d'être* of the discourse," 659.

48. See Michael Osborn, "Rhetorical Depiction," in *Form, Genre, and the Study of Political Discourse,* ed. Herbert. W. Simons and Aram A. Aghazarian, 79. Osborn sees traditional rhetorical concepts as working together within a series of artifacts to create more complex instances of rhetorical depiction.

49. Zarefsky calls this kind of project "the study of historical events from a rhetorical perspective," which examines how "people invented and deployed messages in response to the situation." By studying such events from a rhetorical perspective, he concludes, "one can see significant aspects about those events that other perspectives miss." See David Zarefsky, "Four Senses of Rhetorical History," in *Doing Rhetorical History: Concepts and Cases,* ed. Kathleen J. Turner, 30.

50. The use of a tremendous variety of rhetorical strategies is common in propaganda campaigns. As Jowett and O'Donnell explain, "it would be useful to have a catalog of practices relevant to propaganda that produce effects, but it is not possible." See their *Propaganda,* 200.

51. Edwin Black, "The Second Persona," *Quarterly Journal of Speech* 56 (1970): 113.

52. For instance, on one day in 1943 Gerard and his wife purchased $1,000 in war bonds, an amount equivalent today to more than $10,000. See "$188,850 Reported in War Fund Drive," *New York Times,* Nov. 29, 1943.

53. Ronald E. Rice and Charles K. Atkin, eds., *Public Communication Campaigns,* 2nd ed., 7. See also J. Michael Sproule, "Propaganda: The Ideological Rhetoric," in *Rhetoric and Ideology: Compositions and Criticisms of Power,* ed. Charles W. Kneupper, 94, where he argues that CPI's World War I strategies were the direct precursors of modern public relations campaigns.

54. Charles J. Stewart, Craig Allen Smith, and Robert E. Denton Jr., *Persuasion and Social Movements,* 3rd ed., 4.

55. Ibid.

56. Herbert W. Simons, "Requirements, Problems, and Strategies: A Theory of Persuasion for Social Movements," *Quarterly Journal of Speech* 56 (1970): 6.

57. Stewart, Smith, and Denton, *Social Movements,* 4.

58. Etymologically, the very concept of campaigning is rooted in the act of war. Both wars and campaigns, according to Baus and Ross, "are played in defined theatres; both are fought by tactics of applied weaponry." Social movements share a similarly militarized outlook. Stewart, Smith, and Denton, for instance, describe social movements' "ability to mobilize forces into action." See Herbert M. Baus and William B. Ross, *Politics Battle Plan,* 2; and Stewart, Smith, and Denton, *Social Movements,* 62. While the Treasury's situation differed dramatically from the typical social movement, its strategists chose to respond to their developing situation in a manner reminiscent of social movement strategies. See a similar argument in David Zarefsky, "President Johnson's War on Poverty: The Rhetoric of Three 'Establishment' Movements," *Communication Monographs* 44 (1977): 371.

59. Joanna Bourke, *An Intimate History of Killing: Face-to-Face Killing in Twentieth-Century Warfare,* 59.

60. Anthony Kellett, "The Soldier in Battle: Motivational and Behavioral Aspects of the Combat Experience," in *Psychological Dimensions of War,* ed. Betty Glad, 216–17. Kellett adds the more general category of "mental preparation."

61. Peter Watson, *War on the Mind: The Military Uses and Abuses of Psychology,* 227–30.

62. Stewart, Smith, and Denton, *Social Movements,* 72.

63. "Defense Savings Campaign," Mar. 18, 1941, Box 6, Folder 2, p. 1, Odegard Papers.

64. Jowett and O'Donnell, *Propaganda,* 2, 206.
65. Paul A. Chilton, "The Meaning of Security," in *Post-Realism: The Rhetorical Turn in International Relations,* ed. Francis. A. Beer and Robert Hariman, 197.

Chapter 1

1. Gerhard L. Weinberg, *A World at Arms: A Global History of World War II,* 152. See also Richard Hough, *The Battle of Britain: The Greatest Air Battle of World War II.*
2. See Hadley Cantril, "Public Opinion in Flux," *Annals of the American Academy of Political and Social Sciences* 220 (1942): 136–52. Cantril pointed out that after the 1940 French surrender more than half those polled still said "it was more important for us to stay out of the war than to help Britain," 137.
3. Winkler, *Politics of Propaganda,* 8. In June, 1940, the secretaries of the army and navy presented Roosevelt with a "basic plan for public relations administration," which advocated a CPI-like agency. See discussion of this and other efforts in Steele, "Preparing the Public."
4. Richard W. Steele, *Propaganda in an Open Society: The Roosevelt Administration and the Media, 1933–1941,* 113–14; Blum, *V Was for Victory,* 8, 21. Led by Robert R. McCormick of the *Chicago Tribune,* Roosevelt's media critics were numerous, and they were unafraid of using their platform to criticize him.
5. William L. Langer and S. Everett Gleason, *The Undeclared War, 1940–1941,* 16. The destroyers-for-bases deal was brokered by Churchill, who convinced Roosevelt to help replace Britain's dwindling destroyer fleet by exchanging a ninety-nine-year lease of several sea bases for fifty American destroyers.
6. Morse explains that "the controversy over compulsory vs. voluntary lending was long and at times heated. Until it was resolved, it cast a dark shadow over the entire fiscal program of the Government." See Morse, *Paying for a World War,* 92.
7. See V. R. Cardozier, *The Mobilization of the United States in World War II: How the Government, Military, and Industry Prepared for War.*
8. McAdoo, *Crowded Years,* 372–77. More details on the history of U.S. war finance prior to the twentieth century are available in Lester C. Roig, "Policies of the U.S. Treasury in the Financing of Three Major Wars."
9. Secretary of the Treasury, *Annual Report,* 13–16.
10. Frederick J. Blue, *Salmon P. Chase: A Life in Politics,* 145–56.
11. See Jeffrey A. Cantor and Donald R. Stabile, *A History of the Bureau of the Public Debt, 1940–1990, with Historical Highlights from 1789–1939.*
12. McAdoo, *Crowded Years,* 374.
13. Ibid., 117.
14. Labert St. Clair, *The Story of the Liberty Loans: Being a Record of the Volunteer Liberty Loan Army, Its Personnel, Mobilization and Methods, How America at Home Backed Her Armies in the World War,* 42.
15. McAdoo, *Crowded Years,* 385.
16. George Creel, *How We Advertised America: The First Telling of the Amazing Story of the Committee on Public Information That Carried the Gospel of Americanism to Every Corner of the Globe,* 3, emphasis in original. Creel also explained that for CPI, "moral verdicts took on all the value of military decisions," 3.
17. McAdoo, *Crowded Years,* 378.
18. Hollihan, "Propagandizing," 247.

19. Stephen Vaughn, *Holding Fast the Inner Lines: Democracy, Nationalism, and the Committee on Public Information,* 156.
20. Samuel, *Pledging Allegiance,* 4.
21. Ibid., 7.
22. C. Gilbert, *American Financing,* 117–24; Morse, *Paying for a World War,* 30.
23. Richard Polenberg, *War and Society: The United States, 1941–1945,* 29.
24. Charles W. Smith, "The Selling of America in Oklahoma: The First and Second Liberty Bond Drives," *Chronicles of Oklahoma* 73 (1995/1996): 451.
25. Samuel, *Pledging Allegiance,* 5.
26. Treasury Department, *History.* A centerpiece of Roosevelt's Second New Deal in 1935 was the WPA (Works Progress Administration, later Works Projects Administration). WPA workers built and refurbished a variety of infrastructure projects around the country. The Emergency Relief Appropriation of 1935 allocated $4.8 billion for various employment plans. See William E. Leuchtenburg, *Franklin D. Roosevelt and the New Deal, 1932–1940,* 124–30.
27. John Morton Blum, *From the Morgenthau Diaries: Years of Urgency, 1938–1941,* 301, hereafter cited as Blum, *Years of Urgency.*
28. Eugene W. Sloan to Peter H. Odegard, report, "United States Savings Bonds," Apr. 17, 1944, Box 7, Folder 3, Odegard Papers. The banking holiday began on March 6, 1933—two days after Roosevelt took office for his first term. In his proclamation he halted all banking operations in the country until the federal government could assure that only banks on sound financial ground would reopen. See Susan Eastbrook Kennedy, *The Banking Crisis of 1933,* 155–78.
29. Olney, *War Bond Story,* 1.
30. Treasury Department, Savings Bond Division, *A History of the United States Savings Bonds Program.*
31. Treasury Department, news release, Apr. 27, 1936, Roll 6, Book 22, 67C, Morgenthau Diaries, Franklin D. Roosevelt Presidential Library, Hyde Park, N.Y.
32. Samuel, *Pledging Allegiance,* 9.
33. Sloan, "United States Savings Bonds," Odegard Papers.
34. John Morton Blum, *From the Morgenthau Diaries: Years of Crisis, 1928–1938,* 340–41, hereafter cited as Blum, *Years of Crisis.* See a Treasury scrapbook of baby bond advertisements in Records of the Savings Bond Division (Including Records of Its Predecessor, the War Finance Division), Records of the Field Directors, 1941–47, Publicity Materials, Box 2, General Records of the Department of the Treasury, Record Group 56, National Archives.
35. Blum, *Years of Crisis,* 341.
36. John Maynard Keynes, *How to Pay for the War: A Radical Plan for the Chancellor of the Exchequer,* iv.
37. Blum, *Years of War,* 17. At one point, Morgenthau told FDR that Smith was a "termite undermining the foundation of the Treasury." See "April 15, 1942," personal notes, Box 515, Folder 6, p. 1, Morgenthau Papers, Franklin D. Roosevelt Presidential Library, Hyde Park, N.Y.
38. "Report of Secretary Morgenthau's Press Conference, May 22, 1941," Box 613, Morgenthau Papers. There are no folder numbers in this section of the Morgenthau Papers, as most of the materials are bound into single volumes. The volumes are numbered in a continuation of the system used to number the boxes elsewhere in the collection. To maintain a consistent citation style, I have kept the term "boxes" in notes using such sources. Also quoted in Blum, *Years of Urgency,* 303.

39. Blum, *Years of Urgency,* 300–301.
40. Langer and Gleason, *The Undeclared War,* 200.
41. Steele, *Propaganda in an Open Society,* 83.
42. Steele, "Preparing the Public," 1645.
43. Ibid., 1646.
44. Ibid., 1641.
45. Harold Ickes to Henry Morgenthau Jr., Apr. 11, 1941, Roll 107, Book 388, Morgenthau Diaries.
46. "April 15, 1942," 1, Morgenthau Papers. In this document, Morgenthau recalled his conversation with FDR about the struggle of the war bond program against advocates of compulsory savings: "I said, 'You know, Mr. President, I think it is just as important to use this vehicle to make the country war-minded. . . . [T]here just isn't any other vehicle to do it.' He said, 'You are right.' "
47. Ibid.
48. Blum, *Years of Urgency,* 297. During the summer Roosevelt had already faced vehement charges that he was actively seeking war by supporting conscription, which became law in September 1940.
49. Robert A. Divine, *The Reluctant Belligerent: American Entry into World War II,* 2nd ed., 107–108.
50. U.S. Senate Committee on Finance, Public Debt Act of 1941: Hearings on H.R. 2959, 77th Cong., 1st sess., Feb. 12, 1941, 5.
51. U.S. House Committee on Ways and Means, Public Debt Act of 1941: Hearings on H.R. 2653, 77th Cong., 1st sess., Jan. 29, 1941, 5–6. See also Blum, *Years of Urgency,* 299–300.
52. Blum, *Years of Urgency,* 299.
53. Franklin D. Roosevelt, *Public Papers and Addresses of Franklin D. Roosevelt,* 9:604–15.
54. David Reynolds, *The Creation of the Anglo-American Alliance, 1937–1941,* 160.
55. Olney, *War Bond Story,* 3.
56. Peter H. Odegard and E. Allen Helms, *American Politics: A Study in Political Dynamics,* 771, 545, 549.
57. One private recounting of the bond program's earliest days, for example, gave Odegard primary credit for establishing the Treasury's philosophical direction. See Judy Graves to Peter H. Odegard, report, "Defense Savings Staff," [1944?], Box 6, Folder 2, Odegard Papers.
58. Series F and G were targeted to larger investors, particularly financial institutions. The terms and yield for these bonds were both slightly greater than for the smaller Series E. To help prevent banks from artificially increasing total bond sales (and thus encouraging inflation) no individual or group could purchase more than fifty thousand dollars in bonds.
59. Blum, *Years of Urgency,* 300. See Robert Wm. Kirk, *Earning Their Stripes: The Mobilization of American Children in the Second World War,* 77–101, for an extended discussion of war stamps as used in the nation's elementary and secondary classrooms.
60. Peter H. Odegard to Harford Powel, memorandum, Mar. 7, 1941, Box 8, Folder 2, p. 3, Odegard Papers.
61. Graves to Odegard, Odegard Papers.
62. Graves, "Defense Savings Staff," 7, Odegard Papers. The stricture on flag waving was primarily Odegard's idea. The bond program ultimately found many different flags to wave.

63. Ibid., 4.
64. "Defense Savings Campaign," Odegard Papers.
65. Donald I. Rogers, *Since You Went Away,* 13–28.
66. Houck, *Rhetoric as Currency,* 161, 176. See also Suzanne M. Daughton, "Metaphorical Transcendence: Images of the Holy War in Franklin Roosevelt's First Inaugural," *Quarterly Journal of Speech* 79 (1993): 427–46.
67. Winkler, *Politics of Propaganda,* 22.
68. Brinkley, *Washington,* 123.
69. "Every Time of National Crisis," memorandum, [1941], Box 3, Folder 2, p. 4, Odegard Papers, emphasis in original.
70. See handwritten brainstorming sheets in [Peter H. Odegard], "Literature," manuscript, [1941], Box 8, Folder 3, Odegard Papers.
71. Ibid.
72. "Defense Savings Campaign," 4, Odegard Papers.
73. Olney, *War Bond Story,* 6.
74. Ibid., 7.
75. Sloan, "United States Savings Bonds," 9, Odegard Papers.
76. Peter H. Odegard and Alan Barth, "Millions for Defense," *Public Opinion Quarterly* 5 (1941): 403. See a popularized version of Odegard's Minute Man choice in Jerome Beatty, "Biggest Bargain Sale," *American Magazine,* May, 1943, 108.
77. Cardozier, *Mobilization of the United States.*
78. Indeed, echoing the war-grounded philosophy of Creel's and McAdoo's World War I propaganda efforts, the Treasury very quickly set its sights on mobilizing Americans into a domestic army. Citizens on the home front, the bond program argued, "are as truly enlisted in the defense of democracy as the men who carry rifles." See "Every Time of National Crisis," 4, Odegard Papers.
79. Odegard and Barth, "Millions for Defense," 399.
80. Kellett, "Soldier in Battle," 216.
81. Morse, *Paying for a World War,* 43.
82. Olney, *War Bond Story,* 11.
83. Vincent F. Callahan to Peter H. Odegard, report, Feb. 14, 1945, Box 6, Folder 1, Odegard Papers.
84. "Opening of the Defense Savings Campaign," Roll 109, Book 393, Morgenthau Diaries, 78, 79; ellipsis in original.
85. Olney, *War Bond Story,* 18–19.
86. On this show, Morgenthau insisted that music from jazz to marches to classics be played, so as to appeal "to the various segments of the total audience he wanted to persuade." See Blum, *Years of Urgency,* 303. To help ensure the popularity of Berlin's song, the Treasury arranged for jukebox owners to place the record in first position in their machines (the record in first position is played more often than any other song on a jukebox). See description of this effort in "Any Bonds Today?" *Field Organization News Letter,* 18 Oct. 1941, 15. (With its second volume in March 1942, this publication became the *Minute Man.*)
87. "Will You?" advertisement, *Field Organization News Letter,* 27 Sept. 1941, 32, emphasis in original.
88. Olney, *War Bond Story,* 23.
89. Ibid., 20, 26; Graves, "Defense Savings Staff," 1, Odegard Papers.

90. Odegard and Barth, "Millions for Defense," 404.
91. Quoted without attribution in ibid., 399–400.
92. Cardozier, *Mobilization of the United States,* 18, 20, 12.
93. Hadley Cantril, ed., *Public Opinion: 1935–1946,* 1026.
94. Stanley High, "The U.S. Pocketbook Enlists," *Reader's Digest,* Mar., 1942, 12–14.
95. Morse, *Paying for a World War,* 73.
96. Odegard and Barth, "Millions for Defense," 405.
97. Cantril, *Public Opinion,* 1026.
98. Morse, *Paying for a World War,* 73.
99. James Darsey, "From 'Gay Is Good' to the Scourge of AIDS: The Evolution of Gay Liberation Rhetoric, 1977–1990," *Communication Studies* 42 (1991): 45.
100. Betty Burnett, *St. Louis at War: The Story of a City,* 30.
101. Olney, *War Bond Story,* 30.
102. Henry F. Morgenthau to Stephen Early, Dec. 11, 1941, File 4408, Box 1, Folder 12, Roosevelt Official File, Franklin D. Roosevelt Presidential Library, Hyde Park, N.Y.
103. Kellett, "Soldier in Battle," 217.
104. See Morse, *Paying for a World War,* 75.
105. Cartwright to Odegard, Odegard Papers.
106. Henry C. Murphy, *The National Debt in War and Transition,* 130.
107. Kirk, *Earning Their Stripes,* 81.
108. Ibid., 81.
109. Cartwright to Odegard, Odegard Papers.
110. "Vast Civilian Army in Action: Historic Chicago Meeting Inspires State Leadership," *Defense Savings Staff News,* Jan. 1, 1942, 1.
111. Treasury Department, War Savings Staff, *A Plan for Diverting at Least 10% of America's Payroll into U.S. War Bonds.*
112. "Let's Make Every Pay Day Bond Day," *Defense Savings Staff News,* Jan. 1, 1942, 1.
113. Treasury Department, Defense Savings Staff, *Handbook for Canvassers in the Pledge Campaign,* 1.
114. "April 15, 1942," 1, Morgenthau Papers. See also Blum, *Years of War,* 18.
115. Henry Morgenthau, foreword to *Handbook for Canvassers,* by Treasury Department, Defense Savings Staff, iii.
116. Frank Fox, *Madison Avenue Goes to War: The Strange Military Career of American Advertising, 1941–1945,* 49; and Guy Lemmon, "The Early War Advertising Council Contacts with the U.S. Treasury," Oct., 1944, Box 13, Folder 7, p. 2, Odegard Papers.
117. Thomas Howell, "The Writers' War Board: U.S. Domestic Propaganda in World War II," *Historian* 59 (1997): 796. Morgenthau had a hand in founding WWB, which was an unofficial group of about twenty writers who helped write and place government-initiated propaganda in a variety of media throughout the war.
118. Blum, *Years of War,* 19.
119. Murphy, *The National Debt,* 130.
120. Olney, *War Bond Story,* 39–42.
121. George H. Roeder, *The Censored War: American Visual Experience during World War Two,* 64.

122. *War Victory Comics,* summer, 1942, Box 8, Folder 1, Odegard Papers. The printing figures are from Milburn McCarty Jr., memorandum, August 10, 1942, Box 8, Folder 1, Odegard Papers.

123. Thomas H. Lane, "Evaluation of War Bond Promotion," July 16, 1942, Box 8, Folder 1, p. 15, Odegard Papers.

124. Thomas Lane to Peter H. Odegard, report, "Memorandum No. 3: Growth of the Various Campaigns," Apr. 18, 1944, Box 8, Folder 4, Odegard Papers.

125. Odegard to Hadley Cantril, Mar. 12, 1942, Box 3, Folder 11, Odegard Papers.

126. Henry F. Morgenthau Jr., "A Message from the Secretary," *Minute Man,* June 15, 1942, 3. See also Cantril, *Public Opinion,* 1028, where less than 60 percent of respondents indicated that they had been asked to purchase bonds by a canvasser.

127. Thomas Lane to Peter H. Odegard, report, "Number 1: General," Apr. 12, 1944, Box 8, Folder 4, Odegard Papers.

128. Winkler, *Politics of Propaganda,* 24.

129. Robert E. Sherwood, quoted in ibid., 29.

130. Winkler, *Politics of Propaganda,* 35.

131. Olney, *War Bond Story,* 44, 38.

132. Murphy, *The National Debt,* 130. See also "Quotas Based on Past Sales," *Minute Man,* May 15, 1942, 4.

133. "July 10, 1942," personal notes, Box 515, Folder 7, p. 2, Morgenthau Papers. See also Blum, *Years of War,* 21.

134. S. Weinberg, "What to Tell America," 78.

135. Stanley High, "It Is Not a New Deal War," *Reader's Digest,* Nov. 1942, 26.

136. Murphy, *The National Debt,* 117. Murphy argues that the October financial emergency was the turning point of the financial aspect of the war, 134.

137. Wayne Coy to Franklin D. Roosevelt, memorandum, Aug. 6, 1942, Roll 163, Book 558, 89, Morgenthau Diaries.

138. "August 25, 1942," personal notes, Box 515, Folder 7, p. 1, Morgenthau Papers.

139. "September 2, 1942," meeting with Harold Graves, Roll 166, Book 566, 1, Morgenthau Diaries.

140. For Odegard's viewpoint on the shift to a drive format, see [Peter H. Odegard], "Memorandum on War Bond Advertising," Oct. 27, 1942, Box 8, Folder 5, p. 1, Odegard Papers.

141. Samuel, *Pledging Allegiance,* 45.

142. [Odegard], "Memorandum on War Bond Advertising," 1, Odegard Papers.

Chapter 2

1. Several accounts of World War II describe 1942 as the decisive turning point. See, for example, James Stokesbury, "World War II: An Overview," in *World War II: Personal Accounts: Pearl Harbor to V-J Day,* ed. Gary A. Yarrington and James Stokesbury, 14–17; B. H. Liddell Hart, *History of the Second World War,* 241–394; and Herbert C. O'Neill, *A Short History of the Second World War,* 118–63.

2. Darsey, "Gay Liberation Rhetoric," 45; Stewart, Smith, and Denton, *Social Movements,* 77.

3. Stewart, Smith, and Denton, *Social Movements,* 77, 78, 79.

4. Watson, *War on the Mind,* 227.

5. Morse, *Paying for a World War,* 98–99. Morse offers no citation for this quotation.
6. Ibid., 99.
7. Treasury Department, staff meeting notes, Sept. 11, 1942, Roll 167, Book 568, 113, Morgenthau Diaries.
8. Morse, *Paying for a World War,* 99.
9. Ibid.
10. See the internal discussion in Treasury Department, staff meeting notes, Sept. 11, 1942, 111–21, Morgenthau Diaries.
11. Henry F. Morgenthau Jr., "New Taxes and War Savings," *Minute Man,* Oct. 1, 1942, 3.
12. Winkler, *Politics of Propaganda,* 66.
13. See Polenberg, *War and Society,* 79–84.
14. Winkler, *Politics of Propaganda,* 66. OWI's international activities remained active throughout the conflict.
15. See Lemmon, "Early War Advertising Council Contacts," 5.
16. Callahan to Odegard, 9, Odegard Papers.
17. Thomas Lane to Peter H. Odegard, report, "Memorandum No. 4: Miscellaneous and Anecdotes," Apr. 20, 1944, Box 8, Folder 4, p. 3, Odegard Papers.
18. OWI's Bureau of Campaigns had the general responsibility of assisting various U.S. government offices with national publicity. Although OWI assigned some of its personnel to the Treasury for advising, WSS tried to ignore them at first. When OWI eventually assisted the Treasury, the central bond staff consistently protected their turf by insisting on the approval of any OWI contributions. After the summer of 1943, what was left of the domestic OWI was under strict instructions "to work only through other agencies." For OWI's partial survival beyond June, 1943, see Phillip Nash to Mrs. Sharp, report, Jan. 10, 1952, File 5015, Box 1, Folder 1, Roosevelt Official File. See also Winkler, *Politics of Propaganda,* 71; S. Weinberg, "What to Tell America," 82; and Howell, "Writers' War Board," 797. For a description of the Bureau of Campaigns at work, see "Integrated Drive on for Conservation of Meat: OWI Shows Ability to Coordinate Effort in New Campaign," *Advertising Age,* Oct. 26, 1942, 1.
19. See "Treasury-OWI Relations," Odegard Papers.
20. Robert Griffith, "The Selling of America: The Advertising Council and American Politics, 1942–1960," *Business History Review* 57 (1983): 391.
21. Fox, *Madison Avenue Goes to War,* 49. See also Mark H. Leff, "The Politics of Sacrifice on the American Home Front in World War II," *Journal of American History* 77 (1991): 1312.
22. "Advertising Council Serves to Coordinate War Activities," *Advertising Age,* Dec. 21, 1942, 29.
23. "Newspaper Advertising, the Lane Memoranda, Advertising Statistics, Advertising Operations," report, [1944?], Box 11, Folder 4, p. 8, Odegard Papers.
24. "Basic Copy Policy," [June, 1943], Box 9, Folder 3, Odegard Papers. See also Olney, *War Bond Story,* 23.
25. Samuel, *Pledging Allegiance,* 31.
26. "Top that 10% by New Year's!" *Minute Man,* Nov. 1, 1942, 3. The drive was alternately called "the Victory Loan Drive." There is some confusion about the time periods on this first war loan. Olney, *War Bond Story,* 47, and Morse, *Paying for a World War,* 101, suggest that it started November 30 and ended December 23. Contemporary sources, however, indicate that the drive

took place from November 16 to December 31. In addition to the *Minute Man* just referenced, the issue two weeks later also used these dates. Furthermore, the advertisements associated with the drive suggest that it began in mid-November. See "New Pay-Roll Drive Underway," *Minute Man,* [Nov. 15, 1942], 3. For the internal debate over naming the drive, see Treasury Department, staff meeting notes, Nov. 23, 1942, Roll 173, Book 588, 29–42, Morgenthau Diaries. On OWI's pledge of support for the drive, see Morgenthau to Elmer Davis, telephone conversation transcript, Nov. 9, 1942, Roll 171, Book 582, 190–193, Morgenthau Diaries. On WAC's pledge of support, see Morgenthau to Miller McClintock, telephone conversation transcript, Nov. 9, 1942, Roll 171, Book 582, 194–98, Morgenthau Diaries.

27. Murphy, *The National Debt,* 134.
28. Olney, *War Bond Story,* 47.
29. Blum, *Years of War,* 21.
30. Olney, *War Bond Story,* 47. Treasury bond staffers were insulted by the change, seeing in their rivals an elitist group unknowledgeable about the Treasury's massive bond program. Although the secretary evidently hoped the change would increase sales and thus have a positive impact on public morale, its effect within the Treasury was to cause dissension until the Third War Loan, still a year away. See early discussion of this tension in Treasury Department, staff meeting notes, Nov. 10, 1942, Roll 171, Book 583, 105–17, Morgenthau Diaries.
31. In later years, the initial Victory Fund Drive became known retrospectively as "the first War Loan drive." See, for example, Franklin D. Roosevelt, "Proclamation to the People of the United States," in Treasury Department, *Here's Your AMMUNITION to Back the Attack: Section A, 3rd War Loan Advertising Proof Book for Weeklies* (n.p., [1943]), Box 11, Folder 5, p. 4, Odegard Papers; and Ted R. Gamble, "Financing a War, American Style," *Minute Man,* Sept. 15, 1943, 5. References to this first loan are rare, however (except by implication, as later drives were obviously numbered from this first effort), which reinforces the notion that it was put together at the last moment. An April, 1944, *Minute Man* article, for example, compared the results of the second, third, and fourth drives, but did not mention the first. See "Recommendations Based on Survey," *Minute Man,* April 15, 1944, 6. Moreover, Morgenthau's surprising decision to support a drive system suggests that during this first war loan his staffers were forced to improvise much more than they would need to in later drives.
32. Olney, *War Bond Story,* 47.
33. Morse, *Paying for a World War,* 91.
34. Olney, *War Bond Story,* 47, 48. See "We're Over the Top," *Minute Man,* Dec. 15, 1942, 3–4.
35. Morse, *Paying for a World War,* 119. Morse offers no citation for the study.
36. Olney, *War Bond Story,* 64.
37. Ibid., 65.
38. Ibid., 66. Although I found no historical record of the agreement, apparently part of the compromise was to give each group joint authorship for Second War Loan publications. The internal dissension was mirrored in OWI, where the intellectuals—those who wanted to explain the war in a philosophical vein—were struggling against the advertisers—who were more comfortable with slogans and jingles. In early April the intellectuals quit, foreshadowing OWI's domestic decline in June. See S. Weinberg, "What to Tell America," 81–82.
39. Henry F. Morgenthau Jr., *The Story of America's Greatest War Loan,* Box 9, Folder 2, p. 2, Odegard Papers.

40. Morse, *Paying for a World War,* 145, 156. Although Odegard was no longer serving the Treasury in an official capacity, he continued to advise Morgenthau. On at least some occasions (described in Olney, *War Bond Story,* 93), for example, Odegard attended regional Treasury meetings.

41. For a version of the merger story that omits the rivalry between the two groups, see Gamble, "Financing a War," 4–7.

42. Morse, *Paying for a World War,* 147.

43. Ibid., 148.

44. Olney, *War Bond Story,* 72. For a more in-depth look at the various contributions to the Third War Loan, see "Greatest Promotional Campaign 'Backs the Attack,'" *Minute Man,* Sept. 15, 1943, 8–11.

45. "Third War Loan: Final Score," *Minute Man,* Nov. 1, 1943, 5.

46. Polls suggested that bond drives were the second most important reason that people purchased bonds (behind patriotic reasons). See Cantril, *Public Opinion,* 1030–31.

47. As Stokesbury points out, "by late 1942 the American war machine was at last gearing up for major action. Before Pearl Harbor, it had upset the entire training and mobilization process to send one meager division to occupy Iceland, but now . . . training camps were pouring forth their products." See Stokesbury, "World War II," 15–16.

48. Watson, *War on the Mind,* 227.

49. Black, "Second Persona," 113.

50. [Odegard], "Symbols, Symbol Specialists, and Social Control," 1, Odegard Papers.

51. Treasury Department, staff meeting notes, Nov. 9, 1942, Roll 171, Book 582, 200, Morgenthau Diaries.

52. "Make Your Own Declaration of War," poster, in *Minute Man,* Dec. 1, 1942, 3.

53. Odegard is quoted from a speech he gave to the Newspaper Advertising Executives Association in George A. Brandenburg, "NAEA Hears of Appreciation in Washington for Advertising," *Editor and Publisher,* Oct. 17, 1942, 5.

54. George Lakoff and Mark Johnson, *Metaphors We Live By,* 3.

55. Ibid., 4.

56. Ibid., 5. Throughout this book I follow Lakoff and Johnson in designating concepts or metaphorical domains with small capitals. CIVILIAN, then, refers to the domain surrounding that concept, while "civilian" refers to the flesh and blood version.

57. Roeder describes a similar concept—what he calls the "home front analogy"—as "reassuring visual comparisons of military and home front activities" in which the U.S. government "used images of civilians in military dress and poses to suggest that service station attendants, bus drivers, secretaries, and housewives had a role in the fight." See Roeder, *Censored War,* 59.

58. Treasury Department, *EVERYBODY Top That 10% by New Year!* (n.p., [1942]), Box 8, Folder 7, p. 10, Odegard Papers, emphasis in original. This soldier is similar to those in many war posters, described by Nelson as "the simple image of the generic hero, nearly always a soldier during the war, a figure who rarely varied even between warring countries." Nelson goes on to quote Denis Judd: "Archetypal heroes fix the middle distance with keen (and generally blue) eyes; their square jaws and brawny forearms transcend loyalties and ideologies." See Nelson, *Posters That Won the War,* 116, and Judd, *Posters of World War Two,* 32.

59. Treasury Department, *EVERYBODY Top That 10%,* 11, Odegard Papers.

60. Ibid., 16.

61. Ibid., 8; two-period ellipsis and italics in original.

62. There were some examples of dedicated bond purchases, especially for larger items. Some cities, for instance, were able to target a percentage of their bond investments toward a battleship named after the city. Pacifist groups were allowed to target their bond money toward nonbelligerent causes, including medical supplies for battle. See Roeder, *Censored War,* 60.

63. Treasury Department, *Women's Work in War Finance, 1941–1945,* 9. The National Women's Division director, Harriet Elliott, was responsible for the work of thousands of volunteers at the state and local levels. Under her guidance, the Women's Section established dozens of national promotions, including Women at War Week, the Bomber Campaign, and Bonds for Babies.

64. Treasury Department, War Savings Staff and Victory Fund Committee, *Local Publicity Kit for Second War Loan* (Washington, D.C.: GPO, [1943]), Box 8, Folder 2, p. 36, Odegard Papers.

65. "Battleships and Beanpots Are Purchased with Money Loaned to U.S. Government in 13 Billion Second War Loan Campaign," news release, in Treasury Department, War Savings Staff, and Victory Fund Committee, *A Clipsheet on the Second War Loan of the U.S. Treasury War Finance Committee* (Washington, D.C.: GPO, [1943]), Box 9, Folder 2, p. 3, Odegard Papers.

66. "Copy Fact Sheet," in Treasury Department, War Savings Staff, and Victory Fund Committee, *Local Publicity Kit,* 4, Odegard Papers.

67. See Kirk, *Earning Their Stripes,* 87.

68. "The Way to a Man's Heart Is through His Children," Treasury Department, War Finance Division, *4th War Loan Campaign Book* (Washington: GPO, [1944]), Box 11, Folder 5, p. 39, Odegard Papers. This section of the campaign book is a report on strategies that worked during the Third War Loan.

69. "'Treasure Hunt' by School Children Will be Last-Minute 'Clean-Up' Drive," Treasury Department, War Finance Division, *4th War Loan Campaign Book,* 41, Odegard Papers.

70. [Treasury Department], *3rd War Loan Campaign Book,* Box 9, Folder 3, p. 5, Odegard Papers.

71. "Forward March—America!" advertisement, in Treasury Department, *Here's Your AMMUNITION,* 6, Odegard Papers, emphasis and ellipsis in original.

72. Ibid.

73. Treasury Department, *Here's Your AMMUNITION,* 1, Odegard Papers.

74. Ibid.

75. Paul Messaris, *Visual Persuasion: The Role of Images in Advertising,* 169.

76. I use "juxtapose" to describe this scene because the civilians and the soldier, while close to each other, are not interacting or physically merged. For an example of a civilian factory worker and a soldier shaking hands, see "We're Backing You Up in the 4th War Loan," in Treasury Department, War Finance Division, *4th War Loan: Official Daily Newspaper Advertisements for 4th War Loan* (n.p., [1944]), Box 11, Folder 5, p. 11, Odegard Papers, hereafter referred to as *4th War Loan Newspaper Advertisements,* Odegard Papers. For an example of a civilian and a soldier existing in a merged space between the home front and the battlefront, see McClelland Barclay, "Save Your Cans: Help Pass the Ammunition," poster, n.d., in Roeder, *Censored War,* 111. (In this poster for the tin can salvage effort, a worker's hand extended from beyond the poster's margin and onto the battlefield; the hand held a series of tin cans that morphed into a chain of M-60 ammunition for the soldier's weapon.)

77. This image makes an interesting comparison to a cartoon printed in the predecessor to the *Minute Man* on Oct. 18, 1941. In this pre-Pearl Harbor

cartoon, several soldiers faced the reader with rifles at port arms (tellingly, they were wearing doughboy-style helmets from WWI). Behind them was the expanse of the Atlantic Ocean, and on the American shore appeared several civilians marching purposefully toward the reader with placards: "We're doing our part," "We're buying defense bonds," etc. Uncle Sam, standing behind the soldiers, made the relationship between civilian and soldier clear: "You citizens of America are the second line of defense." By the time of the Third War Loan—two full years later—the metaphoric merging between civilian and soldier was much greater. See the older image in "You, Too, Can Answer Your Country's Call," cartoon, *Field Organization News Letter,* Oct. 18, 1941, 2.

78. "Over the Top! 15 Billion and Lots More," *Minute Man,* Oct. 15, 1943, 4.

79. See Odegard and Helms, *American Politics,* 552, emphasis in original.

80. Chilton, "Meaning of Security," 198.

81. Leonard R. Sillman, "Morale," *War Medicine* 3 (1943): 498.

82. J. Michael Hogan and L. Glen Williams, "Defining 'the Enemy' in Revolutionary America: From the Rhetoric of Protest to the Rhetoric of War," *Southern Communication Journal* 61 (1996): 277–88. See also Kurt W. Ritter and James R. Andrews, *The American Ideology: Reflections of the Revolution in American Rhetoric,* 7–10.

83. Gregory Sieminski, "The Puritan Captivity Narrative and the Politics of the American Revolution," *American Quarterly* 42 (1990): 34–56. See also Richard Slotkin, *Regeneration through Violence: The Mythology of the American Frontier, 1600–1860.*

84. Ronald H. Carpenter, "America's Tragic Metaphor: Our Twentieth-Century Combatants as Frontiersman," *Quarterly Journal of Speech* 76 (1990): 1–22.

85. Robert L. Ivie, "Images of Savagery in American Justifications for War," *Communication Monographs* 47 (1980): 281.

86. Robert L. Ivie, "The Metaphor of Force in Prowar Discourse: The Case of 1812," *Quarterly Journal of Speech* 68 (1982): 240–53; Ivie, "Progressive Form and Mexican Culpability in Polk's Justification for War," *Central States Speech Journal* 30 (1979): 311–20; Ivie, "Images of Savagery"; Ivie, "Literalizing the Metaphor of Soviet Savagery: President Truman's Plain Style," *Southern Speech Communication Journal* 51 (1986): 91–105; and Ivie, *Democracy and America's War on Terror.*

87. Ronald L. Hatzenbuehler and Robert L. Ivie, *Congress Declares War: Rhetoric, Leadership, and Partisanship in the Early Republic,* 115.

88. Odegard and Helms, *American Politics,* 562 (see also 628).

89. [Odegard], "Memorandum on War Bond Advertising," 25, Odegard Papers.

90. Shawn J. Parry-Giles, "Militarizing America's Propaganda Program, 1945–1955," in *Critical Reflections on the Cold War: Linking Rhetoric and History,* ed. Martin L. Medhurst and H. W. Brand, 123.

91. Treasury Department, "What You Buy with Bonds," ad series compilation, [Nov., 1942], Roll 172, Book 585, 179, Morgenthau Diaries.

92. Ibid.

93. "The 9 Billion Dollar Victory Loan Drive Is On!" advertisement, in *Charleston (W.Va.) Gazette,* Dec. 21, 1942, 9.

94. Isabel Cristina Pinedo, *Recreational Terror: Women and the Pleasures of Horror Film Viewing,* 53. Keen argues that "our reluctance to think clearly about the enemy appears to be an unconscious conspiracy. We systematically blur distinctions and insist that the enemy remain faceless." See Sam Keen, *Faces of the Enemy: Reflections of the Hostile Imagination,* 24.

95. Roosevelt, "Proclamation to the People of the United States," advertisement, in Treasury Department, *Here's Your AMMUNITION,* 4, Odegard Papers.

96. "Suggested 5-Minute Speech for State Administration War Savings Staff," in Treasury Department, War Savings Staff, and Victory Fund Committee, *Local Publicity Kit,* 21, Odegard Papers. In several of its drives, the Treasury compiled speakers' handbooks for use by its thousands of local volunteers. Treasury records do not supply evidence that such speeches were used exactly as printed. Still, the widespread dissemination of the Treasury's material suggests that the scripts were quite available in the field. In addition, much like CPI's centralization of the messages of its "Four Minute Men" during World War I, the Treasury's preprinted speeches served to create uniformity in its overall campaign, even if there were slight variations from iteration to iteration. As the Treasury itself advised local workers, "you will find herein material for local radio speeches, which may be delivered by local people either over the radio stations of your county . . . or at luncheon clubs or other meetings." See Vincent F. Callahan to County Chairmen, memorandum, in Treasury Department, War Savings Staff, and Victory Fund Committee, *Local Publicity Kit,* 2, Odegard Papers.

97. "Battleships and Beanpots," 3, Odegard Papers.

98. Treasury Department, War Savings Staff, and Victory Fund Committee, *Local Publicity Kit,* 38, Odegard Papers.

99. "Suggested Speech before Civic Club Luncheon," in Treasury Department, War Savings Staff, and Victory Fund Committee, *Local Publicity Kit,* 26, Odegard Papers.

100. "Suggested 10-Minute Speech for Audience of Working Men and Women," in Treasury Department, War Savings Staff, and Victory Fund Committee, *Local Publicity Kit,* 19, Odegard Papers; all ellipses in original.

101. Cynthia A. Freeland, *The Naked and the Undead: Evil and the Appeal of Horror,* 235, 237.

102. "Suggested 10-Minute Speech," 20, Odegard Papers.

103. Italy had already surrendered at the time of the invasion; the opposition forces in the invasion of the peninsula were well-entrenched divisions of the German army. See Wallace B. Black and Jean F. Blashfield, *Invasion of Italy.*

104. See Gamble, "Financing a War," 7.

105. [Odegard], "Five Possible 3rd War Loan Campaigns," [1943], Box 9, Folder 3, p. 5, Odegard Papers.

106. [Donald Hewitt], "They're Fighting Harder Than Ever," poster, [1943], in Nelson, *Posters That Won the War,* 68, emphasis in original. The Treasury took special pride in its posters, sending its artists to the battlefront to show them war's realities. "Our war posters," bragged the bond newsletter, "are as accurate as military security will allow." See "Behind the Poster Scene," *Minute Man,* June 15, 1944, 21.

107. Barbie Zelizer, "Gender and Atrocity: Women in Holocaust Photographs," in *Visual Culture and the Holocaust,* ed. Barbie Zelizer, 262. See also Gunther Kress and Theo van Leeuwen, *Reading Images: The Grammar of Visual Design,* 66.

108. "It'll Cost You an *Extra* $100 Bond to Look Him in the Eye," advertisement, in Treasury Department, *Here's Your AMMUNITION,* 7, Odegard Papers, emphasis in original title.

109. "You Can't Fail Them Now!" advertisement, in Treasury Department, *Here's Your AMMUNITION,* 8, Odegard Papers, emphasis in original.

110. R. Couillard, "And *WE* Talk about Sacrifice," poster, [1943], Records of the Savings Bond Division (Including Records of its Predecessor, the War Finance Division), Advertising and Promotion Branch, Promotional Records, 1936–51, Box 4, Folder 45, General Records of the Department of the Treasury, Record Group 56, National Archives; ellipsis and emphasis in original.

111. Sieminski, "Puritan Captivity Narrative."

112. See Michael C. McGee, "The Origins of Liberty: A Feminization of Power," *Communication Monographs* 47 (1980): 23–45; Susan Jeffords, "Rape and the New World Order," *Cultural Critique* 19 (1991): 203–15; and Dan F. Hahn and Robert L. Ivie, "'Sex' as Rhetorical Invitation to War," *ETC: A Review of General Semantics* 45 (1988): 16–17.

113. See Zelizer, "Gender and Atrocity," 262, for further discussion of the use of images of women and children to establish culpability in time of war.

114. Robert W. Coyne, "Public Reactions to the Drive," *Minute Man,* Nov. 1, 1943, 3. See chapter 3 for further discussion on the relation of polls to the Treasury's war bond efforts.

115. See Black, "Second Persona."

116. Osborn, "Rhetorical Depiction," 92.

117. Anthony D. Smith, "War and Ethnicity: The Role of Warfare in the Formation, Self-Images, and Cohesion of Ethnic Communities," *Ethnic and Racial Studies* 4 (1981): 391.

Chapter 3

1. Stokesbury, "World War II," 23.
2. Richard W. Steele, "News of the 'Good War': World War II News Management," *Journalism Quarterly* 62 (1985): 712.
3. Polenberg, *War and Society,* 137.
4. "Moods of Wartime," *Life,* Nov. 27, 1944, 28.
5. Fussell, *Wartime,* 139.
6. Steele, "News of the 'Good War,'" 712. While advising radio stations how to sell bonds just after the Third War Loan, another Steele—Alfred—suggested that Americans had moved beyond "defense" and "war" phases and into a victory psychology. But although victory was increasingly assured, discouragement over the growing sacrifices of the war and the elusiveness of the ultimate victory fed public frustration. See Alfred N. Steele, *War Bonds and Radio in 1943–1944* (n.p., 1943), Rare Book and Special Collections Division, Library of Congress, Washington, D.C.
7. "It's Not Over Yet," *Minute Man,* Jan. 15, 1944, 12. Moreover, despite the accomplishments of the first three war loans, the financial need for more drives continued to grow because the war was becoming costlier every month, with expenses in early 1944 running to $250 million per day. Simultaneously, the now-thriving economic engine was placing more money into the public's paychecks, meaning that inflation was an increasing threat. See "Shop Lifting," *Minute Man,* Jan. 1, 1944, 22.
8. Stewart, Smith, and Denton, *Social Movements,* 80.
9. Ibid., 82.
10. Kellett, "Soldier in Battle," 222; Robin M. Williams Jr. and M. Brewster Smith, "General Characteristics of Ground Combat," in *The American Soldier: Combat and Its Aftermath,* vol. 2 of *Studies in Social Psychology in World War II,* ed. Samuel A. Stouffer et al., 80–83.
11. Watson, *War on the Mind,* 229.
12. Kellett, "Soldier in Battle," 230.
13. "Clearing House," *Minute Man,* Dec. 1, 1943, 3.
14. Coyne, "Public Reactions," 3.
15. On the first three drives, the *Minute Man* pointed out that "the year December 1, 1942 to December 1, 1943 was one of great achievement and great

change." Looking ahead to the upcoming drives, it wrote that "in only one month more, the opening guns will blaze for 1944's first big home front attack." See, respectively, "The Year in War Finance," *Minute Man,* Jan. 1, 1944, 3; and "4th War Loan," *Minute Man,* Dec. 15, 1943, 3. Ads for the fourth drive emphasized that the public, too, should treat the new year as something different. See, for example, "This Is 1944!" advertisement, in Treasury Department, *4th War Loan Newspaper Advertisements,* 6, Odegard Papers, which asked the viewer, "What will *you* do to make it the victory year?" emphasis in original.

16. Olney, *War Bond Story,* 77.
17. See "Treasury-OWI Relations," 15–16, Odegard Papers.
18. Ibid., 14–15.
19. Division of Research, Bureau of Special Services, Office of War Information, "Appraisals of the Third War Loan Drive," Oct. 20, 1943, 9, in Materials for Information Campaigns, 1943, Box 1, Folder 9, Records of the Office of War Information, Record Group 208, National Archives.
20. Steele, "News of the 'Good War,'" 707.
21. "Treasury-OWI Relations," 14–15, Odegard Papers.
22. Steele, "News of the 'Good War,'" 712.
23. Lane to Odegard, "Memorandum No. 3," 6–7, Odegard Papers.
24. Olney, *War Bond Story,* 77. The increase in sales was reported in "FINAL RESULTS: 5th War Loan," *Minute Man,* Aug. 15, 1944, 4.
25. "All Secure! 4th Underway—Outlook Bright," *Minute Man,* 1 Feb. 1944, 3.
26. Lane to Odegard, "Memorandum No. 3," 4, Odegard Papers.
27. See introduction of the fourth drive shield in "Promotion Materials," *Minute Man,* Dec. 15, 1943, 20. Service stars in a home's window indicated that a person from the household was serving in the military (blue stars) or had already died in the war (gold stars). One issue of the Treasury's newsletter showed a picture of a home's window boasting a service flag (with two blue stars, meaning that two people from the household were in the service) next to a Fourth War Loan shield. See cover of *Minute Man,* Mar. 1, 1944.
28. See Lane to Odegard, "Memorandum No. 4," 5, Odegard Papers. Of course, this remark does not apply to trademarks advertised since the war.
29. Roeder, *Censored War,* 65.
30. "Survey: NON-FARM People in the 4th," *Minute Man,* April 15, 1944, 4.
31. Cantril, *Public Opinion,* 484.
32. Geoffrey Perrett, *Days of Sadness, Years of Triumph: The American People, 1939–1945,* 274.
33. Robert Sherrod, *Tarawa: The Story of a Battle,* 149, quoted in Fussell, *Wartime,* 13.
34. Perrett, *Days of Sadness,* 275.
35. "5th War Loan: June 12–July 8," *Minute Man,* April 15, 1944, 3.
36. "If Invasion Comes," *Minute Man,* June 1, 1944, 7.
37. "Official 5th War Loan Displays and Sales Materials," *Minute Man,* May 15, 1944, 8. The insignia also used three dots and a dash in its design to symbolize the first few notes of Beethoven's Fifth Symphony (and thus an association with the "fifth" drive) as well as Morse code for the letter *V,* as in victory. Throughout the drive, radio stations across the country regularly played the first notes of the symphony to promote the drive. See "Promotion Highlights," *Minute Man,* May 15, 1944, 11.
38. "Promotion Highlights," 11.

39. "FINAL RESULTS," 3.
40. "Secretary of the Treasury," *Minute Man,* Sept. 1, 1944, 2.
41. "Findings of 5th War Loan Survey," *Minute Man,* Sept. 1, 1944, 3. The Treasury's pollsters went on to conclude that "it may be that 'Back the Attack' has come to serve as a sort of trade-mark for Bonds in general, rather than as a distinguishing part of the Drives," 3.
42. "Key Figures on the Five War Loans," *Minute Man,* Aug. 15, 1944, 4.
43. Steele, "News of the 'Good War,'" 712.
44. Cantril's concerns are described in Polenberg, *War and Society,* 210–11. Among Dewey's divisive comments were that "Roosevelt had 'so weakened and corrupted the Democratic Party that it is subject to capture, and the forces of Communism are, in fact, now capturing it,'" quoted in Polenberg, 208.
45. Ibid., 211, emphasis in original.
46. In fact, the Treasury began planning for "X-day," its code for the day of the coming German surrender. See "National X-day Bond Plans," *Minute Man,* Oct. 1, 1944, 3.
47. Cartwright to Odegard, 14, Odegard Papers. As the Treasury summarized, "it might be desirable to shift the major emphasis from the European theatre to the Asiatic theatre" in the future. See "Findings of 5th War Loan Survey," 4. The Treasury also suggested that Germany was not yet ready to surrender, which turned out to be true. See "National X-day," 3.
48. See "Promotion, Publicity Aids," *Minute Man,* Oct. 15, 1944, 4.
49. Olney, *War Bond Story,* 87, 86.
50. "6th Rolls Up Record for Total Sales," *Minute Man,* Jan. 15, 1945, 3.
51. See "Key Figures on the Six War Loans," *Minute Man,* Jan. 15, 1945, 3.
52. Perrett, *Days of Sadness,* 279.
53. G. Weinberg, *A World at Arms,* 779.
54. Olney, *War Bond Story,* 88–89.
55. Treasury figures showed that E bond sales went from $3.2 billion in the fourth drive to $3 billion in the fifth to $2.9 billion in the sixth. See "Key Figures on the Six War Loans," 3.
56. Cartwright to Odegard, 20, Odegard Papers.
57. Ted R. Gamble, "Of What We May Be Proud," *Minute Man,* Mar. 1, 1944, 3.
58. See, for instance, George Gallup, "How Important Is Public Opinion in Time of War?" *Proceedings of the American Philosophical Association* 85 (1942): 440–44.
59. J. Michael Hogan, "George Gallup and the Rhetoric of Scientific Democracy," *Communication Monographs* 64 (1997): 161–79.
60. See Christopher Simpson, *Science of Coercion: Communication Research and Psychological Warfare, 1945–1960,* 26–27. The polls used in World War II were based on the relatively new "scientific" polling, using random sampling.
61. Coyne, "Public Reactions," 3–4.
62. Guy Lemmon, "October 1942 through the Sixth War Loan," Oct. 1944, Box 13, Folder 7, p. 22, Odegard Papers.
63. Cantril, *Public Opinion,* 484, 1179.
64. This belief was reflected, for example, in Odegard and Helms, *American Politics,* 771.
65. Treasury Department, War Finance Division, *4th War Loan Campaign Book,* 8, Odegard Papers. Roeder discusses *Life*'s controversial publication of the picture. See Roeder, *Censored War,* 14, 34.

66. Lakoff and Johnson, *Metaphors,* 13, emphasis in original.

67. Kenneth Burke, *A Grammar of Motives,* 504.

68. Ibid., 517. As Burke says, "what goes forth as A returns as non-A," 517.

69. Office of War Information, and Treasury Department, *Let's All Back the Attack: Information Program for the Fourth War Loan Drive* (Washington, D.C.: GPO, 1943), Box 9, Folder 6, p. 4, Odegard Papers, emphasis in original.

70. By "ironic conflation" I mean that the two conflated domains have both areas of congruity and areas of incongruity, and that the incongruities are more apparent to the viewing audience. By highlighting the incongruities between civilians and soldiers, then, the Treasury's 1944 propaganda turned its conflation into an ironic conflation.

71. Office of War Information, and Treasury Department, *Let's All Back the Attack,* 4, Odegard Papers; ellipsis in original.

72. "When You Go Home Tonight," advertisement, Records of the Savings Bond Division (Including Records of its Predecessor, the War Finance Division), Records of the Field Directors, 1941–47, vol. 43, General Records of the Department of the Treasury, Record Group 56, National Archives.

73. "This Farm Boy Stopped Bullets," advertisement, in Treasury Department, *4th War Loan Newspaper Advertisements,* 9, Odegard Papers, emphasis and ellipsis in original.

74. See "Who Is Making the Greatest Sacrifice?" advertisement, in Treasury Department, *4th War Loan Newspaper Advertisements,* 10, Odegard Papers.

75. "Sponsored Programs and Spots for 4th War Loan," in Treasury Department, War Finance Division, *4th War Loan Campaign Book,* 13, Odegard Papers, emphasis in original.

76. "The Day You Threw a Party Instead of Buying a Bond," advertisement, Records of the Savings Bond Division (Including Records of its Predecessor, the War Finance Division), Records of the Field Directors, 1941–47, vol. 43, General Records of the Department of the Treasury, Record Group 56, National Archives. Another ad's image depicted two couples out on the town, enjoying a dance performance. The ad's text put a guilt-inducing spin on the illustration: "portrait of some people who said 'I can't afford to buy an extra war bond!'" See "Portrait of Some People," advertisement, in Treasury Department, *4th War Loan Newspaper Advertisements,* 11, Odegard Papers.

77. The fourth drive's propaganda also depicted the inevitable results of American casualties. On the war front, one ad pictured an American soldier's grave marker. The ad's text asked the Treasury's rhetorical question: "And *You* say you 'Can't Afford' an Extra War Bond?" See "And *You* Say You 'Can't Afford' an Extra War Bond?" advertisement, in Treasury Department, *4th War Loan Newspaper Advertisements,* 6, Odegard Papers, emphasis in original. Conversely, one of the drive's posters portrayed the result of casualties on the home front, presenting a picture of a woman who had just opened a letter informing her that her husband was missing in action. As she consoled her young son, her stunned facial expression emphasized the poster's wry text: "buying a bond is no sacrifice." See "Buying a Bond Is No Sacrifice," poster, in *Minute Man,* Jan. 15, 1944, 16. Ironically, such images were not as common as the Treasury's poster implied, since the U.S. government was extremely reluctant to draft men with children, even enacting such a law in 1943. See discussion of the politics behind this issue in Polenberg, *War and Society,* 21.

78. George Gallup, ed., *The Gallup Poll: Public Opinion, 1935–1971,* 438.

79. Treasury Department, War Finance Division, *5th War Loan Campaign Book,* 4.

80. "Do *You* Expect to Be Alive by Dinnertime?" advertisement, in Treasury Department, War Finance Division, *Ammunition! 5th War Loan Official Daily*

Newspaper Ads (n.p., [1944]), Box 11, Folder 5, p. 8, Odegard Papers, emphasis in original, hereafter referred to as *Ammunition!* Odegard Papers.

81. "I Died Today," advertisement, in Treasury Department, War Finance Division, *Ammunition!* 9, Odegard Papers, emphasis in original.
82. Messaris, *Visual Persuasion,* 131.
83. Barbie Zelizer, *Remembering to Forget: Holocaust Memory through the Camera's Eye,* 86.
84. "So You Can't Buy Another War Bond," advertisement, in Treasury Department, War Finance Division, *5th War Loan Campaign Book,* 27.
85. Ibid.
86. Zelizer, *Remembering to Forget,* 86.
87. "Thinking of Buying a Bond?" advertisement, in Treasury Department, War Finance Division, *Ammunition!* 7, Odegard Papers.
88. "Tired of Lending?" advertisement, in Treasury Department, War Finance Division, *Ammunition!* 8, Odegard Papers.
89. See "I Died Today," advertisement, and "This Beachhead Is Big Enough for *All* of Us," advertisement, both in Treasury Department, War Finance Division, *Ammunition!* 8, Odegard Papers, emphasis in originals.
90. Burke, *Grammar,* 515.
91. "Key Figures on the Five War Loans," 4.
92. Steele, "News of the 'Good War,'" 712.
93. "A Prayer," advertisement, in Treasury Department, War Finance Division, and Office of War Information, *Information Program on the 6th War Loan Drive* (Washington, D.C.: GPO, [1945]), Box 11, Folder 5, p. 16, Odegard Papers, emphasis and ellipses in original.
94. "THEY Still Die—Will YOU Buy?" advertisement, in Treasury Department, War Finance Division, *6th War Loan Campaign Book,* 26, Odegard Papers, emphasis in original.
95. "*Next* Year Isn't Soon Enough for Them," advertisement, in Treasury Department, War Finance Division, and Office of War Information, *Information Program on the 6th War Loan,* 16, Odegard Papers, emphasis in original.
96. "Our Part Has Been Easy," advertisement, in Treasury Department, War Finance Division, *6th War Loan Campaign Book,* 26, Odegard Papers, emphasis in original.
97. "They *Can't* Come Back till It's Over over There!" advertisement, in Treasury Department, War Finance Division, *6th War Loan Campaign Book,* 25, Odegard Papers, emphasis in original.
98. "So Sorry, Nips, You're Blocking the Road," advertisement, in *Montgomery Advertiser,* December 5, 1944, 10.
99. "You Can't Afford It?" advertisement, in Treasury Department, War Finance Division, *You and the 6th War Loan,* 7, Odegard Papers.
100. Burke, *Grammar,* 504.
101. Black, "Second Persona."
102. According to Burke, "a given terminology"—such as the Treasury's civilian-soldier conflation—may contain "various *implications,* and there is a corresponding 'perfectionist' tendency for men to attempt carrying out those implications." See Kenneth Burke, *Language as Symbolic Action: Essays on Life, Literature, and Method,* 19, emphasis in original.
103. Irving L. Janis, "Effects of Fear Arousal on Attitude Change: Recent Developments in Theory and Research," in *Advances in Experimental Social Psychology,* vol. 3, ed. Leonard Berkowitz, 293.

104. Robert L. Ivie, "Metaphor and the Rhetorical Invention of Cold War 'Idealists,'" *Communication Monographs* 54 (1987): 178.

105. Peter H. Odegard to Harold Graves, report, Apr. 12, 1941, Box 4, Folder 2, p. 1, Odegard Papers.

106. Ivie, "Images of Savagery," 281.

107. Perrett, *Days of Sadness,* 299.

108. "Down the Home Stretch," *Minute Man,* Feb. 15, 1944, 3.

109. Paul R. Pillar, "Ending Limited War: The Psychological Dynamics of the Termination Process," in Glad, *Psychological Dimensions of War,* 253.

110. "It's Not Over Yet," 12, emphasis in original.

111. Jürgen Link, "Fanatics, Fundamentalists, Lunatics, and Drug Traffickers: The New Southern Enemy Image," *Cultural Critique* 19 (Fall, 1991): 33–53.

112. I use "his" purposely here, as Link's research suggests that rhetorical enemies are typically seen as either masculine ("he") or sexless ("it").

113. Link, "Southern Enemy Image," 40.

114. Ibid.

115. Ibid.

116. Ibid., 41.

117. Soon after the war, Nevins reinforced this dichotomy. "Emotions forgotten since our most savage Indian wars," he wrote, "were reawakened by the ferocities of Japanese commanders," 13. In contrast, he said that "if it could not be said that the German people as a whole came to be hated, certainly the German *system* was detested." The Nazi system, he continued, was a "satanic cancer," 14. See Allan Nevins, "How We Felt about the War," in *While You Were Gone: A Report on Wartime Life in the United States,* ed. Jack Goodman, emphasis in original.

118. There were, to be sure, a few isolated cases of a personified enemy in this drive. One ad, for example, featured pictures of both Hitler and Hirohito, proclaiming "they haven't quit yet . . . HAVE YOU?" Another ad showed an American soldier surrounded by dead enemy bodies, angrily yelling, "Come on, America! It's 1944!" Although the dead soldiers were clearly German, the artist gave them peaceful, humanizing positions in death, as if they were sleeping. See "They Haven't Quit Yet," advertisement, in Treasury Department, *4th War Loan Newspaper Advertisements,* 8, Odegard Papers, emphasis and ellipsis in original; and "Come On, America!" advertisement, in Treasury Department, *4th War Loan Newspaper Advertisements,* 10, Odegard Papers.

119. Messaris, *Visual Persuasion,* 27.

120. Bernard Perlin, "Let 'Em Have It," poster, [1944], Records of the Savings Bond Division (Including Records of its Predecessor, the War Finance Division), Advertising and Promotion Branch, Promotional Records, 1936–51, Box 4, Folder 236, General Records of the Department of the Treasury, Record Group 56, National Archives.

121. Messaris, *Visual Persuasion,* 32.

122. "Let's All Back the Attack," billboard, [1944], in Treasury Department, War Finance Division, *4th War Loan Campaign Book,* 22, Odegard Papers.

123. "While Your $100 Nestled in the Bank," advertisement, in Treasury Department, *4th War Loan Newspaper Advertisements,* 8, Odegard Papers.

124. Pinedo, *Recreational Terror,* 52.

125. J. P. Telotte, "Faith and Idolatry in the Horror Film," *Literature/Film Quarterly* 8 (1980): 147.

126. Treasury Department, War Finance Division, *These Are Their Words on Freedom vs. Tyranny,* 2.

127. Ibid. Typical was Hitler's statement, "My will—that must be the creed of all of us. Everything that you are, you are through me!" juxtaposed with Thomas Jefferson's "Resistance to tyrants is obedience to God," 6. Although the Japanese were not given a voice in this booklet, Mussolini (already deposed after Italy's surrender in 1943) had two quotations.

128. Link, "Southern Enemy Image," 40–41. Part of this disparity, of course, was due to the fact that the Japanese initiated an unprovoked attack on American forces while on American territory. The memory of Pearl Harbor was a strong motivation for hatred toward the Japanese throughout the war. As Dower's work suggests, however, the Pearl Harbor motivation was only one part of Americans' dehumanization of the Japanese adversary. In his words, "the Japanese were more hated than the Germans before as well as after Pearl Harbor." See John Dower, *War without Mercy: Race and Power in the Pacific War,* 8.

129. "Hell Diving's *His* Job . . Lending Is Yours!" advertisement, Records of the Savings Bond Division (Including Records of its Predecessor, the War Finance Division), Records of the Field Directors, 1941–47, vol. 43, General Records of the Department of the Treasury, Record Group 56, National Archives, emphasis and two-period ellipsis in original.

130. "Drive It Home!" advertisement, in Treasury Department, War Finance Division, *Ammunition!* 11, Odegard Papers.

131. Link, "Southern Enemy Image," 40.

132. "Drive It Home!" *Ammunition!* 11, Odegard Papers.

133. "Are *Your Pockets* Stripped for Action?" advertisement, Records of the Savings Bond Division (Including Records of its Predecessor, the War Finance Division), Records of the Field Directors, 1941–47, vol. 43, General Records of the Department of the Treasury, Record Group 56, National Archives, emphasis in original.

134. Link, "Southern Enemy Image," 41.

135. "Now for the Big Push!" advertisement, in Treasury Department, War Finance Division, *Ammunition!* 10, Odegard Papers.

136. "They *Can't* Come Back till It's Over over There," 25, Odegard Papers, emphasis and ellipses in original.

137. "Now Let's Give the Sons of Heaven . . . Hell!" advertisement, in Treasury Department, War Finance Division, and Office of War Information, *Information Program on the 6th War Loan,* 15, Odegard Papers, ellipsis in original.

138. "Next!" poster, [1944], in Nelson, *Posters That Won the War,* 124.

139. "Copy Policy for Sixth War Loan Drive," in Treasury Department, War Finance Division, and Office of War Information, *6th War Loan Campaign Book,* 4, Odegard Papers.

140. "There's More to Remember Than Pearl Harbor!" advertisement, in Treasury Department, War Finance Division, and Office of War Information, *Information Program on the 6th War Loan,* 11, Odegard Papers.

141. "Help Stamp Out this Snake-in-the-Grass," advertisement, Records of the Savings Bond Division (Including Records of its Predecessor, the War Finance Division), Records of the Field Directors, 1941–47, vol. 42, General Records of the Department of the Treasury, Record Group 56, National Archives.

142. "They Stabbed Us in the Back; Let's Give It to Them Face to Face," advertisement, ibid., emphasis in original.

143. See "While Our Farm Boys Harvest Japs," advertisement, and "The Best INSURANCE a Farmer Can Buy," advertisement, both in ibid., emphasis in original.

144. "It Costs $5,000 to Kill a Jap," advertisement, in Treasury Department, War Finance Division, and Office of War Information, *Information Program on*

the 6th War Loan, 11, Odegard Papers. Text for this ad is duplicated in the same booklet, 12.

145. Link, "Southern Enemy Image."
146. Black, "Second Persona," 113.
147. Of course, the Treasury's depictions of the Japanese were one important part of a larger milieu of racist attitudes. According to one account, "All Japanese people were lumped together as a misshapen, ugly, stupid dwarf people. They were like . . . Mr. Tolkien's orcs in *The Lord of the Rings,* creations of a people of sheer malevolence and hideousness." See Peter Calvocoressi, Guy Wint, and John Pritchard, *Total War: The Causes and Courses of the Second World War,* rev. ed., 966.
148. Blum, *V Was for Victory,* 20.
149. Additional factors were probably involved in the decrease in E bond sales during 1944. As the Treasury's pollsters found, Americans gave many reasons why they could not purchase more bonds than they were already buying. See Cartwright to Odegard, Odegard Papers.
150. Americans were strongly in favor of the "unconditional surrender" demand upon Japan, to the point that public perception of the issue essentially demanded that Truman use atomic weapons rather than answer tentative Japanese peace initiatives that were less than unconditional. See this argument in James W. Hikins, "The Rhetoric of 'Unconditional Surrender' and the Decision to Drop the Atomic Bomb," *Quarterly Journal of Speech* 69 (1983): 379–400.
151. [Odegard], "Literature," 5, Odegard Papers.

Chapter 4

1. Perrett, *Days of Sadness,* 415.
2. The Yalta Conference took place from February 4 to February 11, 1945. Here the three Allied leaders hoped to sketch out postwar plans for occupation and reparations. The strongest memory of the conference, however, is of Stalin's insistence that the Soviet Union would maintain its control over Poland and other areas then controlled by its forces. See description and background on the conference in G. Weinberg, *A World at Arms,* 802–806.
3. Ibid., 803.
4. Watson, *War on the Mind,* 230.
5. Stewart, Smith, and Denton, *Social Movements,* 83, use a similar label for the final stage of a social movement: "termination."
6. In the classic war movie, of course, this scenario becomes the general's rousing speech to the troops. Grossman argues that such "military officers . . . have tremendous potential to cause their soldiers to overcome individual resistance and reluctance in combat," 145. Moreover, he suggests, "the primary factor in ensuring the will to fight is identification with the direct commanding officer," 144. See the discussion about combat and authority in Dave Grossman, *On Killing: The Psychological Cost of Learning to Kill in War and Society,* 143–46.
7. Stewart, Smith, and Denton, *Social Movements,* 84.
8. Ibid., 84–85.
9. Watson, *War on the Mind,* 241.
10. Dane Archer and Rosemary Gartner, "Violent Acts and Violent Times: A Comparative Approach to Postwar Homicide Rates," *American Sociological Review* 41 (1976): 960.
11. Perrett, *Days of Sadness,* 415.

12. Lisle A. Rose, *Dubious Victory: The United States and the End of World War II,* 364–65.
13. Gallup, *The Gallup Poll,* 483.
14. John Morton Blum, *Roosevelt and Morgenthau,* 585. For background on the Morgenthau Plan, see John H. Backer, *The Decision to Divide Germany: American Foreign Policy in Transition.*
15. Loyd E. Lee, *War Years: A Global History of the Second World War,* 256–57.
16. Gar Alperovitz, *The Decision to Use the Atomic Bomb and the Architecture of an American Myth,* 282.
17. G. Weinberg, *A World at Arms,* 847–49.
18. Martha Byrd Hoyle, *A World in Flames: A History of World War II,* 307.
19. See "To Inspire a Mighty 7th!" *Minute Man,* May 15, 1945, 2. Olney writes that the three surviving marines, upon their return to the home front, became celebrities in the war bond campaign. See Olney, *War Bond Story,* 93.
20. Stokesbury, "World War II," 38.
21. Ibid., 32.
22. Henry F. Morgenthau Jr., "Back to Serious Business," *Minute Man,* June 1, 1945, 2. This issue printed excerpts from Morgenthau's May 14, 1945, address on the first day of the Mighty Seventh.
23. Morse, *Paying for a World War,* 279.
24. The front cover of the June 15, 1945, *Minute Man* showed a magazine vendor displaying many of these covers at his stand. For the full text of the letter, see "To the American People," advertisement, in Treasury Department, War Finance Division, *The Mighty Seventh War Loan Information Program* (Washington, D.C.: GPO, 1945), 2, in Records of the Savings Bond Division (Including Records of its Predecessor, the War Finance Division), Records of the Field Directors, 1941–47, Publicity Materials, vol. 13, enc. 2, General Records of the Department of the Treasury, Record Group 56, National Archives.
25. Treasury Department, *Art for Bonds;* Morse, *Paying for a World War,* 281. See also "7th Swings into High," *Minute Man,* June 15, 1945, 3–4.
26. Robert James Maddox, *Weapons for Victory: The Hiroshima Decision Fifty Years Later,* 20.
27. Blum, *Roosevelt and Morgenthau,* 638–42.
28. Ibid., 642–43.
29. On the acrimony between Morgenthau and Vinson, see Blum, *Roosevelt and Morgenthau,* 449. Once free of his obligations to President Truman, Morgenthau completed a book detailing the Morgenthau Plan, which was published later in 1945. See Henry F. Morgenthau Jr., *Germany Is Our Problem.*
30. Olney, *War Bond Story,* 96.
31. Although the new secretary was not welcomed with open arms by the bond staff, he was introduced with an emphasis on "his long and distinguished career in the United States Government." See "An Old Hand," *Minute Man,* Aug. 1, 1945, 2.
32. Neither Morse nor Olney mention any personnel changes in 1945, with the exception of the new secretary. As the bond program's ongoing manager, Gamble, along with his staff, thus represented a continuity for the campaign despite the departure of Morgenthau.
33. Olney, *War Bond Story,* 95–96.
34. Dennis D. Wainstock, *The Decision to Drop the Atomic Bomb,* 69–70.
35. Blum, *V Was for Victory,* 301.
36. Perrett, *Days of Sadness,* 427.

37. "Announcing the Victory Loan," *Minute Man,* Aug. 15, 1945, 3. This issue went to press several weeks late so as to include the news about the end of war and the new victory bonds.
38. Perrett, *Days of Sadness,* 424–25.
39. Lee, *War Years,* 312–14.
40. Leonard S. Cottrell Jr., "The Aftermath of Hostilities," in *The American Soldier: Combat and Its Aftermath,* vol. 2 of *Studies in Social Psychology in World War II,* ed. Samuel A. Stouffer et al., 552–53.
41. Bourke, *Intimate History of Killing,* 338.
42. Cottrell, "Aftermath of Hostilities," 587.
43. Nevins, "How We Felt about the War," 6. As Bourke asks, "Is the combatant so different from the non-combatant? . . . Is the gap between 'them' and 'us' really so wide?" See Bourke, *Intimate History of Killing,* 338.
44. See Maddox, *Weapons for Victory,* 152–53.
45. Lane Fenrich, "Mass Death in Miniature: How Americans Became Victims of the Bomb," in Lauren Hein and Mark Selden, eds., *Living with the Bomb: American and Japanese Cultural Conflicts in the Nuclear Age,* 126. On the widespread dissemination of Holocaust atrocity photos in America, see Zelizer, *Remembering to Forget,* 89–94.
46. Rose (51) explains that public "criticism of the Soviet Union and its practices . . . increased steadily if slowly in the United States between 1943 and 1945." Accordingly, Adler and Paterson argue that the emerging Soviet enemy swiftly replaced the German enemy in America's postwar popular imagination. See Rose, *Dubious Victory,* 51; and Les K. Adler and Thomas G. Patterson, "Red Fascism: The Merger of Nazi Germany and Soviet Russia in the American Image of Totalitarianism, 1930s–1950s," *American Historical Review* 75 (1970): 1046–64.
47. Perrett, *Days of Sadness,* 428.
48. Charles C. Alexander, *Nationalism in American Thought, 1930 –1945,* 228. See also John Fousek, *To Lead the Free World: American Nationalism and the Cultural Roots of the Cold War,* 16.
49. "The Roosevelt Bond," *Minute Man,* Sept. 15, 1945, 16.
50. Olney, *War Bond Story,* 96.
51. "Victory Loan a Success," *Minute Man,* Jan., 1946, 3. After 1945 this newsletter became a monthly publication. It folded in 1947.
52. "Challenge of the Victory Loan," *Minute Man,* Jan., 1946, 3.
53. Treasury Department, War Finance Division, *Forward to the Seventh War Loan* (Washington, D.C.: Treasury Department, [1945]), 11, in Records of the Savings Bond Division (Including Records of its Predecessor, the War Finance Division), Records of the Field Directors, 1941–47, Publicity Materials, vol. 13, enc. 4, General Records of the Department of the Treasury, Record Group 56, National Archives.
54. "How Could *He* Afford *This*?" advertisement, in Treasury Department, War Finance Division, *The Mighty Seventh,* 8, General Records of the Department of the Treasury, emphasis in original.
55. Messaris, *Visual Persuasion,* 7.
56. "Every Sixty Seconds, One of Us Comes Home," advertisement, in Treasury Department, War Finance Division, *The Mighty Seventh,* 15, General Records of the Department of the Treasury.
57. "The Bond between Us," billboard, in Records of the Savings Bond Division (Including Records of its Predecessor, the War Finance Division), Records of the Field Directors, 1941–1947, Publicity Materials, vol. 48, General Records of the Department of the Treasury, Record Group 56, National Archives.

58. Kress and van Leeuwen, *Reading Images,* 43.
59. Messaris, *Visual Persuasion,* 23.
60. Kress and van Leeuwen, *Reading Images,* 123.
61. "To the American People," 2, General Records of the Department of the Treasury.
62. "For Some of Them, It May Take a Year," photograph, *Minute Man,* Sept. 1, 1945, 16.
63. "Is This Man Worth Reconverting?" advertisement, in U.S. Treasury, War Finance Division, *Victory Loan Portfolio for Daily Newspapers* [Washington, DC: GPO, 1945], 11, in Records of the Savings Bond Division (Including Records of its Predecessor, the War Finance Division), Advertising and Promotion Branch, Promotional Records, 1936–51, Box 7, Folder 110, General Records of the Department of the Treasury, Record Group 56, National Archives.
64. Norman Rockwell, "Hasten the Homecoming: Buy Victory Bonds," poster, [1945], in ibid., Folder 38.
65. Nelson, *Posters That Won the War,* 119.
66. On narratives within images, see Kress and van Leeuwen, *Reading Images,* 56–58.
67. Rockwell, "Hasten the Homecoming," General Records of the Department of the Treasury.
68. "Our Pledge on Armistice Day," advertisement, in *Minute Man,* Oct. 15, 1945, 7.
69. "Remember Pearl Harbor!" advertisement, in *Minute Man,* Oct. 15, 1945, 7.
70. Black, "Second Persona."
71. See "Seventh War Loan Drive," copy policy, in Treasury Department, War Finance Division, *The Mighty Seventh,* 4, General Records of the Department of the Treasury.
72. "They're Fighting *Two* Battles on *One* Beachhead!" advertisement, in ibid., emphasis in original.
73. "This Time—Go All Out!" advertisement, in ibid., 9.
74. Paul Kecskemeti, *Strategic Surrender: The Politics of Victory and Defeat,* 23. See also Rune Ottosen, "Enemy Images and the Journalistic Process," *Journal of Peace Research* 32 (1995): 97. Ottosen suggests that the use of dehumanizing images tapers off as relationships between enemy nations improve.
75. Jonathan A. Becker, "A Disappearing Enemy: The Image of the United States in Soviet Political Cartoons," *Journalism and Mass Communication Quarterly* 73 (1996): 609. Ottosen confirms that "major changes on the international scene" can frequently "cause existing enemy images to fade." See Ottosen, "Enemy Images and the Journalistic Process," 97.
76. Becker, "Disappearing Enemy," 616.
77. John D. Chappell, *Before the Bomb: How America Approached the End of the Pacific War,* 18–19.
78. As Rose points out, "In such an atmosphere [of total dehumanization] talk of a negotiated settlement short of the unconditional surrender doctrine propounded at Casablanca two years before was deemed unthinkable." See Rose, *Dubious Victory,* 59.
79. Wainstock, *Decision to Drop,* 14. See also Maddox, *Weapons for Victory,* 70, 82.
80. In Pillar's words, "leaders . . . are apt to find it difficult to talk about a peace settlement, much less to take steps toward reaching one, without undermining the will to fight." See Pillar, "Ending Limited War," 254.

81. Maddox, *Weapons for Victory,* 16.
82. See, for example, scenes of battle in "For the Last Time, America—Buy *Extra* Bonds!" advertisement, in *Bismarck Tribune,* Nov. 3, 1945, 2, emphasis in original.
83. For an example, see "What Are You Doing for Them?" advertisement, in *Washington Evening Star,* Nov. 12, 1945, evening edition.
84. Ibid.; ellipsis in original. Note the slightly different wording—used interchangeably with this wording—in Figure 4.2.
85. "Our War's Over—But Theirs Isn't!" advertisement, in *Bismarck Tribune,* Nov. 10, 1945, 6.
86. See Vamik D. Volkan, *The Need to Have Enemies and Allies,* 194.
87. See Keen, *Faces of the Enemy,* 158–59.
88. See James J. Kimble, "Feminine Style and the Rehumanization of the Enemy: Peacemaking Discourse in *Ladies Home Journal,* 1945–1946," *Women and Language* 27 (2004): 65–70.
89. Chappell, *Before the Bomb,* 38. See also Dower, *War without Mercy,* 140–42. Pillar adds: "The expectation of peace may lead people at war, buoyed by the belief that their pain and suffering will soon be over, to support even more painful measures in a last-ditch effort to obtain their objectives." See Pillar, "Ending Limited War," 253.
90. Hikins, "The Rhetoric of 'Unconditional Surrender,'" 379.
91. Ellul, for example, argues that nationalism is a powerful appeal for propagandists, particularly in time of war. See Jacques Ellul, *Propaganda: The Formation of Men's Attitudes,* 37–38.
92. Paul C. Stern, "Why Do People Sacrifice for their Nations?" in *Perspectives on Nationalism and War,* ed. John L. Comaroff and Paul C. Stern, 101.
93. John Breuilly, "Nationalism and the State," in *Nationality, Patriotism, and Nationalism in Liberal Democratic Societies,* ed. Roger Michener, 21.
94. Anthony D. Smith, *National Identity,* 17.
95. Barry R. Posen, "Nationalism, the Mass Army, and Military Power," in Comaroff and Stern, *Perspectives on Nationalism and War,* 168.
96. Stern, "Why Do People Sacrifice," 101.
97. See, for example, "130,000,000 Americans . . . with *One Thought— One Purpose—VICTORY!*" advertisement, in *Des Moines Register,* Dec. 3, 1942, morning edition, emphasis and ellipsis in original.
98. See, for example,"What You Will Be Asked to Do," advertisement, in Treasury Department, *Here's Your AMMUNITION,* 5, Odegard Papers.
99. "Forward with the Mighty 7th War Loan," advertisement, in Treasury Department, War Finance Division, *The Mighty Seventh,* 1, General Records of the Department of the Treasury 3.
100. "The Biggest Drive in America's History," advertisement, in *Bismarck Tribune,* May 14, 1945, 2.
101. See Kress and van Leeuwen, *Reading Images,* 96–97, where they analyze a similar image with a winding series of depictions.
102. "The Biggest Drive," *Bismarck Tribune,* May 14, 1945, 2, emphasis in original.
103. "7th War Loan: Now—All Together," poster, [1945], in Box 35, Folder 5, Odegard Papers.
104. A series of Marine Corps photographs from the Iwo Jima flag-raising (including one that is a match for Rosenthal's famous shot) are reprinted in "To Inspire a Mighty 7th!" 2.

105. Kress and van Leeuwen, *Reading Images,* 55. See also Janice L. Edwards and Carol K. Winkler, "Representative Form and the Visual Ideograph: The Iwo Jima Image in Editorial Cartoons," *Quarterly Journal of Speech* 83 (1997): 291. For discussions about implied stories in still images, see Messaris, *Visual Persuasion,* 102–105, and Kress and van Leeuwen, *Reading Images,* 56–58.

106. Arnold Whittick, *Symbols: Signs and Their Meaning and Uses in Design,* 2nd ed., 18.

107. Edwards and Winkler analyze the Iwo Jima image as used in editorial cartoons several decades after the war. They describe the image as a representative form, still recognizable to most Americans despite the fact that relatively few viewers actually remember the war years. My analysis suggests that the Treasury was among the first to adapt Rosenthal's picture for its own purposes, a strategic move that took place only weeks after the photograph was taken. See Edwards and Winkler, "Representative Form."

108. Ibid., 291.

109. Roeder, *Censored War,* 80.

110. Messaris, *Visual Persuasion,* 34–38.

111. Roeder, *Censored War,* 80.

112. "Americans! *Victory Can't Wait!*" advertisement, in *Bismarck Tribune,* May 19, 1945, 7, emphasis in original.

113. Kress and van Leeuwen, *Reading Images,* 62.

114. "Let's Prove We're All in This Together! Back Them Up in the Big Seventh!" advertisement, in Treasury Department, War Finance Division, *The Mighty Seventh,* General Records of the Department of the Treasury, 12.

115. "LET'S GO . . . Put the Big Drive Over!" advertisement, in ibid., 15, emphasis and ellipsis in original.

116. Martin Gilbert, *The Day the War Ended: May 8, 1945—Victory in Europe,* 405.

117. Fousek, *To Lead the Free World,* 16.

118. Stewart, Smith, and Denton, *Social Movements,* 84.

119. Stewart, Smith, and Denton offer little detail about "perfecting myths," although their sense of "myth" is clearly more limited than the sort studied in structuralist anthropology. In this project, I borrow some of Roderick Hart's perspective, treating perfecting myths as "moral guides" (315), which create both "a heightened sense of coherence" (320) and "a heightened sense of community" (320) as a group's experiences are converted into memory. Hart would likely call the Treasury's perfecting myth a fantasy theme, which he defines as "mythic shorthand," a narrative "describing an idealized . . . past, present, or future" (329). Indeed, Bormann argues that in the wake of the Civil War, Lincoln's second inaugural used a cultural "fantasy type" to "rebuild and restore a sense of national community." As Bormann describes it, that inaugural's cleansing function in the wake of postwar revulsion is very similar to my view of the Treasury's perfecting myth and its function in the post–World War II mood of revulsion. See Roderick P. Hart, *Modern Rhetorical Criticism,* and Ernest G. Bormann, "Fetching Good Out of Evil," *Quarterly Journal of Speech* 63 (1977): 139.

120. "For the Last Time, America," *Bismarck Tribune,* Nov. 3, 1945, 2.

121. Ibid.

122. A full-size reproduction of the Roosevelt bond is in *Minute Man,* Sept. 15, 1945, 16.

123. See, for instance, Blum, *Roosevelt and Morgenthau,* 620, 626, 628.

124. "The Roosevelt Bond," 16, emphasis in original.

125. Ibid.

126. "In the Strength of Great Hope," poster, *Minute Man,* Oct. 1, 1945, 1.
127. Whittick, *Symbols,* 226.
128. "The Roosevelt Bond," 16.
129. "Victory—Now You Can Invest in It," poster, [1945], in Records of the Savings Bond Division (Including Records of its Predecessor, the War Finance Division), Advertising and Promotion Branch, Promotional Records, 1936–51, Box 7, Folder 92, General Records of the Department of the Treasury, Record Group 56, National Archives.
130. On low angles in images, see Messaris, *Visual Persuasion,* 34–38.
131. "Victory—Now You Can Invest in It," General Records of the Department of the Treasury.
132. Whittick, *Symbols,* 311.
133. Michael C. C. Adams, *The Best War Ever: America and World War II,* 2.
134. Matthew S. Hirshberg, "The Self-Perpetuating National Self-Image: Cognitive Biases in Perceptions of International Interventions," *Political Psychology* 14 (1993): 79–80.
135. See, for example, Adams, *Best War Ever.*
136. Black, "Second Persona."
137. "The Plow Remains," *Minute Man,* June, 1946, 1.
138. "In This Issue," *Minute Man,* June, 1946, 2.
139. "Carry On!" *Minute Man,* June, 1946, 2.

Chapter 5

1. Tom Brokaw, *An Album of Memories: Personal Histories from the Greatest Generation.*
2. See Terkel, *Good War;* and Richard Polenberg, "The Good War? A Reappraisal of How World War II Affected American Society," *Virginia Magazine of History and Biography* 100 (1992): 295–322.
3. Warren I. Susman, "History and the American Intellectual: Uses of a Usable Past," in *Culture as History: The Transformation of American Society in the Twentieth Century,* 7–26.
4. See, for example, Penny Walker, "Vets Share Memories of WWII in 'Valor,'" *Arizona Republic,* June 6, 2001, final edition; Rafiah Davis, "Honoring Corporal Lobas," *(Cleveland) Plain Dealer,* May 31, 2001, final edition; and Jack Cowan, "Many Aging Veterans Are Still Quietly Modest," *Columbus Dispatch,* May 28, 2001.
5. Adams, *Best War Ever,* 156.
6. Of course, the administration's *international* propaganda thrived throughout the war. See Winkler, *Politics of Propaganda;* Fitzhugh Green, *American Propaganda Abroad;* and Clayton D. Laurie, *The Propaganda Warriors: America's Crusade against Nazi Germany.*
7. OCD, OFF, and OWI faced resistance from the American public and from Congress based on their status as propaganda agencies. Although the Treasury's domestic operations were in fact much broader than these programs, its messages were apparently never attacked as propaganda. Instead, contemporary accounts of the bond program inevitably discussed its financial goals and accomplishments. See, for example, High, "The U.S. Pocketbook Enlists"; Beatty, "Biggest Bargain Sale"; and "Buy Bonds! U.S. Spurs Drive to Draw in a Billion a Month," *Newsweek,* July 6, 1942, 44.
8. Perrett, *Days of Sadness,* 10. See also Lotchin, who argues that our knowledge of the home front in World War II is still quite fragmented. Roger W. Lotchin,

"The Historians' War or the Home Front's War? Some Thoughts for Western Historians," *Western Historical Quarterly* 26 (1995): 185–96.

9. See, for example, Green, *American Propaganda Abroad,* and Laurie, *Propaganda Warriors.* One recent exception is Steven Casey, *Cautious Crusade: Franklin D. Roosevelt, American Public Opinion, and the War against Nazi Germany.*
10. Winkler, *Politics of Propaganda.* S. Weinberg reinforces this notion when she suggests that the curtailment of OWI's domestic branch in the summer of 1943 was the end of the administration's propaganda efforts. See S. Weinberg, "What to Tell America." W. O'Neill references what he calls "Washington's lack of interest in propaganda" during World War II. See William O'Neill, *A Democracy at War: America's Fight at Home and Abroad in World War II,* 141.
11. Even before Pearl Harbor, for instance, 97 percent of the public was aware of the defense bond program. See Cantril, *Public Opinion,* 1026.
12. Samuel, *Pledging Allegiance,* 214.
13. Ibid.
14. "Forward March—America!" 6.
15. "Attack! Attack! Attack!" advertisement, in Treasury Department, *In Line with the New Restrictions on Paper, the Treasury Department Recommends to Magazine Publishers Interested in Furthering the Sale of U.S. War Bonds the Following Ideas* (Washington: GPO, [1942]), Box 8, Folder 7, p. 9, Odegard Papers.
16. "Carry On!" 2.
17. "This Is Your 'Battle Flag' Here at Home," advertisement, in Treasury Department, *4th War Loan Newspaper Advertisements,* 10, Odegard Papers.
18. Ellen Herman, *The Romance of American Psychology: Political Culture in the Age of Experts,* 48.
19. Odegard, "Tentative Outline," book proposal (typescript), Box 7, Folder 3, p. 8, Odegard Papers.
20. According to Cantor and Stabile, the Treasury was "aware of the 'propaganda value' of the Savings Bond Program in fostering patriotism and national unity, and many of the savings bonds sales campaigns reinforced other patriotic appeals." See Cantor and Stabile, *History of the Bureau of the Public Debt,* 92.
21. Fox, *Madison Avenue Goes to War,* 58. On the Treasury-WAC connection, see Lemmon, "Early War Advertising Council Contacts."
22. "For Joe and Pete and Jack and Harry," advertisement, *Saturday Evening Post,* Feb. 5, 1944, 4. Similar comparisons are available in Derek Nelson, *The Ads That Won the War.* The Treasury was well aware of independent advertisements that echoed its own message. In one publication, the bond staff reprinted several such ads, commenting below one: "Here is shown a War Bond ad which could have been signed by the Treasury Department . . . But it's by Oldsmobile of General Motors"; ellipsis in original. See *War Savings Staff News, National Advertisers Edition,* April, 1943, 17, in Records of the Savings Bond Division (Including Records of its Predecessor, the War Finance Division), Records of the Field Directors, 1941–1947, Publicity Materials, Box 2, General Records of the Department of the Treasury, Record Group 56, National Archives.
23. Schoolchildren, for instance, were encouraged to gather loose change and convert the coins into bond stamps, and ultimately into war bonds. See Kirk, *Earning Their Stripes,* 77–101. The military significance of even these small purchases was evident in one of the Treasury's newspaper fillers: "A Stamp's a bullet, A bond's a gun / Buy them both till the War is won," quoted in Treasury Department, *In Line with the New Restrictions,* 8, Odegard Papers.

24. Michael S. Sherry, *In the Shadow of War: The United States since the 1930s*, 95.
25. Ibid.
26. Gamble, "Of What We May Be Proud," 3.
27. Coyne, "Public Reactions," 3.
28. "Home Front Beach Head," cartoon, *Los Angeles Times*, June 14, 1944, morning edition.
29. "60,000,000 Americans Can't Be Wrong," *New York Times Magazine*, June 11, 1944, 20. See also "Worst Fight Ahead, President Asserts in War Loan Plea," *New York Times*, Jan. 19, 1944, late city edition; High, "The U.S. Pocketbook Enlists"; and "Buy Bonds! U.S. Spurs Drive."
30. Treasury Department, *EVERYBODY Top That 10%*, 11, Odegard Papers.
31. Messaris, *Visual Persuasion*, 34.
32. Black, "Second Persona," 113.
33. Consider, for instance, that the Seventh War Loan by itself sold more bonds ($26.3 billion) than were sold during the entire World War I bond campaign ($21.5 billion). For these figures, see Samuel, *Pledging Allegiance*, 8. Or consider that the Treasury's wartime posters achieved a greater level of prominence in the nation's store windows than for all other government campaigns combined. See Cartwright to Odegard, Odegard Papers.
34. See Cartwright to Odegard, Odegard Papers, for an extensive discussion of the Treasury's reliance on statistical sampling during the war.
35. Fousek, *To Lead the Free World*, 7. See also Sherry, *In the Shadow of War*, 124, 498.
36. Parry-Giles, "Militarizing America's Propaganda," 107.
37. Ibid., 110.
38. Laura McEnaney, *Civil Defense Begins at Home: Militarization Meets Everyday Life in the Fifties*, 5, emphasis in original.
39. The various histories of the Treasury Department offer no evidence that it participated in widespread propaganda efforts after World War II. See, for instance, the postwar history in Cantor and Stabile, *History of the Bureau of the Public Debt*.
40. Patrick M. Regan, "War Toys, War Movies, and the Militarization of the United States, 1900–1985," *Journal of Peace Research* 31 (1994): 56, 55.
41. Diane J. Garsombke, "Organizational Culture Dons the Mantle of Militarism," *Organizational Dynamics* 17 (1988): 47.
42. Cynthia Enloe, *Maneuvers: The International Politics of Militarizing Women's Lives*, 4.
43. Sherry, *In the Shadow of War*, 349.
44. Ibid., 504.
45. Enloe, *Maneuvers*, 3.
46. Regan, "War Toys," 45.
47. Adams, *Best War Ever*, 2.
48. Odegard, "Tentative Outline," 3, Odegard Papers.
49. Kecskemeti, *Strategic Surrender*, 26. See also Ivie, "Images of Savagery"; Keen, *Faces of the Enemy;* Hogan and Williams, "Defining 'the Enemy'"; and Carpenter, "America's Tragic Metaphor."
50. Philip Wander, "The Rhetoric of American Foreign Policy," *Quarterly Journal of Speech* 70 (1984): 353.
51. Kecskemeti, *Strategic Surrender*, 26.
52. Ivie, "Images of Savagery," 294.

53. Hans Speier, "The American Soldier and the Sociology of Military Organization," in *Continuities in Social Research: Studies in the Scope and Method of "the American Soldier,"* ed. Robert K. Merton and Paul F. Lazarsfeld, 119.
54. Keen, *Faces of the Enemy,* 12.
55. See Chilton, "Meaning of Security," 197.
56. Link, "Southern Enemy Image," 48, 47.
57. Kecskemeti, *Strategic Surrender,* 23.
58. Keen, *Faces of the Enemy,* 18; Grossman, *On Killing,* 158. As Grossman suggests, the revulsion often produced by a GI's first kill may be "rooted in a sense of identification or an empathy for the humanity of their victim," 237. In World War II, the military was well aware of the need to avoid humanizing the enemy. According to Roeder, "military authorities censored photographs showing American soldiers treating wounded Japanese soldiers, perhaps because these images of one human being helping another blurred the visual distinctions considered necessary to a win-the-war attitude." See Roeder, *Censored War,* 87. Dower adds that in 1945 "the Pentagon was still blue-penciling [documentary] scripts on the grounds that the passages in question would evoke 'too much sympathy for the Jap people.'" See Dower, *War without Mercy,* 19. See also Volkan, *The Need to Have Enemies,* 173.
59. Grossman, *On Killing,* 161.
60. For example, by August, 1945, 50 percent of U.S. occupation troops gave Germans "very favorable" or "fairly favorable" evaluations, compared to their opinion of the French (45 percent) and the English (75 percent). See Cottrell, "Aftermath of Hostilities," 566.
61. Robert MacDougall, "Red, Brown, and Yellow Perils: Images of the American Enemy in the 1940s and 1950s," *Journal of Popular Culture* 32 (1999): 65.
62. Faris R. Kirkland, "Can Soldiers Keep Peace? A Study of the Recent History of the Psychological Dimensions of the U.S. Army," *Journal of Psychohistory* 23 (1996): 435.
63. Christopher Thorne, "Racial Aspects of the Far Eastern War of 1941–1945," *Proceedings of the British Academy* 66 (1980): 350.
64. James Weingartner, "War against Subhumans: Comparisons between the German War against the Soviet Union and the American War against Japan, 1941–1945," *Historian* 58 (1996): 572.
65. MacDougall, "Red, Brown, and Yellow Perils," 65.
66. Rose, *Dubious Victory,* 367.
67. Ronald Takaki, "50 Years after Hiroshima," *Dissent* 42 (1995): 328.
68. Susan D. Moeller, "Pictures of the Enemy: Fifty Years of Images of Japan in the American Press, 1941–1992," *Journal of American Culture* 19 (1996): 32.
69. Peter Stanley, "Our Good China/Bad Japan Syndrome," *New Republic,* Feb. 17, 1979, 21.
70. MacDougall, "Red, Brown, and Yellow Perils," 72.
71. Dower, *War without Mercy,* 309.
72. Keen, *Faces of the Enemy,* 26.
73. Ibid.
74. Thorne, "Racial Aspects," 376.
75. Fussell, *Wartime,* 7–8; Roeder, *Censored War,* 25.
76. MacDougall, "Red, Brown, and Yellow Perils," 63.
77. Ralph K. White, "Hitler, Roosevelt, and the Nature of War Propaganda," *Journal of Abnormal and Social Psychology* 44 (1949): 170, emphasis in original.
78. Osborn, "Rhetorical Depiction," 79.

79. Zelizer, *Remembering to Forget,* 154.
80. Roeder, *Censored War,* 128.
81. Ibid., 130.
82. MacDougall, "Red, Brown, and Yellow Perils," 63.
83. Gerald Parshall, "The Face of Victory," *U.S. News and World Report,* Dec. 2, 1991, 52.
84. Roeder, *Censored War,* 3.
85. Fussell, *Wartime,* 267.
86. Anne Ford to Truman, Aug. 9, 1945, quoted in Rose, *Dubious Victory,* 363.
87. Hanson Baldwin, quoted in ibid., 362.
88. Simon Serfaty, *The Elusive Enemy: American Foreign Policy since World War II,* 30.
89. Stewart, Smith, and Denton, *Social Movements,* 84.
90. Terkel, *Good War.*
91. "Believe It or Not! Victory Costs More Than You Think!" advertisement, in *Bismarck Tribune,* Oct. 27, 1945, 2.
92. Burke, *Language as Symbolic,* 45.
93. Adams, *Best War Ever,* 7.
94. Fousek, *To Lead the Free World,* 46.
95. Rose, *Dubious Victory,* 365.
96. Ibid., 43.
97. Philip Gleason, "Americans All: World War II and the Shaping of American Identity," *Review of Politics* 43 (1981): 511.
98. Fousek, *To Lead the Free World,* 36.
99. Ibid., 2.
100. Ibid.
101. Samuel, *Pledging Allegiance,* 209.
102. Gerald F. Linderman, *Embattled Courage: The Experience of Combat in the American Civil War,* 1.
103. Brokaw, *Album of Memories.*

BIBLIOGRAPHY

This bibliography is divided into two sections. The first cites general information about manuscript collections; specific source locations are in the chapter endnotes. The second section lists all other published works used in the book, including publications of the U.S. Treasury Department that are available outside of manuscript collections. These include GPO (Government Printing Office) material as authorized by the Treasury, but individual posters, appeals, and other advertisements are not cited. Specific source locations for these materials are in the endnotes.

Manuscript Collections

General Records of the Department of the Treasury. National Archives, College Park, Md.

Morgenthau Diaries. Franklin D. Roosevelt Presidential Library, Hyde Park, N.Y.

Morgenthau Papers. Franklin D. Roosevelt Presidential Library, Hyde Park, N.Y.

Odegard Papers. Franklin D. Roosevelt Presidential Library, Hyde Park, N.Y.

Rare Book and Special Collections Division. Library of Congress, Washington, D.C.

Records of the Office of War Information. National Archives, College Park, Md.

Roosevelt Official File. Franklin D. Roosevelt Presidential Library, Hyde Park, N.Y.

Published Works

Adams, Michael C. C. *The Best War Ever: America and World War II.* Baltimore, Md.: Johns Hopkins University Press, 1994.

Adler, Les K., and Thomas G. Patterson. "Red Fascism: The Merger of Nazi Germany and Soviet Russia in the American Image of Totalitarianism, 1930s–1950s." *American Historical Review* 75 (1970): 1046–64.

"Advertising Council Serves to Coordinate War Activities." *Advertising Age,* Dec. 21, 1942, 24, 26, 28–30.

Alexander, Charles C. *Nationalism in American Thought, 1930–1945.* Chicago: Rand McNally, 1969.

"All Secure! 4th Underway—Outlook Bright." *Minute Man,* Feb. 1, 1944, 3.

Alperovitz, Gar. *The Decision to Use the Atomic Bomb and the Architecture of an American Myth.* New York: Alfred A. Knopf, 1995.

"Announcing the Victory Loan." *Minute Man,* Aug. 15, 1945, 3.

"Any Bonds Today?" *Field Organization News Letter,* Oct. 18, 1941, 15.

Archer, Dane, and Rosemary Gartner. "Violent Acts and Violent Times: A Comparative Approach to Postwar Homicide Rates." *American Sociological Review* 41 (1976): 937–63.

Backer, John H. *The Decision to Divide Germany: American Foreign Policy in Transition.* Durham, N.C.: Duke University Press, 1978.

Baus, Herbert M., and William B. Ross. *Politics Battle Plan.* New York: Macmillan, 1968.

Beatty, Jerome. "Biggest Bargain Sale." *American Magazine,* May, 1943, 108.

Becker, Jonathan A. "A Disappearing Enemy: The Image of the United States in Soviet Political Cartoons." *Journalism and Mass Communication Quarterly* 73 (1996): 609–19.

"Behind the Poster Scene." *Minute Man,* June 15, 1944, 20–21.

Black, Edwin. "The Second Persona." *Quarterly Journal of Speech* 56 (1970): 109–19.

Black, Wallace B., and Jean F. Blashfield. *Invasion of Italy.* New York: Crestwood House, 1992.

Blue, Frederick J. *Salmon P. Chase: A Life in Politics.* Kent, Ohio: Kent State University Press, 1987.

Blum, John Morton. *From the Morgenthau Diaries: Years of Crisis, 1928–1938.* Boston: Houghton Mifflin, 1959.

———. *From the Morgenthau Diaries: Years of Urgency, 1938–1941.* Boston: Houghton Mifflin, 1965.

———. *From the Morgenthau Diaries: Years of War, 1941–1945.* Boston: Houghton Mifflin, 1967.

———. *Roosevelt and Morgenthau.* Boston: Houghton Mifflin, 1972.

———. *V Was for Victory: Politics and American Culture during World War II.* New York: Harcourt Brace Jovanovich, 1976.

Bormann, Ernest G. "Fetching Good out of Evil." *Quarterly Journal of Speech* 63 (1977): 130–39.

Bourke, Joanna. *An Intimate History of Killing: Face-to-Face Killing in Twentieth-Century Warfare.* New York: Basic Books, 1999.

Brandenburg, George A. "NAEA Hears of Appreciation in Washington for Advertising." *Editor and Publisher,* Oct. 17, 1942, 5, 34, 36.

Braverman, Jordan. *To Hasten the Homecoming: How Americans Fought World War II through the Media.* Lanham, Md.: Madison Books, 1996.

Breuilly, John. "Nationalism and the State." In *Nationality, Patriotism, and Nationalism in Liberal Democratic Societies,* ed. Roger Michener, 19–48. St. Paul, Minn.: Paragon House, 1993.

Brinkley, David. *Washington Goes to War.* New York: Ballantine Books, 1988.

Brokaw, Tom. *An Album of Memories: Personal Histories from the Greatest Generation.* New York: Random House, 2001.

Burke, Kenneth. *A Grammar of Motives.* Berkeley: University of California Press, 1969.

———. *Language as Symbolic Action: Essays on Life, Literature, and Method.* Berkeley: University of California Press, 1966.

Burnett, Betty. *St. Louis at War: The Story of a City.* St. Louis, Mo.: Patrice Press, 1987.

"Buy Bonds! U.S. Spurs Drive to Draw in a Billion a Month." *Newsweek,* July 6, 1942, 44.

Calvocoressi, Peter, Guy Wint, and John Pritchard. *Total War: The Causes and Courses of the Second World War,* rev. ed. New York: Pantheon, 1989.

Cantor, Jeffrey A., and Donald R. Stabile. *A History of the Bureau of the Public Debt, 1940–1990, with Historical Highlights from 1789–1939.* Danbury, Conn.: CH Associates, 1990.

Cantril, Hadley. "Public Opinion in Flux." *Annals of the American Academy of Political and Social Sciences* 220 (1942): 136–52.

———, ed. *Public Opinion: 1935–1946.* Princeton, N.J.: Princeton University Press, 1951.

Cardozier, V. R. *The Mobilization of the United States in World War II: How the Government, Military, and Industry Prepared for War.* Jefferson, N.C.: McFarland, 1995.

Carpenter, Ronald H. "America's Tragic Metaphor: Our Twentieth-Century Combatants as Frontiersmen." *Quarterly Journal of Speech* 76 (1990): 1–22.

"Carry On!" *Minute Man,* June, 1946, 2.

Casey, Steven. *Cautious Crusade: Franklin D. Roosevelt, American Public Opinion, and the War against Nazi Germany.* New York: Oxford University Press, 2001.

"Challenge of the Victory Loan." *Minute Man,* Jan., 1946, 3.

Chappell, John D. *Before the Bomb: How America Approached the End of the Pacific War.* Lexington: University Press of Kentucky, 1997.

Chilton, Paul A. "The Meaning of Security." In *Post-Realism: The Rhetorical Turn in International Relations,* ed. Francis. A. Beer and Robert Hariman, 193–216. East Lansing: Michigan State University Press, 1996.

"Clearing House." *Minute Man,* Dec. 1, 1943, 3.

Conner, William H., and Leon de Valinger Jr. *Delaware's Role in World War II: 1940–1946.* Vol. 2. Dover, Del.: Public Archives Commission, 1955.

Cottrell, Leonard S., Jr. "The Aftermath of Hostilities." In *The American Soldier: Combat and Its Aftermath,* 549–95. Vol. 2 of *Studies in Social Psychology in World War II,* ed. Samuel A. Stouffer et al. Princeton, N.J.: Princeton University Press, 1949.

Coyne, Robert W. "Public Reactions to the Drive." *Minute Man,* Nov. 1, 1943, 3–4.

Creel, George. *How We Advertised America: The First Telling of the Amazing Story of the Committee on Public Information That Carried the Gospel of Americanism to Every Corner of the Globe.* New York: Harper and Brothers, 1920.

Darsey, James. "From 'Gay Is Good' to the Scourge of AIDS: The Evolution of Gay Liberation Rhetoric, 1977–1990." *Communication Studies* 42 (1991): 43–66.

Daughton, Suzanne M. "Metaphorical Transcendence: Images of the Holy War in Franklin Roosevelt's First Inaugural." *Quarterly Journal of Speech* 79 (1993): 427–46.

Dewey, John. "The New Paternalism." *New Republic,* Dec. 21, 1918, 216–17.

Divine, Robert A. *The Reluctant Belligerent: American Entry into World War II.* 2nd ed. New York: John Wiley, 1979.

Dower, John. *War without Mercy: Race and Power in the Pacific War.* New York: Pantheon Books, 1986.

"Down the Home Stretch." *Minute Man,* Feb. 15, 1944, 3.

Edwards, Janice L., and Carol K. Winkler. "Representative Form and the Visual Ideograph: The Iwo Jima Image in Editorial Cartoons." *Quarterly Journal of Speech* 83 (1997): 289–310.

Ellul, Jacques. *Propaganda: The Formation of Men's Attitudes.* New York: Alfred A. Knopf, 1965.

Enloe, Cynthia. *Maneuvers: The International Politics of Militarizing Women's Lives.* Berkeley: University of California Press, 2000.

Fenrich, Lane. "Mass Death in Miniature: How Americans Became Victims of the Bomb." In *Living with the Bomb: American and Japanese Cultural Conflicts in the Nuclear Age,* ed. Lauren Hein and Mark Selden, 122–33. Armonk, N.Y.: M. E. Sharpe, 1997.

"5th War Loan: June 12–July 8." *Minute Man,* April 15, 1944, 3.

"FINAL RESULTS: 5th War Loan." *Minute Man,* Aug. 15, 1944, 3–5.

"Findings of 5th War Loan Survey." *Minute Man,* Sept. 1, 1944, 3.

Flynn, George Q. *The Mess in Washington: Manpower Mobilization in World War II.* Westport, Conn.: Greenwood Press, 1979.

"4th War Loan." *Minute Man,* Dec. 15, 1943, 3.

Fousek, John. *To Lead the Free World: American Nationalism and the Cultural Roots of the Cold War.* Chapel Hill: University of North Carolina Press, 2000.

Fox, Frank. *Madison Avenue Goes to War: The Strange Military Career of American Advertising, 1941–1945.* Provo, Utah: Brigham Young University Press, 1975.

Freeland, Cynthia A. *The Naked and the Undead: Evil and the Appeal of Horror.* New York: Westview Press, 2000.

Fussell, Paul. *Wartime: Understanding and Behavior in the Second World War.* New York: Oxford University Press, 1989.

Gallup, George. "How Important Is Public Opinion in Time of War?" *Proceedings of the American Philosophical Association* 85 (1942): 440–44.

———, ed. *The Gallup Poll: Public Opinion, 1935–1971.* New York: Random House, 1972.

Gamble, Ted R. "Financing a War, American Style." *Minute Man,* Sept. 15, 1943, 4–7.

———. "Of What We May Be Proud." *Minute Man,* Mar. 1, 1944, 3.

Garsombke, Diane J. "Organizational Culture Dons the Mantle of Militarism." *Organizational Dynamics* 17 (1988): 46–56.

Gerard, James W. *Face to Face with Kaiserism.* New York: George H. Doran, 1918.

Gibbs, Philip. *Now It Can Be Told.* New York: Harper and Brothers, 1920.

Gilbert, Charles. *American Financing of World War I.* Westport, Conn.: Greenwood Press, 1970.

Gilbert, Martin. *The Day the War Ended: May 8, 1945—Victory in Europe.* New York: Henry Holt, 1995.

Gleason, Philip. "Americans All: World War II and the Shaping of American Identity." *Review of Politics* 43 (1981): 483–518.

Goodwin, Doris K. *No Ordinary Time: Franklin and Eleanor Roosevelt: The Home Front in World War II.* New York: Simon and Schuster, 1994.

"Greatest Promotional Campaign 'Backs the Attack.'" *Minute Man,* Sept. 15, 1943, 8–11.

Green, Fitzhugh. *American Propaganda Abroad.* New York: Hippocrene Books, 1988.

Griffith, Robert. "The Selling of America: The Advertising Council and American Politics, 1942–1960." *Business History Review* 57 (1983): 388–412.

Grossman, Dave. *On Killing: The Psychological Cost of Learning to Kill in War and Society.* New York: Little, Brown, 1995.

Hahn, Dan F., and Robert L. Ivie. "'Sex' as Rhetorical Invitation to War." *ETC: A Review of General Semantics* 45 (1988): 15–21.

Hart, B. H. Liddell. *History of the Second World War.* New York: Perigee, 1982.

Hart, Roderick P. *Modern Rhetorical Criticism.* Glenview, Ill.: Scott, Foresman/Little, 1990.

Hatzenbuehler, Ronald L., and Robert L. Ivie. *Congress Declares War: Rhetoric, Leadership, and Partisanship in the Early Republic.* Kent, Ohio: Kent State University Press, 1983.

Herman, Ellen. *The Romance of American Psychology: Political Culture in the Age of Experts.* Berkeley: University of California Press, 1995.

High, Stanley. "It is Not a New Deal War." *Reader's Digest,* Nov., 1942, 26.

———. "The U.S. Pocketbook Enlists." *Reader's Digest,* Mar., 1942, 13.

Hikins, James W. "The Rhetoric of 'Unconditional Surrender' and the Decision to Drop the Atomic Bomb." *Quarterly Journal of Speech* 69 (1983): 379–400.

Hirshberg, Matthew S. "The Self-Perpetuating National Self-Image: Cognitive Biases in Perceptions of International Interventions." *Political Psychology* 14 (1993): 77–98.

Hogan, J. Michael. "George Gallup and the Rhetoric of Scientific Democracy." *Communication Monographs* 64 (1997): 161–79.

Hogan, J. Michael, and L. Glen Williams. "Defining 'the Enemy' in Revolutionary America: From the Rhetoric of Protest to the Rhetoric of War." *Southern Communication Journal* 61 (1996): 277–88.

Hollihan, Thomas. A. "Propagandizing in the Interest of War: A Rhetorical Study of the Committee on Public Information." *Southern Speech Communication Journal* 49 (1984): 241–57.

Houck, Davis W. *Rhetoric as Currency: Hoover, Roosevelt, and the Great Depression.* College Station: Texas A&M University Press, 2001.

Hough, Richard. *The Battle of Britain: The Greatest Air Battle of World War II.* New York: W. W. Norton, 1989.

Howell, Thomas. "The Writers' War Board: U.S. Domestic Propaganda in World War II." *Historian* 59 (1997): 795–813.

Hoyle, Martha Byrd. *A World in Flames: A History of World War II.* New York: Atheneum, 1970.

"If Invasion Comes." *Minute Man,* June 1, 1944, 7.

"Integrated Drive on for Conservation of Meat: OWI Shows Ability to Coordinate Effort in New Campaign." *Advertising Age,* Oct. 26, 1942, 1.

"In This Issue." *Minute Man,* June, 1946, 2.

"It's Not Over Yet." *Minute Man,* Jan. 15, 1944, 12.

Ivie, Robert L. *Democracy and America's War on Terror.* Tuscaloosa: University of Alabama Press, 2005.

———. "Images of Savagery in American Justifications for War." *Communication Monographs* 47 (1980): 279–94.

———. "Literalizing the Metaphor of Soviet Savagery: President Truman's Plain Style." *Southern Speech Communication Journal* 51 (1986): 91–105.

———. "Metaphor and the Rhetorical Invention of Cold War 'Idealists.'" *Communication Monographs* 54 (1987): 165–82.

———. "The Metaphor of Force in Prowar Discourse: The Case of 1812." *Quarterly Journal of Speech* 68 (1982): 240–53.

———. "Progressive Form and Mexican Culpability in Polk's Justification for War." *Central States Speech Journal* 30 (1979): 311–20.

Jackall, Robert, and Janice M. Hirota. "America's First Propaganda Ministry: The Committee on Public Information during the Great War." In *Propaganda,* ed. Robert Jackall, 137–73. New York: New York University Press, 1995.

Janis, Irving L. "Effects of Fear Arousal on Attitude Change: Recent Developments in Theory and Research." In *Advances in Experimental Social Psychology,* vol. 3, ed. Leonard Berkowitz, 293–315. New York: Academic Press, 1967.

Jeffords, Susan. "Rape and the New World Order." *Cultural Critique* 19 (1991): 203–15.

Jowett, Garth S., and Victoria O'Donnell. *Propaganda and Persuasion.* 3rd ed. Newbury Park, Calif.: Sage Publications, 1999.

Judd, Denis. *Posters of World War Two.* New York: St. Martins, 1973.

Kecskemeti, Paul. *Strategic Surrender: The Politics of Victory and Defeat.* New York: Atheneum, 1964.

Keen, Sam. *Faces of the Enemy: Reflections of the Hostile Imagination.* San Francisco: Harper and Row, 1986.

Kellett, Anthony. "The Soldier in Battle: Motivational and Behavioral Aspects of the Combat Experience." In *Psychological Dimensions of War,* ed. Betty Glad, 215–35. Newbury Park, Calif.: Sage Publications, 1990.

Kennedy, Susan Eastbrook. *The Banking Crisis of 1933.* Lexington, Ky.: 1973.

"Key Figures on the Five War Loans." *Minute Man,* Aug. 15, 1944, 4.

"Key Figures on the Six War Loans." *Minute Man,* Jan. 15, 1945, 3.

Keynes, John Maynard. *How to Pay for the War: A Radical Plan for the Chancellor of the Exchequer.* New York: Harcourt Brace, 1940.

Kimble, James J. "Feminine Style and the Rehumanization of the Enemy: Peacemaking Discourse in *Ladies Home Journal,* 1945–1946." *Women and Language* 27 (2004): 65–70.

Kirk, Robert Wm. *Earning Their Stripes: The Mobilization of American Children in the Second World War.* New York: Peter Lang, 1994.

Kirkland, Faris R. "Can Soldiers Keep Peace? A Study of the Recent History of the Psychological Dimensions of the U.S. Army." *Journal of Psychohistory* 23 (1996): 427–37.

Kress, Gunther, and Theo van Leeuwen. *Reading Images: The Grammar of Visual Design.* New York: Routledge, 1996.

Lakoff, George, and Mark Johnson. *Metaphors We Live By.* Chicago: University of Chicago Press, 1980.

Langer, William L., and S. Everett Gleason. *The Undeclared War, 1940–1941.* New York: Harper and Brothers, 1953.

Lasswell, Harold D. *Propaganda Technique in World War I.* Cambridge, Mass.: Massachusetts Institute of Technology, 1927.

Laurie, Clayton D. *The Propaganda Warriors: America's Crusade against Nazi Germany.* Lawrence: University Press of Kansas, 1996.

Lee, Loyd E. *War Years: A Global History of the Second World War.* Boston: Unwin Hyman, 1989.

Leff, Mark H. "The Politics of Sacrifice on the American Home Front in World War II." *Journal of American History* 77 (1991): 1296–318.

"Let's Make Every Pay Day Bond Day." *Defense Savings Staff News,* Jan. 1, 1942, 1.

Leuchtenburg, William E. *Franklin D. Roosevelt and the New Deal, 1932–1940.* New York: Harper and Row, 1963.

Linderman, Gerald F. *Embattled Courage: The Experience of Combat in the American Civil War.* New York: Free Press, 1987.

Link, Jürgen. "Fanatics, Fundamentalists, Lunatics, and Drug Traffickers: The New Southern Enemy Image." *Cultural Critique* 19 (Fall, 1991): 33–53.

Lippmann, Walter. *Public Opinion.* New York: Harcourt, Brace, 1922.

Lotchin, Roger W. "The Historians' War or the Home Front's War? Some Thoughts for Western Historians." *Western Historical Quarterly* 26 (1995): 185–96.

MacDougall, Robert. "Red, Brown, and Yellow Perils: Images of the American Enemy in the 1940s and 1950s." *Journal of Popular Culture* 32 (1999): 59–75.

Maddox, Robert James. *Weapons for Victory: The Hiroshima Decision Fifty Years Later.* Columbia: University of Missouri Press, 1995.

McAdoo, William G. *Crowded Years.* Boston: Houghton Mifflin, 1931.

McEnaney, Laura. *Civil Defense Begins at Home: Militarization Meets Everyday Life in the Fifties.* Princeton, N.J.: Princeton University Press, 2000.

McGee, Michael C. "The Origins of Liberty: A Feminization of Power." *Communication Monographs* 47 (1980): 23–45.

Medhurst, Martin J. "Eisenhower and the Crusade for Freedom: The Rhetorical Origins of a Cold War Campaign." *Presidential Studies Quarterly* 27 (1997): 646–61.

Messaris, Paul. *Visual Persuasion: The Role of Images in Advertising.* Thousand Oaks, Calif.: Sage Publications, 1997.

Mock, James. R., and Cedric Larson. *Words That Won the War: The Story of the Committee on Public Information, 1917–1919.* Princeton, N.J.: Princeton University Press, 1939.

Moeller, Susan D. "Pictures of the Enemy: Fifty Years of Images of Japan in the American Press, 1941–1992." *Journal of American Culture* 19 (1996): 29–42.

"Moods of Wartime." *Life,* Nov. 27, 1944, 28.

Morgenthau, Henry F., Jr. "Back to Serious Business." *Minute Man,* June 1, 1945, 2.

———. Foreword to *Handbook for Canvassers in the Pledge Campaign,* by Treasury Department, Defense Savings Staff, 1. Washington, D.C.: GPO, 1942.

———. *Germany Is Our Problem.* New York: Harper and Brothers, 1945.

———. "A Message from the Secretary." *Minute Man,* June 15, 1942, 3.

———. "New Taxes and War Savings." *Minute Man,* Oct. 1, 1942, 3.

———. *War Finance Policies: Excerpts from Three Addresses by Henry Morgenthau, Jr., Secretary of the Treasury.* Washington, D.C.: GPO, 1944.

Morse, Jarvis M. *Paying for a World War: The United States Financing of World War II.* Washington, D.C.: U.S. Savings Bond Division, 1971.

Murphy, Henry C. *The National Debt in War and Transition.* New York: McGraw-Hill, 1950.

"National X-Day Bond Plans." *Minute Man,* Oct. 1, 1944, 3.

Nelson, Derek. *The Ads That Won the War.* Osceola, Wis.: Motorbooks International, 1992.

———. *The Posters That Won the War.* Osceola, Wis.: Motorbooks International, 1991.

Nevins, Allan. "How We Felt about the War." In *While You Were Gone: A Report on Wartime Life in the United States,* ed. Jack Goodman, 3–27. New York: Da Capo Press, 1946.

"New Pay-Roll Drive Underway." *Minute Man,* [Nov. 15, 1942], 3.

Odegard, Peter H. "The Spirit of '76." Review of *Propaganda and the American Revolution,* by Philip Davidson. *Saturday Review of Literature,* Mar. 7, 1942, 5-6, 23.

Odegard, Peter H., and Alan Barth. "Millions for Defense." *Public Opinion Quarterly* 5 (1941): 399–411.

Odegard, Peter H., and E. Allen Helms. *American Politics: A Study in Political Dynamics.* New York: Harper and Brothers, 1938.

"Official 5th War Loan Displays and Sales Materials." *Minute Man,* May 15, 1944, 8–9.

"An Old Hand." *Minute Man,* Aug. 1, 1945, 2.

Olney, Laurence M. *The War Bond Story.* Washington, D.C.: U.S. Savings Bonds Division, 1971.

O'Neill, Herbert C. *A Short History of the Second World War.* New York: Praeger, 1950.

O'Neill, William. *A Democracy at War: America's Fight at Home and Abroad in World War II.* New York: Free Press, 1993.

Osborn, Michael. "Rhetorical Depiction." In *Form, Genre, and the Study of Political Discourse,* ed. Herbert. W. Simons and Aram A. Aghazarian, 79–107. Columbia: University of South Carolina Press, 1986.

Ottosen, Rune. "Enemy Images and the Journalistic Process." *Journal of Peace Research* 32 (1995): 97–112.

"Over the Top! 15 Billion and Lots More." *Minute Man,* Oct. 15, 1943, 3–5.

Parry-Giles, Shawn J. "'Camouflaged' Propaganda: The Truman and Eisenhower Administrations' Covert Manipulation of News." *Western Journal of Communication* 60 (1996): 146–67.

———. "Militarizing America's Propaganda Program, 1945–1955." In *Critical Reflections on the Cold War: Linking Rhetoric and History,* ed. Martin J. Medhurst and H. W. Brand, 95–132. College Station: Texas A&M University Press, 2000.

Parshall, Gerald. "The Face of Victory." *U.S. News and World Report,* Dec. 2, 1991, 52.

Perrett, Geoffrey. *Days of Sadness, Years of Triumph: The American People, 1939–1945.* New York: Coward, McCann, and Geoghegan, 1973.

Pillar, Paul R. "Ending Limited War: The Psychological Dynamics of the Termination Process." In *Psychological Dimensions of War,* ed. Betty Glad, 252–63. Newbury Park, Calif.: Sage Publications, 1990.

Pinedo, Isabel Cristina. *Recreational Terror: Women and the Pleasures of Horror Film Viewing.* New York: State University of New York Press, 1997.

"The Plow Remains." *Minute Man,* June, 1946, 1.

Polenberg, Richard. "The Good War? A Reappraisal of How World War II Affected American Society." *Virginia Magazine of History and Biography* 100 (1992): 295–322.

———. *War and Society: The United States, 1941–1945.* Philadelphia: J. B. Lippincott, 1972.

Posen, Barry R. "Nationalism, the Mass Army, and Military Power." In *Perspectives on Nationalism and War,* ed. John L. Comaroff and Paul C. Stern, 135–85. New York: Gordon and Breach, 1995.

"Promotion Highlights." *Minute Man,* May 15, 1944, 11.

"Promotion Materials." *Minute Man,* Dec. 15, 1943, 20.

"Promotion, Publicity Aids." *Minute Man,* Oct. 15, 1944, 4.

"Quotas Based on Past Sales." *Minute Man,* May 15, 1942, 4.

"Recommendations Based on Survey." *Minute Man,* April 15, 1944, 6.

Regan, Patrick M. "War Toys, War Movies, and the Militarization of the United States, 1900–1985." *Journal of Peace Research* 31 (1994): 45–58.

Reynolds, David. *The Creation of the Anglo-American Alliance, 1937–1941.* Chapel Hill: University of North Carolina Press, 1982.

Rice, Ronald E., and Charles K. Atkin, eds. *Public Communication Campaigns.* 2nd ed. Newbury Park, Calif.: Sage Publications, 1989.

Ritter, Kurt W., and James R. Andrews. *The American Ideology: Reflections of the Revolution in American Rhetoric.* Falls Church, Va.: Speech Communication Association, 1978.

Roeder, George H. *The Censored War: American Visual Experience during World War Two.* New Haven, Conn.: Yale University Press, 1993.

Rogers, Donald I. *Since You Went Away.* New Rochelle, N.Y.: Arlington House, 1973.

Roig, Lester C. "Policies of the U.S. Treasury in the Financing of Three Major Wars." Ph.D. diss., Bowling Green University, 1950.

Roosevelt, Franklin D. *Public Papers and Addresses of Franklin D. Roosevelt.* Vol. 9. New York: Macmillan, 1941.

———. *Public Papers and Addresses of Franklin D. Roosevelt.* Vol. 12. New York: Harper Brothers, 1943.

"The Roosevelt Bond." *Minute Man,* Sept. 15, 1945, 16.

Rose, Lisle A. *Dubious Victory: The United States and the End of World War II.* Kent, Ohio: Kent State University Press, 1973.

Samuel, Lawrence R. *Pledging Allegiance: American Identity and the Bond Drive of World War II.* Washington, D.C.: Smithsonian Institution, 1997.

Secretary of the Treasury. *Annual Report.* Washington, D.C.: Treasury Department, 1863.

"Secretary of the Treasury." *Minute Man,* Sept. 1, 1944, 2.

Serfaty, Simon. *The Elusive Enemy: American Foreign Policy since World War II.* Boston: Little, Brown, 1972.

"7th Swings into High." *Minute Man,* June 15, 1945, 3–4.

Sherrod, Robert. *Tarawa: The Story of a Battle.* New York: Duell, Sloan, and Pearce, 1944. Quoted in Paul Fussell, *Wartime: Understanding and Behavior in the Second World War,* 13. New York: Oxford University Press, 1989.

Sherry, Michael S. *In the Shadow of War: The United States since the 1930s.* New Haven, Conn.: Yale University Press, 1995.

"Shop Lifting." *Minute Man,* Jan. 1, 1944, 22.

Sieminski, Gregory. "The Puritan Captivity Narrative and the Politics of the American Revolution." *American Quarterly* 42 (1990): 34–56.

Sillman, Leonard R. "Morale." *War Medicine* 3 (1943): 498–502.

Silverstein, Brett. "Toward a Science of Propaganda." *Political Psychology* 8 (1987): 49–59.

Simons, Herbert W. "Requirements, Problems, and Strategies: A Theory of Persuasion for Social Movements." *Quarterly Journal of Speech* 56 (1970): 1–11.

Simpson, Christopher. *Science of Coercion: Communication Research and Psychological Warfare, 1945–1960.* New York: Oxford University Press, 1994.

"6th Rolls Up Record for Total Sales." *Minute Man,* Jan. 15, 1945, 3.

"60,000,000 Americans Can't Be Wrong." *New York Times Magazine,* June 11, 1944, 20.

Slotkin, Richard. *Regeneration through Violence: The Mythology of the American Frontier, 1600–1860.* Middletown, Conn.: Wesleyan, 1973

Smith, Anthony D. *National Identity.* Reno: University of Nevada Press, 1991.

———. "War and Ethnicity: The Role of Warfare in the Formation, Self-Images, and Cohesion of Ethnic Communities." *Ethnic and Racial Studies* 4 (1981): 375–97.

Smith, Charles W. "The Selling of America in Oklahoma: The First and Second Liberty Bond Drives." *Chronicles of Oklahoma* 73 (1995/1996): 438–53.

Speier, Hans. "The American Soldier and the Sociology of Military Organization." In *Continuities in Social Research: Studies in the Scope and Method of "the American Soldier,"* ed. Robert K. Merton and Paul F. Lazarsfeld, 106–32. Glencoe, Ill.: Free Press, 1950.

Sproule, J. Michael. "Propaganda Studies in American Social Science: The Rise and Fall of the Critical Paradigm." *Quarterly Journal of Speech* 73 (1987): 60–78.

———. "Propaganda: The Ideological Rhetoric." In *Rhetoric and Ideology: Compositions and Criticisms of Power,* ed. Charles W. Kneupper, 90–97. Arlington, Tex.: Rhetoric Society of America, 1989.

———. "Social Responses to Twentieth-Century Propaganda." In *Propaganda: A Pluralistic Perspective,* ed. Ted J. Smith III, 5–22. New York: Praeger, 1989.

Stanley, Peter. "Our Good China/Bad Japan Syndrome." *New Republic,* Feb. 17, 1979, 21.

St. Clair, Labert. *The Story of the Liberty Loans: Being a Record of the Volunteer Liberty Loan Army, Its Personnel, Mobilization and Methods, How America at Home Backed Her Armies in the World War.* Washington, D.C.: James William Bryan Press, 1919.

Steele, Richard W. "News of the 'Good War': World War II News Management." *Journalism Quarterly* 62 (1985).

———. "Preparing the Public for War: Efforts to Establish a National Propaganda Agency." *American Historical Review* 75 (1970): 1640–53.

———. *Propaganda in an Open Society: The Roosevelt Administration and the Media, 1933–1941.* Westford, Conn.: 1985.

Stern, Paul C. "Why Do People Sacrifice for Their Nations?" In *Perspectives on Nationalism and War,* ed. John L. Comaroff and Paul C. Stern, 99–121. New York: Gordon and Breach, 1995.

Stewart, Charles J., Craig Allen Smith, and Robert E. Denton Jr. *Persuasion and Social Movements.* 3rd ed. Prospect Heights, Ill.: Waveland, 1994.

Stokesbury, James. "World War II: An Overview." In *World War II: Personal Accounts: Pearl Harbor to V-J Day,* ed. Gary. A. Yarrington and James Stokesbury, 1–45. Austin, Tex.: LBJ Foundation, 1992.

"Survey: NON-FARM People in the 4th." *Minute Man,* April 15, 1944, 4.

Susman, Warren I. "History and the American Intellectual: Uses of a Usable Past." In *Culture as History: The Transformation of American Society in the Twentieth Century,* 7–26. New York: Pantheon Books, 1984.

Takaki, Ronald. "50 Years after Hiroshima." *Dissent* 42 (1995): 328–30.

Telotte, J. P. "Faith and Idolatry in the Horror Film." *Literature/Film Quarterly* 8 (1980): 143–55.

Terkel, Studs. *"The Good War": An Oral History of World War II.* New York: Pantheon Books, 1984.

"Third War Loan: Final Score." *Minute Man,* Nov. 1, 1943, 5.

Thorne, Christopher. "Racial Aspects of the Far Eastern War of 1941–1945." *Proceedings of the British Academy* 66 (1980): 329–77.

"To Inspire a Mighty 7th!" *Minute Man,* May 15, 1945, 2.

"Top That 10% by New Year's!" *Minute Man,* Nov. 1, 1942, 3.

Treasury Department. *Art for Bonds: Posters from the Bureau of the Public Debt.* Washington, D.C.: N.p., 1996.

———. *A History of the United States Savings Bond Program.* Washington, D.C.: GPO, 1984.

———. *Women's Work in War Finance, 1941–1945.* Washington, D.C.: Treasury Department, 1946.

———. Defense Savings Staff. *Handbook for Canvassers in the Pledge Campaign.* Washington, D.C.: GPO, 1942.

———. Office of Public Affairs. U.S. Savings Bond Division. *50 Questions and Answers on U.S. Savings Bonds.* Washington, D.C.: U.S. Savings Bond Division, [1983].

———. Savings Bond Division. *A History of the United States Savings Bonds Program.* Washington, D.C.: Savings Bond Division, 1991.

———. War Finance Division. *5th War Loan Campaign Book.* Washington, D.C.: GPO, [1944].

———. War Finance Division. *4th War Loan Campaign Book.* Washington, D.C.: GPO, [1944].

———. War Finance Division. *These Are Their Words on Freedom vs. Tyranny.* Washington, D.C.: GPO, [1944].

———. War Savings Staff. *A Plan for Diverting at Least 10% of America's Payroll into U.S. War Bonds.* Washington, D.C.: GPO, 1942.

U. S. House Committee on Ways and Means. Public Debt Act of 1941: Hearings on H.R. 2653. 77th Cong., 1st sess., 29 Jan. 1941.

U.S. Senate Committee on Finance. Public Debt Act of 1941: Hearings on H.R. 2959. 77th Cong., 1st sess., 12 Feb. 1941.

"Vast Civilian Army in Action: Historic Chicago Meeting Inspires State Leadership." *Defense Savings Staff News,* Jan. 1, 1942, 1.

Vaughn, Stephen. *Holding Fast the Inner Lines: Democracy, Nationalism, and the Committee on Public Information.* Chapel Hill: University of North Carolina Press, 1980.

"Victory Loan a Success." *Minute Man,* Jan., 1946, 3.

Volkan, Vamik D. *The Need to Have Enemies and Allies.* Northvale, N.J.: Jason Aronson, 1988.

Wainstock, Dennis D. *The Decision to Drop the Atomic Bomb.* Westport, Conn.: Praeger, 1996.

Walton, Douglas. "What Is Propaganda, and What Exactly Is Wrong with It? *Public Affairs Quarterly* 11 (1997): 1–31.

Wander, Philip. "The Rhetoric of American Foreign Policy." *Quarterly Journal of Speech* 70 (1984): 339–61.

Watson, Peter. *War on the Mind: The Military Uses and Abuses of Psychology.* New York: Basic Books, 1978.

Weinberg, Gerhard L. *A World at Arms: A Global History of World War II.* Cambridge, Eng.: Cambridge University Press, 1994.

Weinberg, Sydney. "What to Tell America: The Writers' Quarrel in the Office of War Information." *Journal of American History* 55 (1968): 73–89.

Weingartner, James. "War against Subhumans: Comparisons between the German War against the Soviet Union and the American War against Japan, 1941–1945." *Historian* 58 (1996): 557–73.

"We're Over the Top." *Minute Man,* Dec. 15, 1942, 3–4.

White, Ralph K. "Hitler, Roosevelt, and the Nature of War Propaganda." *Journal of Abnormal and Social Psychology* 44 (1949): 157–74.

Whittick, Arnold. *Symbols: Signs and Their Meaning and Uses in Design.* 2nd ed. London: Leonard Hill, 1971.

Williams, Robin M., and M. Brewster Smith. "General Characteristics of Ground Combat." In *The American Soldier: Combat and Its Aftermath,* 59–104. Vol. 2 of *Studies in Social Psychology in World War II,* ed. Samuel A. Stouffer et al. Princeton, N.J.: Princeton University Press, 1949.

Winkler, Allan M. *The Politics of Propaganda: The Office of War Information, 1942–1945.* New Haven, Conn.: Yale University Press, 1978.

"The Year in War Finance." *Minute Man,* Jan. 1, 1944, 3.

Zarefsky, David. "Four Senses of Rhetorical History." In *Doing Rhetorical History: Concepts and Cases,* ed. Kathleen J. Turner, 19–32. Tuscaloosa: University of Alabama Press, 1998.

———. "President Johnson's War on Poverty: The Rhetoric of Three 'Establishment' Movements." *Communication Monographs* 44 (1977): 352–73.

Zelizer, Barbie. "Gender and Atrocity: Women in Holocaust Photographs." In *Visual Culture and the Holocaust,* ed. Barbie Zelizer, 247–71. New Brunswick, N.J.: Rutgers University Press, 2001.

———. *Remembering to Forget: Holocaust Memory through the Camera's Eye.* Chicago: University of Chicago Press, 1998.

INDEX